The Violin

Its Famous Makers and Their Imitators

George Hart

Alpha Editions

This edition published in 2024

ISBN : 9789362991584

Design and Setting By
Alpha Editions
www.alphaedis.com
Email - info@alphaedis.com

As per information held with us this book is in Public Domain.
This book is a reproduction of an important historical work. Alpha Editions uses the best technology to reproduce historical work in the same manner it was first published to preserve its original nature. Any marks or number seen are left intentionally to preserve its true form.

Contents

PREFACE TO THE ENLARGED AND REVISED EDITION .- 1 -
PREFATORY NOTE BY THE EDITORS ....- 4 -
SECTION I ....- 5 -
SECTION II ....- 20 -
SECTION III ....- 30 -
SECTION IV ....- 39 -
SECTION V ....- 48 -
SECTION VI ....- 52 -
SECTION VII ....- 141 -
SECTION VIII ....- 145 -
SECTION IX ....- 164 -
SECTION X ....- 166 -
SECTION XI ....- 185 -
SECTION XII ....- 190 -
SECTION XIII ....- 216 -
SECTION XIV ....- 241 -
SECTION XV ....- 260 -

PREFACE TO THE ENLARGED AND REVISED EDITION

The favourable reception accorded to the previous editions of this work has not only added greatly to the pleasure attending the preparation of a new and revised edition, but has encouraged me to spare no effort within my power to render the volume as interesting and complete as possible. In making these endeavours, the bulk of the book has been necessarily increased by additional information, spread over all the sections of the work, but chiefly on those which treat of the Early History of the leading instrument, and the Italian branches of the subject.

It is in connection with the Italian divisions of the book that the reader will discover, I venture to hope, information which he will regard as interesting in its character, besides being of some historical value. The greater part of this new matter has been obtained from original MSS. belonging to the trustees of the Civic Museum at Cremona, which Institution is located in the palace bequeathed to the citizens, together with its contents, by the Marchese Ponzoni. In the year 1872, Dr. F. Robolotti, the learned historiographer of the town, and a distinguished physician, and the Marchese Senatore Araldi Erizzo, presented to the Institution referred to an important collection of rare books and documents illustrative of the history of the City of Cremona. Among these are two sets of MSS., numbered respectively 729 and 431, the contents of which shed much light on the Italian sections of our subject, and constitute the source of the principal portion of the additional information contained in the following pages. The first-named MS. is the work of Don Desiderio Arisi, a monk of the order of St. Jerome, who in the quiet of his cell in the Convent of St. Sigismondo set himself the task of writing brief notices of Cremonese worthies. The MS. is dated 1720, and includes a most interesting account of the patronage enjoyed by Antonio Stradivari, together with several items of information of more or less worth, relative to the famous Violin-maker. In passing, it may be mentioned that Don Desiderio Arisi was intimate with Stradivari, and gained his knowledge of the facts he recorded from the artist himself. The second-named MSS., from which extracts have been made, are dated 1823. These contain references to the principal makers of Cremona, combined with critical remarks on their works from the pen of Vincenzo Lancetti, a Cremonese poet and biographer. The information contained in these MSS. was chiefly received from Count Cozio di Salabue in the course of correspondence between him and Lancetti.

Nearly the whole of the extracts to which the reader's attention has been directed were given to me as far back as the year 1875, when the original edition of this work was in the press. Finding it impossible to make adequate use of them, in consequence of the volume being partly printed, I decided to insert a few items at the end of the notice of Antonio Stradivari, and to hold over the remainder in order to distribute the information among the notices of the several makers in a future edition.

I am indebted for the knowledge of the existence of the Arisi and Lancetti MSS., and for their contents, to my friend Signor Federico Sacchi,[1] who during his researches among the Robolotti collection had free access to all the original documents, and whose family has long lived near the house occupied by Stradivari. With these advantages, it is almost needless to remark that my friend possessed ample means of aiding me in my endeavours to learn much concerning the makers of his native city. Taking as he does a deep and enthusiastic interest in the past history of Cremonese art, he spared no effort to obtain for me all the information possible. To him I am also indebted for the contents of the correspondence relative to the purchase, by Count Cozio di Salabue, of the tools used by Antonio Stradivari, and for the same having been placed at my disposal by the Marquis dalla Valle. In making these acknowledgments, I desire to tender Signor Sacchi my warmest thanks for the interest he has taken in my undertaking.[2]

> 1 Signor Sacchi is the author of—
>
> 1. "Cenni sulla vita e le opere di Agostino Aglio pittor Cremonese." Cremona, 1868. 8vo.
> 2. "Notizie pittoriche Cremonesi." Cremona, 1872. 4to.
> 3. "I Tipografi Ebrei di Soncino." Cremona, 1877. 4to.
> 4. "Annali Tipografici della Cittàe provincia di Cremona,"
>
> and many other memoirs on Cremonese printers and painters.
>
> 2 Signor Sacchi died in 1902.—ED.

The Section containing the Anecdotes has been recruited by additional Miscellanea, including "Hudibras and the Champion Crowdero." In placing this piece of wit and humour before my readers, I have endeavoured to do so in a form as connected as possible, by the selection of passages likely to conduce to that end, without trespassing too much on space, and on the reader's patience.

I am indebted to Mr. G. D. Bishopp for the table containing the amount of tension of Violin strings, and their downward pressure. The information therein contained will doubtless be acceptable to many of my readers.

I owe to M. le Chevalier Kraus, of Florence, the pleasure of including among the engravings those of the instruments made by Antonio Stradivari for the Grand Duke of Florence, he having obtained for me the necessary photographs.

In conclusion, I have to thank my young friend Mr. Allan Fea for the two illustrations forming the head and tail pieces to "Hudibras and the Champion Crowdero."

   28, *Wardour Street, London*, 1884.

PREFATORY NOTE BY THE EDITORS

Pending the completion of a more costly revised version of the late Mr. Hart's work, the editors, in compliance with what seems to be a widespread public desire, have decided to reprint the volume, as issued in popular form and finally corrected by the author in 1887, but with additions and certain emendations desirable in order to bring it into accord with the present state of knowledge, and to enhance its value as a work of reference. To this end the names of a considerable number of makers, either unknown at the time, or not deemed of sufficient prominence for insertion in the edition of 1887, have been incorporated in the text, together with particulars of the distinctive features of their work; and the notices relating to others have, where needful, been modified or recast. In other respects the book remains substantially as the author left it.

28 *Wardour Street*
    November, 1909.

SECTION I

The Early History of the Violin

1.

The early history of the Violin is involved in obscurity, and in consequence, much diversity of opinion exists with regard to it. The chief object of the writer of these pages is to throw light upon the instrument in its perfected state. It is, therefore, unnecessary to enter at great length upon the vexed question of its origin. The increased research attendant upon the development of musical history generally could hardly fail to discover facts of more or less importance relative to the origin of instruments played with a bow; but although our knowledge in this direction is both deeper and wider, the light shed upon the subject has not served to dissipate the darkness attending it. Certain parts have been illumined, and conclusions of more or less worth have been drawn therefrom; for the rest, all remains more hopelessly obscured and doubtful than the identity of the "Man in the Iron Mask" or the writer of the "Letters of Junius."

It is satisfactory to know that the most valuable and interesting part of our subject is comparatively free from that doubt and tradition which necessarily attaches to the portion belonging to the Dark or Middle Ages. When we reflect that Music—as we understand it—is a modern art, and that all instruments of the Viol and Fiddle type, as far as the end of the fifteenth century, were rude if not barbarous, it can scarcely excite surprise that our interest should with difficulty be awakened in subtle questions pertaining to the archæology of bowed instruments.

The views taken of the early history of the leading instrument have not been more multiform than remote. The Violin has been made to figure in history sacred and profane, and in lore classic and barbaric. That an instrument which is at once the most perfect and the most difficult, and withal the most beautiful and the most strangely interesting, should have been thus glorified, hardly admits of wonder. Enthusiasm is a noble passion, when tempered with reason. It cannot be said, however, that the necessity of this qualification has been invariably recognised by enthusiastic inquirers into the history of instruments played with a bow. We have a curious instance of its non-recognition in a treatise on the Viol,[1] written by a distinguished old French Violist named Jean Rousseau. The author, bent upon going to the root of his subject, begins with the Creation, and speaks of Adam as a Violist. Perhaps Rousseau based his belief in the existence of Fiddling at this early period of the world's history on the words "and his brother's name was Jubal; from him descended the Flute players and Fiddlers," as rendered by Luther.

    1 "Traité de la Viole," Paris, 1687.

The parts Orpheus and Apollo have been made to play in infantile Fiddle history have necessarily been dependent upon the licence and the imagination of the sculptor and the medallist. Inferences of antiquity, however, have been drawn from such representations. Tracings of a bow among the sculpture of the ancients have been sought for in vain: no piece is known upon which a bow is distinguishable. A century since, an important discovery was thought to have been made by musical antiquarians in the Grand Duke's Tribuna at Florence, wherein was a small figure of Apollo playing on a kind of Violin with something of the nature of a bow. Inquiry, however, made it clear that the figure belonged to modern art. Orpheus has been represented holding a Violin in one hand and a bow in the other; inquiry again showed that the Violin and the bow were added by the restorer of the statue.

The views held by musical historians regarding the origin of the Violin may be described by the terms Asiatic and Scandinavian. The Eastern view, it need scarcely be said, is the most prolonged, exceeding some five thousand years along the vista of time, where little else is discoverable but what is visionary, mythical, and unsubstantial. It is related—traditionally of course—that some three thousand years before our era there lived a King of Ceylon named Ravanon,[2] who invented a four-stringed instrument played with a bow, and which was named after the inventor "the Ravanastron." If it were possible to identify the instrument of that name, now known to the Hindoos, as identical with that of King Ravanon—as M. Sonnerat declares it to be—the Eastern view of our subject would be singularly clear and defined. A declaration, however, resting on tradition, necessarily makes the gathering of evidence in support of it a task both dubious and difficult.[3]

    2 M. Sonnerat, "Voyage aux Indes Orientales," 1806.

    3 In Mr. Engel's "Researches into the Early History of the Violin Family," 1883—a book containing much valuable evidence on the subject—the author rightly remarks: "Now, this may be true; still it is likewise true that most of the Asiatic nations are gifted with a remarkably powerful imagination, which evidently induces them sometimes to assign a fabulously high age to any antiquity of theirs the origin of which dates back to a period where history merges in myth. At the present day the Hindoos possess, among their numerous rude instruments of the Fiddle class, an extraordinarily primitive contrivance, which they believe to

> be the instrument invented by Ravanon. Their opinion has actually been adopted by some of our modern musical historians as if it were a well established truth."

It is said that Sanscrit scholars have met with names for the bow in Sanscrit writings dating back nearly two thousand years. If this information could be supplemented by reliable monumental evidence of the existence of a bow of some rude kind among the nations of the East about the commencement of the Christian era, its value would necessarily be complete. In the absence of such evidence we are left in doubt as to what was intended to be understood by the reported references to a bow in ancient Sanscrit literature. The difficulty of understanding what Greek and Roman authors meant, in reference to the same subject, must be greatly intensified in the works of ancient Eastern writers.[4]

> 4 In the "Reflections" at the end of Vol. I., "Burney's History of Music," we read, "The ancients had instead of a bow, the Plectrum." "It appears too clumsy to produce from the strings tones that had either the sweetness or brilliancy of such as are drawn from them by means of the bow or quill. But, notwithstanding it is represented so massive, I should rather suppose it to have been a quill, or piece of ivory in imitation of one, than a stick or blunt piece of wood or ivory."

The inquiry is simplified from the point of view of a Violinist if we reject all bow-progenitors but those which have been strung with fibre, silk, hair, or other material, the properties of which would permit of the production of sustained sounds. Implements less developed belong to a separate order of sound-producing contrivances, namely plectra, and may be described as permitting strumming by striking in place of twanging or twitching the strings. The imperfect knowledge we have of instruments of the Fiddle kind in Europe, belonging to a period many centuries later than that we are now considering, points to their having been struck or strummed, and not bowed with a view to the sounds being sustained.

The oldest known representation of a contrivance or instrument upon which a string is stretched with a peg to adjust its tension, is probably that described by Dr. Burney as having been seen by him at Rome on an Egyptian obelisk. In a notice of Claudius Ptolemeus, an Egyptian, who wrote upon harmonic sounds about the middle of the second century, we have an illustration of an instrument of a similar character to that found on the obelisk above noticed.[5] In all probability neither of these contrivances was intended to be used as a musical instrument further than for scientific purposes, as a means of testing the tension of strings and the division of the scale: in short, they were monochords and dichords.

5 Sir John Hawkins' History.

In following the Eastern branch of our subject, it is necessary to refer to the suggested Arabian origin of the Ribeca of the Italians and the Rebec of the French—a little bowed instrument, shaped like the half of a pear, and having therefore something of the character of the mandoline. We have early mention of this particular view of Violin history among the valuable and interesting manuscript notes of Sir John Hawkins.[6] The author states that the Rebab was taken to Spain by the Moors, "from whence it passed to Italy, and obtained the appellation of Ribeca." He also refers to a work entitled "Shaw's Travels," in which mention is made of the Rebeb or Rebab as an instrument common in the East in the eighteenth century. It is, however, upon turning to the dissertation on the invention and improvement of stringed instruments by John Gunn, published in 1793, that we first find a lucid account of Eastern influence in connection with bowed instruments.[7] The author refers to the monochord as the invention of the Arabians: he then says, "The early acquaintance which it is probable the Egyptians had of the science and practice of music, was the source whence the Arabians might derive their knowledge. There is a remarkable correspondence between the dichord of the Egyptians and an instrument of the like number of strings of the Arabians. This instrument was played with a bow, and was probably introduced into Europe by the Arabians of Spain, and well known from the Middle Ages down to the last century by the name of the Rebec; it had probably, on its first introduction, only two strings, as it still has among the Moors, and soon after had the number increased to three. Dr. Shaw, who had seen it, calls it a Violin with three strings, which is played on with a bow, and called by the Moors Rebebb." In passing it may be said that the translators of the Bible, historians, painters, and poets have in many instances contributed greatly to the confusion attending the history of bowed instruments from their inability to correctly name and depict corded instruments. About a century after the publication of Dr. Shaw's "Travels in the East," appeared Lane's "Modern Egypt," wherein reference is made to an instrument named Rebab. It is described as being made partly of parchment, and mounted with one or two strings, played on with a bow. These instruments appear to be identical. We do not usually look to the East for progressiveness, and would therefore not expect to discover much difference between a Rebab of the nineteenth century and one of the eighth century. In taking this view we may therefore assume that the existing Rebab has nearly all in common with its Eastern namesake of the eighth century. The rude and gross character of the instrument is remarkable, and renders any connection between it and the Rebec of Europe in the Middle Ages somewhat difficult to realise. Having no certain knowledge of the form of the ancient Rebab, our views regarding its connection with the Rebec must necessarily be speculative, and mainly dependent upon the etymological thread which is drawn between the words Rebec and Rebab. It is worthy of notice in relation to the opinion held by Sir John Hawkins and many other musical historians as to a bowed instrument of the Fiddle kind having been introduced into Spain from the East in the eighth century, that we possess no certain evidence of bowed instrument cultivation in Spain between the eighth and twelfth centuries, whilst we have proof of the use of bowed instruments both in Germany and in England within that period.[8] The evidence we have of the use of a description of Viol at that time, from the carvings on the Portico della Gloria of the Church of Santiago da Compostella, does not carry conviction that a bow was used, since none is represented.[9]

> 6 Hawkins' "History of Music" was published in the year 1776. The MS. notes, which are attached to the author's copy in the British Museum, were included in the edition published in 1853 by Novello & Co.
>
> 7 It may be remarked that nineteen years prior to the publication of John Gunn's dissertation was published the valuable work of Martinus Gerbertus, "De Cantu et Musicâ Sacrâ," dated 1774. The volumes of Gerbertus were evidently perused with care and attention by Gunn. The references of John Gunn to the work are the earliest I have met with.
>
> 8 Mention is made by Ash-Shakandi, who wrote on Moorish music in Spain in the thirteenth century, of the Rebab. If this instrument was not more developed than its modern namesake, we have evidence of the Saxons being in possession of bowed instruments infinitely superior at a much earlier date.
>
> 9 In "The Violin and its Music," 1881, page 50, I have assumed their use by the performers on the above mentioned arch, believing it not improbable that the use of the bow was introduced by the settlers in Spain from the North.

That the Spanish were influenced by their Moorish conquerors with regard to music, minstrelsy, and dancing is certain. The origin of such movements as the Saraband, the Morisca (or Morris dance), and the Chaconne,[10] has been traced to the East. That such dances should have been accompanied by instruments of Eastern origin of the Lute kind may be assumed. Both in

Spain and southern France accompanying instruments struck with plectra or twanged with the fingers were adopted at a very early period, and the people of those parts attained to a high state of proficiency—so much so indeed as to have rendered the cultivation of this description of music a national characteristic with them in the use of such instruments. The usage of the bow, however, does not appear to have been cultivated sufficiently, if at all, to leave its traces in history, until about the twelfth century, when the Troubadours sought the aid of the Trouvères and Jongleurs. The Trouvères were minstrel poets belonging to Northern France. The Jongleurs entertained their patrons with jests and arch sayings, and were often joined by the Gigeours of Germany, to accompany their lays with their Geigen and kindred instruments.

> 10 It need scarcely be said that the Eastern and Spanish ancestor of Bach's Chaconne was terpsichorean, and was unconnected with any kind of scientific musical treatment.

The foregoing remarks point to the absence of reliable evidence of the existence of a bow—worthy of the name from the point of view of a Violinist—among the Asiatic nations in the early centuries of our era. The Ravanastron of India, the Rebab of Arabia, and other stringed instruments used by the Persians and the Chinese, hardly admit of being looked upon as links in the genealogical Fiddle chain. Whatever the shape and use of ancient Eastern instruments—having something in common with the European Violin—may have been, the slight apparent affinity is accidental, and no real relationship exists between the European and the Asiatic Fiddle.[11]

> 11 Mr. Engel, "Researches into the Early History of the Violin Family," page 104, remarks: "It is rarely that the name of an Asiatic musical instrument can be traced to a European origin. There are, however, one or two instances in which this seems to be possible. Thus, the Chinese name Ye-Yia, by which they occasionally designate their Fiddle, may possibly be a corruption of *giga* or *geige*, considering that the common name of the Chinese Fiddle is Unheen, and that Macao, where this instrument is said to be called Ye-Yin, has been above three hundred years in the possession of the Portuguese, and in constant communication with European nations." This seems to deprive the argument of the Eastern origin of the Fiddle of weight, and favours the already strong evidence of Scandinavian origin centred in the word Geige.

2.

The survey of the early history of bowed instruments in the North of Europe necessarily discovers a broader field of ostensible data than is possible to be found in the Asiatic view of the subject. Tradition, accompanied by its attendant uncertainties, gives place to facts recorded in illuminated manuscripts of the Middle Ages, on sculptured stone, on engraved brasses, in the lay of the minstrel, in the song of the poet, and, finally, in the works of the painter and of the musician. The information obtainable from these several sources is often of the slightest kind, and admits of little else than a rude historical outline being drawn. The varied character of the evidence, however, serves in some instances to counterbalance the lack of detail.

Enquiry into the history of any science seldom fails to make us acquainted with men whose views and opinions were formulated prior to the production of well-digested evidence in favour of their premises—a condition of things resulting oftentimes in their judgments being post-dated, and their names in consequence severed from them; in short—

"Elder times have worn the same,
Though new ones get the name."

In relation to our subject, the Hon. Roger North, Attorney-General to King James the Second, occupies a position of the kind described. In his work entitled "Memoirs of Music," written in the early part of the eighteenth century, we have the ingenious author's views as to the source from whence sprung the progenitor of the long line of Fiddle and Viol. His treatment of the subject displays a truly commendable amount of skill and judgment, and more so when we consider the limited sources of information at his disposal in comparison with those at the service of subsequent musical authors. He says, "There is no hint where the Viol kind came first in use." "But as to the invention which is so perfectly novel as not to have been heard of before Augustulus, the last of the Roman Emperors, I cannot but esteem it perfectly Gothic." "I suppose that at first it was like its native country, rude and gross, and at the early importation it was of the lesser kind which they called Viola da Bracchia, and since the Violin." He concludes by expressing his belief that the Hebrews did not sound their "lutes and guitars with the scratch of an horse-tail bow." These opinions of Roger North are for the most part identical with those held by well-known promoters of the Northern view of our subject.[12]

> 12 Paul Lacroix remarks, in "The Arts of the Middle Ages": "Stringed instruments that were played on by means of bows were not known before the fifth century, and

belonged to the Northern races." Sir Gore Ouseley, in his English edition of Naumann's "History of Music," commenting upon the author's statement that "the Rebab was introduced by Arabs into Southern Europe, and may be the precursor of all our modern stringed instruments," says, "From this view I am compelled to dissent," and speaks in favour of the Northern origin. William Chappell, "Popular Music of the Olden Times," remarks: "I will not follow M. Fétis in his newly adopted Eastern theory of the bow. The only evidence he adduces is its present use in the East, and the primitive form of Eastern instruments." "I would ask how comes it that the bow was unknown to the Greeks and the Romans? Did not Alexander the Great conquer India and Persia? And were not those countries better known to the ancients than to the modern until within the last three hundred years? The Spaniards derived their instruments from the Moors, but the bow was not among them."

About fifty years later than the date of North's "Memoirs of Music" appeared the famous work of Martinus Gerbertus, entitled, "De Cantu et Musicâ Sacrâ." Among the valuable manuscripts referred to by the author is one which supplies the earliest known representation of a bow instrument of the Fiddle kind, and which may be accepted as a description of German Fiddle. The date of this particular manuscript has been ascribed by M. Fétis to the ninth century. It may possibly have belonged to an earlier period.[13]

> 13 As the manuscript was destroyed by the fire which burnt nearly the whole of the buildings, Abbey, Church, and Library of St. Blasius in the Black Forest in 1768, the language of Gerbertus, who examined the original manuscript, is worthy of some attention. After referring to certain plates, copied from a manuscript of the year 600, he says that "the other twenty-three representations on the following eighth plate" (in which is included the early German Fiddle) "are from a manuscript a *little more recent.*" Whether the period of three centuries named by M. Fétis can be considered recent is at least questionable. The information taken from this manuscript is of paramount importance, with reference to the Asiatic and Northern views of the origin of the Violin. The view taken by some authorities, that the Europeans received their earliest instructions in infantile Fiddling from the Moors, when they conquered Spain in the eighth century, is already

overclouded by the representation of a Fiddle and bow on this German Manuscript, even assuming it to be of the ninth century; but if its date be given prior to the appearance of the Moors in Europe, the Eastern view of the subject is naturally further darkened.

The instrument was described in the manuscript of St. Blasius as a Lyre. Gerbertus rightly observes that it has only one string, and is more like a Cheli.[14] He quotes writers of different epochs relative to the meaning of the word Lyre as used by them, the tendency of his remarks apparently being to establish a connection between the German Fiddle named a Lyre in the manuscript and the Rebec. The representation we have of the instrument certainly conveys the idea of its having been a progenitor of the Rebec of the French, the Ribeca of the Italians, and the Fithele and the Geige of the Germans. The mention of an instrument of the kind in a German manuscript, discovered in an ancient German monastery, together with the record being dated by Gerbertus as not far removed from the sixth century, lends much weight to the opinion of Roger North with regard to the part played by the Teutonic race in the early history of bowed instruments.

> 14 The ancient name of corded instruments of the Lute, Mandoline, and Guitar kinds. Tradition has it that the Nile, having overflowed Egypt, left on shore a dead *Cheli* (tortoise), the flesh of which being dried in the sun, nothing was left within the shell but nerves and cartilages, and these being braced and contracted were rendered sonorous. Mercury, in walking, struck his foot against the shell of the tortoise, and was delighted with the sound produced, which gave him the idea of a Lyre that he later constructed in the form of a tortoise, and strung with the dried sinews of dead animals. This account of the origin of Lutes, Fiddles, and catgut is classic and picturesque. Tradition and myth have played parts of much consequence in the work of civilisation: they have, however, at length fallen upon a critical and remarkably sceptical age, and rapidly fade and die under the inquisitorial torture of modern inquiry—a result at least to be expected from the contact of their own dreamy and delicate nature with unromantic matter. It is perhaps safer to refer the origin of the name Cheli or tortoise, as applied to corded instruments, to the fact of their having sound chambers, constructed with tortoise-shell, as was the case with the Greek Lyre, or to the circumstance of the bodies of the instruments being shaped like the tortoise. The Germans used the word Chelys to

designate their Viols; and Christopher Simpson, in his famous treatise on the "Viol da Gamba," names it Chelys. The application of the word Chelys to bowed instruments is suggestive of their remote connection with the ancient Lyre.

ANTONIO STRADIVARI VIOLA.
1672.

Plate I.

It is now necessary to refer to the well-known representation of a Saxon Fiddle contained in the Cottonian manuscripts in the British Museum. Strutt, in his "Sports and Pastimes," supplies us with a copy of the illustration, which is that of a juggler throwing balls and knives to the accompaniment of an instrument of the Fiddle kind. Strutt ascribes the manuscript to the tenth century. The form of this Fiddle is in advance of that supplied in the St. Blasius manuscript, there being four strings, but there is no bridge indicated, and, had there been, it would not have evidenced a Saxon knowledge of tuning the strings to given intervals, and playing upon each string. The little light which has been thrown on the condition of instrumental music at the time renders it doubtful whether any bowed instrument was used, other than for the purpose of rendering a rude extemporaneous accompaniment to the voice or the dance.

The chief authorities upon ancient minstrelsy agree that the Saxon's love of music was cultivated for centuries with ardour by his Saxon ancestors; it would therefore be reasonable to believe that his knowledge of rude Fiddles was derived from the land of his forefathers, and not from any instrument he discovered in Britain.[15] The similarity of the instrument of the St. Blasius manuscript and of that in the hands of the Saxon Gleeman in the Cottonian manuscript is evidence of Teutonic origin. It is, moreover, strengthened by the fact of the use of the word Fithele by the Anglo-Saxons for nearly two centuries after the Norman Conquest, which name was adopted with but little variation by the whole of the Teutonic race.[16] In Germany the word was used as late as the twelfth century. About this period the word Geige appears to have been applied in Germany to designate a Fiddle. It is described as an improved Rebec, and strung with three strings.[17] The use of the word Geige in Germany instead of Fithele in the twelfth century, is worthy of attention as bearing upon Teutonic origin. The earliest information we have of the use of the Geige in France is in connection with the Jongleurs. The Geige was popular in France until the fifteenth century, when, as M. Lacroix says, it disappeared, leaving its name "as the designation of a joyous dance, which for a considerable period was enlivened by the sound of the instrument." The word Geige, I am inclined to think, is important as furnishing evidence of historical value in relation to the ancestry of the Violin. Lacroix believes that Germany created the Geige; other authorities are of opinion that it originated among the people of Provence. The former view is supported by the strongest evidence. Some inquirers derive the word Geige from the French and Italian words for leg of mutton.[18] Wigand, however, supposes it to be derived from the old northern word *Geiga*, meaning trembling, or from *Gigel*, to quiver. If we consider the nature and character of the instrument, this view of the derivation of the word appears both ingenious and correct. Roger North shrewdly conjectured that the "rude and gross" Gothic Fiddle "used to stir up the vulgar to dancing, or perhaps to solemnise their idolatrous sacrifices." In the Dark Ages dancing may have been regarded as bi-pedal trembling. I have remarked in another place,[19] "In the early ages of mankind dancing or jigging must have been done to the sound of the voice, next to that of the pipe, and, when the bow was discovered, to that of a stringed instrument which was named the Geige from its primary association with dancing." The evidence we have of the use to which the leading instrument was put in the days of its adolescence is indicative of its having grown up among dancers, jugglers, and buffoons. In Germany its players gave fame and name to a distinct class of itinerant minstrels named the Gigeours, who were often associated with the Jongleurs in their perambulations. In France, from the days of the Jongleurs to those of Henry IV., and later to those of Louis XIV., the instrument was wedded to the dance. In England to the time of Charles II. it was in the hands of the Fiddler, who accompanied the jig, the hornpipe, the round, and the North Country frisk.

> 15 In Carl Engel's "Researches into the Early History of the Violin Family," 1883, the author disbelieves in the Crwth having been the lineal ancestor of the Violin, and there can be but little doubt of the correctness of his opinion.
>
> 16 It is worthy of remark that the Northmen, who invaded and gave their name to Normandy, carried from their Scandinavian homes a love of minstrelsy.
>
> 17 Sebastian Wirdung, a priest, published a work in 1511, in which he describes the bow instruments of his time by the names Gross-Geigen and Klein-Geigen. The illustration of the Klein-Geige differs but little from the Rebec; it has three strings, whilst the Gross-Geige has nine. Further information is supplied by the work of Martin Agricola, published in 1529.—*Mendel's German Musical Dictionary, article "Violine."*
>
> 18 "Almost all our musical writers state, as if it were a well-ascertained fact, that the German word Geige is derived from the *Gigue* of the French Minstrels, who, during the 13th and 14th centuries, had a sort of *Rebec* which they called by that name, and which, according to some commentators, resembled in outward appearance the shank of a goat or ram, called *Gigot*, and hence the origin of all the similar words occurring in different European languages. These commentators have, however, neglected to prove that the old French word Gigue occurs before the 13th century, or that it is earlier than the Middle High German Gige."—*Engel's "Researches into the History of the Violin Family."*
>
> 19 "The Violin and its Music," 1881, page 19.

In pursuing the course of our subject, our inquiries have hitherto been mainly concerned with the leading instrument in a barbarous and semi-barbarous state. We now reach what may be termed the transition stage of the question. The information relative to the appearance of the Geige, or Violin tuned in fifths, is of the slenderest kind. To obtain evidence of much worth it is necessary to reflect upon the condition of instrumental music about the sixteenth century, together with the form and character of bowed instruments belonging to the same period. The manners and customs of peoples have also to be considered. We have hitherto found the Geige or Fiddle among minstrels and itinerant musicians in countries where music and minstrelsy had become an institution with the people. The instrument was rude and gross, and its office was to play extemporaneous accompaniments, with considerable licence. At length domestic music began to be zealously cultivated in Germany and the Low Countries, to which important circumstance the rapid development of stringed instruments is traceable. Viols of various kinds supported the voices, and an important manufacture of such instruments took root in Nuremberg and other German cities. In following the history of the Madrigal much light is thrown upon that of the Viol, to which it is necessary to give attention in order to follow in some degree the development of the Violin.

The condition of music in Italy previous to the time when the father of the Madrigal, Adrian Willaert, followed in the steps of his countrymen and made Italy his home, presents a great contrast to the state of the art in Germany and the Netherlands about the same period. The love of music in these countries had been growing among the people from the days of their minstrel poets and their wandering musicians. In Italy minstrelsy received but little attention or encouragement. The effect of this was probably felt when that extraordinary love of culture and admiration for art manifested itself amid the courts of her princes, about the middle of the fifteenth century. The love of melody then, as now, was deeply rooted in the nature of her people. Musical composition, however, of a high order, and able executants, were to be found elsewhere, and in Flanders in particular, and there the principal music and musicians were sought by the Italian *dilettanti*. To this fortuitous combination of melody and musical learning we owe the greatest achievements in the art of music. Upon it was raised the work of Palestrina, Scarlatti, and Corelli, which their distinguished followers utilised with such judgment and effect. The progress and development of the Madrigal in Italy may be said to have been co-equal with that of the Viol, for which its music served, and to which the Italians gave the same beauty of form and exquisite refinement. The ingenuity and skilfulness of the early German Viol makers was not less speedily recognised by the Italians than was the learning and power manifested by the Flemish motet writers. The work of the Italians with regard to both the Madrigal and the Viol was artistic in the highest degree, and such as could alone have been accomplished by men nourished on the teachings of the Renaissance, and surrounded by its chief glories.

There is evidence of German influence over the Italian Viol manufacture at the end of the fifteenth century, in the German-sounding names of makers located in Italy, and likewise in the character and construction of the oldest Italian Viols: notably, there is the crescent-shaped sound-hole common to the German Grosse-Geige and Klein-Geige. The most ancient Viols in existence are those by Hieronymus Brensius of Bologna, two of which are in the Museum of the Academy of Music at Bologna, and a third is in my possession. They have labels printed in Roman letters, and doubtless belong to the end of the fifteenth century. These instruments serve to illustrate the condition of the art of Viol-making in Italy at that period. They are rude in form and workmanship, and present a marked contrast to the high artistic work associated with the Italians in other branches of industry. This rudeness is indicative of this particular manufacture being of recent importation, and of its having been received from Germany, and partly perhaps from the Low Countries, where instrumental music was cultivated chiefly by the people, in which case utility would naturally have priority of design and workmanship. With the introduction of Viols, in connection with the Madrigal, into the palaces of Italy, together with their increased use in connection with the service of the Church, a demand speedily arose for instruments of elegant design and finished workmanship, in keeping with the high standard raised by Italian artists in every direction. The work on the Viol by Silvestro Ganassi, published at Venice in 1543, furnishes us with ample proof of the advance made by the Italians in Viol-making since Brensius worked. We see from a representation of a Viol in the above-mentioned work that the sound-holes are better formed, the scroll is artistically designed, and the whole harmonious. These steps towards perfection were mounted by Duiffoprugcar and Gasparo da Salò, both of whom rapidly developed the art. With Gasparo da Salò, or a contemporary, was witnessed the rejection of the crescent-formed sound-hole, and the adoption of that which has held its own for upwards of three centuries. The sound-holes of the Amati and of Stradivari are but those of Gasparo and his contemporaries, marked with their own individuality. All Viols until about 1520 were furnished with pieces of gut tied round the neck and fingerboard to mark the divisions of the scale—in short, were fretted. From the work of Ganassi we learn that the use of these divisions was optional, thus supplying us with authentic information of considerable value with regard to the gradual emancipation of this class of instrument from frets, and foreshadowing the union of the Geige or Fiddle with the Viol. Passing to the question of form given by the Italians, early in the sixteenth century, to Viols, we find the Violono or Bass Viol with its upper and lower sides, middle bouts, belly, and sound-holes almost identical with those of the Tenor Viols, the chief difference being in the back of the latter, which is modelled, whilst the former is flat. This was the form given to the Violono by Gasparo da Salò, and which has been changed in the upper portion of the body of the instrument, to permit of modern passages being executed with greater facility. The original fingerboard was short, and generally fretted. The number of strings was five or more, and not as we now string them with three or four. It will be seen that this form of instrument gives us what Mr. Charles Reade describes as the invention of Italy, namely "the four corners."[20] The same author in speaking of the order of invention remarks that he is puzzled "to time the Violono, or as we childishly call it (after its known descendant) the Double Bass. If I were so presumptuous as to trust to my eye alone, I should say it was the first of them all." With this opinion I entirely agree, and I am also in unison with Mr. Reade in believing that the large Viola (played on or between the knees) was the next creation, the design of which was that of the Violono or Double Bass already referred to. The next and most important step was in all probability to make the common Geige or three-stringed Fiddle of the same shape as these Tenor and Contralto Viols, thus handing to us the present-shaped Violin. In the MS. notes of Lancetti, reference is made to a three-stringed Violin in the collection of Count Cozio di Salabue, which throws some light upon the question as to three-stringed Violins, of the form of the Italian Viola, having been made prior to the introduction of those with four strings tuned in fifths. The instrument to which Lancetti refers was dated 1546, and was attributed to Andrea Amati. Until the beginning of the present century, this instrument remained in its original condition, when it was altered by the Brothers Mantegazza of Milan into a Violin with four strings. Mention of this curious and valuable fact furnishes us with the sole record of a three-stringed Violin having been in existence during the nineteenth century, and also supplies the link needful to connect the old type of Fiddle with the perfect instrument of the great Italian makers. When or where the four-stringed Violin tuned in fifths first appeared in Italy is a question the answer to which must ever remain buried in the past. It may have seen the light in Mantua, Bologna, or Brescia. The last-mentioned town is usually associated with its advent, and to Gasparo da Salò is given the credit of its authorship.

> 20 "Cremona Violins," *Pall Mall Gazette*, 1872. This reference applies to the corners and corner-blocks as made by Gasparo and all makers to the present time, in contradistinction to those seen in the Viol da Gamba and early German Viols.

SECTION II

The Construction of the Violin

The construction of the present form of the Violin has occupied the attention of many scientific men. It cannot be denied that the subject possesses a charm sufficiently powerful to induce research, as endeavour is made to discover the causes for the vast superiority of the Violin of the seventeenth century over the many other forms of bow instruments which it has survived. The characteristic differences of the Violin have been obtained at the cost of many experiments in changing the outline and placing the sound-holes in various incongruous positions. These, and the many similar freaks of inventors in their search after perfection, have signally failed, a result to be expected when it is considered that the changes mentioned were unmeaning, and had nothing but novelty to recommend them. But what is far more extraordinary is the failure of the copyist, who, vainly supposing that he has truthfully followed the dimensions and general features of the Old Masters, at last discovers that he is quite unable to construct an instrument in any way deserving of comparison with the works of the period referred to. The Violin has thus hitherto baffled all attempts to force it into the "march of progress" which most things are destined to follow. It seems to scorn complication in its structure, and successfully holds its own in its simplicity. There is in the Violin, as perfected by the great Cremonese masters, a simplicity combined with elegance of design, which readily courts the attention of thoughtful minds, and gives to it an air of mystery that cannot be explained to those outside the Fiddle world. Few objects possess so charming a display of curved lines as the members of the Violin family. Here we have Hogarth's famous line of beauty worked to perfection in the upper bouts,[1] in the lower bouts, in the outer line of the scroll, in the sound-hole. Everywhere the perfection of the graceful curve is to be seen. It has been asserted by Hogarth's enemies that he borrowed the famous line from an Italian writer named Lomazzo, who introduced it in a treatise on the Fine Arts. We will be more charitable, and say that he obtained it from the contemplation of the beauties of a Cremonese Violin.

1 A technical term for the sides.

In looking at a Violin we are struck with admiration at a sight of consummate order and grace; but it is the grace of nature rather than of mechanical art. The flow of curved lines which the eye detects upon its varied surface, one leading to another, and all duly proportioned to the whole figure, may remind us of the winding of a gentle stream, or the twine of tendrils in the trellised vine.

Often is the question asked, What can there be in a simple Violin to attract so much notice? What is it that causes men to treat this instrument as no other, to view it as an art picture, to dilate upon its form, colour, and date? To the uninitiated such devotion appears to be a species of monomania, and attributable to a desire of singularity. It needs but little to show the inaccuracy of such hypotheses. In the first place, the true study of the Violin is a taste which needs as much cultivation as a taste for poetry or any other art, a due appreciation of which is impossible without such cultivation. Secondly, it needs, equally with these arts, in order to produce proficiency, that spark commonly known as *genius*, without which, cultivation, strictly speaking, is impossible, there being nothing to cultivate. We find that the most ardent admiration for the Violin regarded as a work of art, has ever been found to emanate from those who possessed tastes for kindred arts. Painters, musicians, and men of refined minds have generally been foremost among the admirers of the Violin. Much interest attaches to it from the fact of its being the sole instrument incapable of improvement, whether in form or in any other material feature. The only difference between the Violin of the sixteenth century and that of the nineteenth lies in the arrangement of the sound-bar (which is now longer, in order to bear the increased pressure caused by the diapason being higher than in former times), and the comparatively longer neck, so ordered to obtain increased length of string. These variations can scarcely be regarded as inventions, but simply as arrangements. The object of them was the need of adapting the instrument to modern requirements, so that it might be used in concert with others that have been improved, and allow the diapason to be raised. Lastly, it must be said that, above all, the Violin awakens the interest of its admirers by the tones which it can be made to utter in the hands of a skilful performer. It is, without doubt, marvellous that such sounds should be derivable from so small and simple-looking an instrument. Its expressiveness, power, and the extraordinary combinations which its stringing admits of, truly constitute it the king of musical instruments. These somewhat desultory remarks may suffice to trace the origin of the value set upon the Violin both as a work of art and as a musical instrument.

We will now proceed to consider the acoustical properties of the Violin. These are, in every particular, surprisingly great, and are the results of many tests, the chief of which has been the adoption of several varieties of wood in its construction. In Brescia, which was in all probability the cradle of Violin manufacture, the selection of the material of the sides and back from the pear, lemon, and ash trees was very general, and there is every reason to believe that Brescia was the first place where such woods were used. It is possible that the makers who chose them for the sides and backs of their instruments considered it desirable to have material more akin to that adopted for the bellies, which was the finest description of pine, and that the result was found to be a tone of great mellowness. If they used these woods with this intention, their calculations were undoubtedly correct. They appear to have worked these woods with but few exceptions for their Tenors, Violoncellos, and Double Basses, while they adopted the harder woods for their Violins, all which facts tend to show that these rare old makers did not consider soft wood eligible for the back and sides of the leading instrument; and later experiment has shown them to have arrived at a correct conclusion on this point. The experiments necessary to obtain these results have been effected by cutting woods of several kinds and qualities into various sizes, so as to give the sounds of the diatonic scale. By comparing the intensity and quality of tone produced by each sample of wood, plane-tree[2] and sycamore have been found to surpass the rest. The Cremonese makers seem to have adhered chiefly to the use of maple, varying the manner of cutting it. First, they made the back in one piece, technically known as a "whole back"; secondly, the back in two parts; thirdly, the cutting known as the "slab back." There being considerable doubt as to the mode of dividing the timber, the woodcuts given will assist the reader to understand it. Fig. 1 represents the cutting for the back in two pieces—the piece which is separated from the log is divided. Fig. 2 shows the method adopted to obtain the slab form.

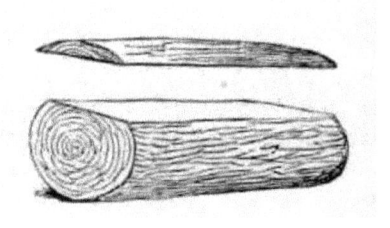

FIG. 1.   FIG. 2.

2 The Germans call the plane-tree *morgenländischer ahorn*— *i.e.*, "oriental maple." From the German word *ahorn* is probably derived the term "air wood," often corrupted into "hair-wood." Thomas Mace says, respecting the lute, "the air-wood is absolutely the best, and next to that our English maple."—*Engel* ("Researches into the Early History of the Violin Family").

JACOBUS STAINER.
Date 1669.

GIUSEPPE GUARNERI DEL GESÙ.
(THE "VIEUXTEMPS.")

NICCOLÒ AMATI.
Grand Pattern. Date 1641.
(J. S. COOKE, ESQ.)

Plate II.

This mode of cutting is constantly met with in the works of the Brescian makers, and likewise in those of the early Cremonese. Andrea Amati invariably adopted this form. Stradivari rarely cut his wood slab-form. Joseph Guarneri made a few Violins of his best epoch with this cutting, the varnish on which is of an exquisite orange colour, so transparent that the curls of the wood beneath resemble richly illuminated clouds.

There can be no doubt whatever that the Cremonese and Brescian makers were exceedingly choice in the selection of their material, and their discrimination in this particular does not appear to have risen so much from a regard to the beauty as to the acoustic properties of the wood, to which they very properly gave the first place in their consideration. We have evidence of much weight upon this interesting question in the frequent piecings found on the works of Cremona makers, pointing to a seeming preference on their part to retain a piece of wood of known acoustic properties rather than to work in a larger or better preserved portion at the probable expense of tone. The time and care required for such a delicate operation must have been sufficient to have enabled the maker, had he been so minded, to have made a complete instrument. There is also ample proof that Joseph Guarneri possessed wood to the exceptional qualities of which he was fully alive, and the same may be said of Stradivari, Ruggeri, and others. It is scarcely reasonable to suppose that in the seventeenth century there was a dearth in Italy of timber suitable for the manufacture of Violins, and that in consequence these eminent makers were compelled to patch and join their material to suit their purpose. They were men who were in the enjoyment of a patronage certainly sufficient to enable them to follow their calling without privation of any kind. Scarcity of pine and sycamore, good or bad, could not have been the cause, since we find Italian cabinet-work of great beauty that was manufactured at this same period. The plane-tree and pine used by the Amati, Stradivari, and the chief masters in Italy, was usually of foreign growth, and was taken from the Tyrol and Istria. Its value was, therefore, in advance of Italian wood, but hardly so much as to place it beyond the reach of the Cremonese masters. It is, further, improbable that these masters of the art should have expended such marvellous care and toil over their work, pieced as it frequently was like mosaic, when for a trifling sum they could have avoided such a task to their ingenuity by purchasing fresh wood. We are therefore forced to admit that there must have been some cause of great weight which induced them to apply so much time and labour, and that the problem can only be accounted for by the solution before proposed, viz., that external appearance was of less importance than the possession of acoustic properties thoroughly adapted to the old makers' purpose, and that the scarcity of suitable wood was such as to make them hoard and make use of every particle. The selection of material was hence considered to be of prime importance by these makers; and by careful study they brought it to a state of great perfection. The knowledge they gained of this vital branch of their art is enveloped in a similar obscurity to that which conceals their famous varnish, and in these branches of Violin manufacture rests the secret of the Italian success, and until it is rediscovered the Cremonese will remain unequalled in the manufacture of Violins.

We may now pass to the consideration of the various constituent parts of a Violin. It will be found, if a Violin be taken to pieces, that it is constructed of no less than fifty-eight separate parts, an astonishing number of factors for so small and simple-looking an instrument. The back is made of maple or sycamore, in one or two parts; the belly of the finest quality of Swiss pine, and from a piece usually divided; the sides, like the back, of maple, in six pieces, bent to the required form by means of a heated iron; the linings, which are used to secure the back and belly to the sides, are twelve in number, sometimes made of lime-tree, but also of pine. The bass or sound-bar is of pine, placed under the left foot of the bridge in a slightly oblique position, in order to facilitate the vibrating by giving about the same position as the line of the strings. The divergence is usually one-twelfth of an inch, throughout its entire length of ten inches. It is curious to discover that this system of placing the bar was adopted by Brensius of Bologna, a Viol-maker of the fifteenth century, and by Gasparo da Salò. The later Violin-makers, however, for the most part, do not appear to have followed the example, they having placed it in a straight line, thus leaving the system to be re-discovered. The bar of the Violin not only serves the purpose of strengthening the instrument in that part where the pressure of the bridge is greatest, but forms a portion of the structure at once curious and deeply interesting; it may indeed be called the nervous system of the Violin, so exquisitely sensitive is it to external touch. The slightest alteration in its position will effect such changes in the tone as often to make a good Violin worthless. Those troublesome notes technically known as "wolf notes" by its delicate adjustment are sometimes removed, or passed to intervals where the disagreeable sound is felt with less intensity. Numerous attempts have been made to reduce these features to a philosophy, but the realisation of the coveted discovery appears as distant as ever. The most minute variation in the construction of the instrument necessitates a different treatment of this active agent as regards its conjunction with the bridge; and when it is considered that scarcely two Violins can be found of exactly identical structure, it must be admitted that the difficulties in the way of laying down any set of hard and fast rules for their regulation seem to be insuperable.

The next important feature of the internal organism is the sound-post, which serves many purposes. It is the medium by which the vibratory powers of the instrument are set in motion; it gives support to the right side of the belly, it transmits vibrations, and regulates both the power and quality of tone. The terms used for this vital factor of a Violin on the Continent at once prove its importance. The Italians and French call it the "Soul," and the Germans the "Voice." If we accept the bass-bar as the nervous system of a Violin, the sound-post may be said to perform the functions of the heart with unerring regularity. The pulsations of sound are regulated by this admirable contrivance. If mellowness of quality be sought, a slight alteration of its position or form will produce a favourable change of singular extent; if intensity of tone be requisite, the sound-post is again the regulator. It must, of course, be understood that its power of changing the quality of the tone is limited in proportion to the constitutional powers of the instrument in each case. It is not pretended that a badly constructed instrument can be made a good one by means of this subtle regulator, any more than a naturally weak person can be made robust by diet and hygiene.

The position of the sound-post is usually one-eighth to three-eighths of an inch behind the right foot of the bridge, the distance being variable according to the model of the instrument. If the Violin be high-built, the post requires to be nearer the bridge, that its action may be stronger; whilst flat-modelled instruments require that the post be set further away from the bridge. It is not possible to have any uniform arrangement of the sound-post in all instruments; as we have remarked before in reference to the bass-bar, the variations in the thickness, outline, model, &c., of the Violin are so frequent as to defy identity of treatment; uniformity has been sought for, but without success.

The post can only be adjusted by a skilful workman, who either plays himself or has the advantage of having the various adjustments tested by a performer. The necessity of leaving this exceedingly delicate matter in practised hands cannot be too strongly impressed upon the amateur, for the damage done in consequence of want of skill is often irreparable.

There are two methods of setting the sound-post in the instrument: the first fixes it in such a position as to place the grain of the post parallel with the grain of the belly; the second sets it crosswise.

The next important feature to be mentioned is the bridge, which forms no small part of the vibrating mechanism of the instrument, and needs the utmost skill in its arrangement. Its usual position is exactly between the two small niches marked in each sound-hole, but this arrangement is sometimes altered in the case of the stop being longer or shorter. Many forms of bridges have been in use at different periods, but that now adopted is, without doubt, the best. In selecting a bridge great care is requisite that the wood be suitable to the constitution of the Violin. If the instrument is wanting in brilliancy, a bridge having solidity of fibre is necessary; if wanting in mellowness, one possessing soft qualities should be selected.

We now pass to the neck of the Violin, which is made of sycamore or plane-tree. Its length has been increased since the days of the great Italian masters, who seem to have paid but little attention to this portion of the instrument, in regard to its appearance and as to the wood used for its manufacture, which was of the plainest description. It may be observed that in those times the florid passages which we now hear in Violin music were in their infancy, the first and second positions being those chiefly used; hence the little attention paid to the handle of the instrument. Modern requirements have made it imperative that the neck should be well shaped, neither too flat nor too round, but of a happy medium. The difficulties of execution are sensibly lessened when due attention is paid to this requirement.

The finger-board is of ebony, and varies a little in length according to the position of the sound-holes. To form the board properly is a delicate operation, for if it be not carefully made the strings jar against it, and the movements of the bow are impeded. The nut, or rest, is that small piece of ebony over which the strings pass on the finger-board.

The purfling is composed of three strips of lime-tree, two of which are stained black. Whalebone purfling has been frequently used, particularly by the old Amsterdam makers.

The principal parts of the instrument have now been described, and there remain only the pegs, blocks, strings, and tail-piece, the sum of which makes up the number of fifty-eight constituent parts as before mentioned. There is still, however, one item of the construction to be mentioned which does not form a separate portion of the Violin, but which is certainly worthy of notice, viz., the button, which is that small piece of wood against which the heel of the neck rests. The difficulty of making this apparently insignificant piece can only be understood by those who have gone through the various stages of Violin manufacture. The amount of finish given to the button affects in a great measure the whole instrument, and if there is any defect of style it is sure to be apparent here. It is a prominent feature, and the eye naturally rests upon it: as the key-stone to the arch, so is the button to the Violin.

The sound-holes, or *f*-holes, it is almost needless to remark, are features of vital importance. Upon the form given to them, and the manner of cutting them, largely depend the volume and quality of tone. The Italian makers of Brescia and Cremona appear to have been aware of the singular influence the formation of the sound-hole has upon the production and quality of sound. The variety of original shapes they gave to them is evidence of their knowledge. Appearance in keeping with the outline of their design may have influenced them in some measure, but not entirely. Most makers used patterns from which to cut their sound-holes; Joseph Guarneri and some others appear to have drawn them on the belly, and cut them accordingly.

From the foregoing remarks upon the various portions of the Violin it may be assumed that the reader has gained sufficient insight into the process of its manufacture to enable him to dispense with a more minute description of each stage.

In conclusion, I cannot refrain from cautioning possessors of good instruments against entrusting them into the barbaric hands of pretended repairers, who endeavour to persuade them into the belief that it is necessary to do this, that, and the other for their benefit. The quack doctors of the Violin are legion—they are found in every town and city, ready to prey upon the credulity of the lovers of Fiddles, and the injury they inflict on their helpless patients is frequently irreparable. Unfortunately, amateurs are often prone to be continually unsettling their instruments by trying different bars, sound-posts, &c., without considering the danger they run of damaging their property instead of improving it. Should your instrument need any alteration, no matter how slight, consult only those who have made the subject a special study. There are a few such men to be found in the chief cities of Europe, men whose love for the instrument is of such a nature that it would not permit them to recommend alterations prejudicial to its well-being.

SECTION III

Italian and other Strings

Upon the strings of the Violin depends in a great measure the successful regulation of the instrument. If, after the careful adjustment of bridge, sound-post, and bass-bar, strings are added which have not been selected with due care and regard to their relative proportion, the labour expended upon the important parts named is at once rendered useless. Frequently the strings are the objects least considered when the regulation of a Violin is attempted; but if this be the case, results anything but satisfactory ensue. It is, therefore, important that every Violinist should endeavour to make himself acquainted with the different varieties and powers of strings, that he may arrange his instrument with due facility.

The remarkable conservatism attending the structural formation of the Violin exists more or less in the appliances necessary for the awakening of its dormant music. If we turn to its pegs, we find them of the same character as the peg of its far-removed ancestor, the monochord; and if we compare the Italian peg of the seventeenth century with a modern one, the chief difference lies in the latter being more gross and ugly. Upon turning to the bridge, we see that the bridge of to-day is almost identical with the bridge of Stradivari; and when we come to the strings of the Violin, we discover that we have added but little, if anything, to the store of information regarding them possessed by our forefathers.

In, perhaps, the earliest book on the Lute, that of Adrian Le Roy, published in Paris in 1570, and translated into English in 1574,[1] we read: "I will not omit to give you to understand how to know strings." "It is needful to prove them between the hands in the manner set forth in the figures hereafter pictured, which show on the finger and to the eye the difference from the true with the false." The instructions here given, it will be seen, are those set forth by Louis Spohr in his "Violin School." In the famous musical work of Merseene, published in 1648, we find an interesting account of strings; he says they are of "metal, and the intestines of sheep." "The thicker chords of the great Viols and of Lutes are made of thirty or forty single intestines, and the best are made in Rome and some other cities in Italy. This superiority is owing to the air, the water, or the herbage on which the sheep of Italy feed." He adds that "chords may be made of silk, flax, or other material," but that "animal chords are far the best." The experience of upwards of two centuries has not shaken the soundness of Merseene's opinion of the superiority of gut strings over those made of silk and steel. Although strings of steel and silk are made to some extent on account of their durability and their fitness for warm climates, no Violinist familiar with the true quality of tone belonging to his instrument is likely to torture his ears with the sound of strings made with thread or iron. Continuing our inquiries among the old musical writers in reference to the subject of strings, we find Doni says in his musical treatise, published in 1647: "There are many particulars relating to the construction of instruments which are unknown to modern artificers, as, namely, that the best strings are made when the north and the worst when the south wind blows," a truism well understood by experienced string manufacturers. Thomas Mace, in his curious book on the Lute, enters at some length into the question of strings, and speaks in glowing terms of his *Venetian Catlins*. The above references to strings, met with in the writers of the sixteenth and seventeenth centuries, indicate a full knowledge of the most important facts concerning them on the part of the musicians and makers of those days; and notwithstanding our superior mechanical contrivances in the manufacture, it is doubtful whether modern strings are generally equal to those made in times when leisure waited on quality, in lieu of speed on quantity.

> 1 Fétis, in his notice of Le Roy, states that the first edition of this rare book was published in 1557, and was translated by J. Alford into English in 1568.

Musical strings are manufactured in Italy, Germany, France, and England. The Italians rank first, as in past times, in this manufacture, their proficiency being evident in the three chief requisites for string, viz., high finish, great durability, and purity of sound. There are manufactories at Rome, Naples, Padua, and Verona, the separate characteristics of which are definitely marked in their produce. Those strings which are manufactured at Rome are exceedingly hard and brilliant, and exhibit a slight roughness of finish. The Neapolitan samples are smoother and softer than the Roman, and also whiter in appearance. Those of Padua are highly polished and durable, but frequently false. The Veronese strings are softer than the Paduan, and deeper in colour. The variations described are distinct, and the more remarkable that all the four kinds are produced by one and the same nation; as, however, the raw material is identical throughout Italy, the process of manufacture must be looked upon as the real cause of the difference noticed. The German strings now rank next to the Italian, Saxony being the seat of manufacture. They may be described as very white and smooth, the better kinds being very durable. Their chief fault arises from their being over-bleached, and hence faulty in sound. The French take the third place in the manufacture. Their strings are carefully made, and those of the larger sizes answer well; but the smaller strings are wanting in durability. The English manufacture all qualities, but chiefly the cheaper kinds; they are durable, but unevenly made, and have a dark appearance.

The cause of variation in quality of the several kinds enumerated arises simply from the difference of climate. In Italy an important part of the manufacture is carried on in the open air, and the beautiful climate is made to effect that which has to be done artificially in other countries. Hence the Italian superiority. Southern Germany adopts, to some extent, similar means in making strings; France, to a less degree; while England is obliged to rely solely on artificial processes. It therefore amounts to this—the further from Italy the seat of manufacture, the more inferior the string.

From the foregoing references we find that strings, although called "catgut," are not made from the intestines of that domestic animal. Whether they were originally so made, and hence derive their name, it is impossible to learn. Marston, the old dramatist, says:

> "How the musicians
> Hover with nimble sticks o'er squeaking Crowds,[2]
> Tickling the dried guts of a mewing cat."

We may be sure, however, that had the raw material been drawn from that source up to the present time, there would have been no need to check the supply of the feline race by destroying nine kittens out of ten; on the contrary, the rearing of cats would indeed have been a lucrative occupation. A time-honoured error is thus commemorated in a word, the origin of which must be ascribed to want of thought. If the number of cats requisite for the string manufacture be considered for a moment, it is easy to see that Shylock's "harmless necessary" domestics are under no contribution in this matter. Strings are made from the intestines of the sheep and goat, chiefly of the former. The best qualities are made from the intestines of the lamb, the strength of which is very great if compared with those of a sheep more than a year old. This being so, the chief manufacture of the year is carried on in the month of September, the September string-makings being analogous to October brewings. The demand for strings made at this particular season far exceeds the supply, and notably is this the case with regard to strings of small size, which have to bear so great a strain that if they were not made of the best material there would be little chance of their endurance. To enter into a description of the various processes of the manufacture is unnecessary, as it would form a subject of little interest to the general reader; we may therefore conclude this brief notice of strings by a few rules to be observed in their selection.

    2 The old English name for a Fiddle.

Endeavour to obtain strings of uniform thickness throughout, a requisite which can only be insured by careful gauging. In selecting the E string, choose those that are most transparent; the seconds and thirds, as they are made with several threads, are seldom very clear. The firsts never have more than a few threads in them, and hence, absence of transparency in their case denotes inferior material. Before putting on the first string, in particular, in order to test its purity it will be well to follow Le Roy's advice, which is to hold between the fingers of each hand a portion of the string sufficient to stretch from the bridge to the nut, and to set it in vibration. If two lines only be apparent, the string is free from falseness; but if a third line be produced, the contrary conclusion must be assumed. In the case of seconds and thirds we cannot always rely on this test, as the number of threads used in their manufacture frequently prevents the line from being perfectly clear. The last precaution of moment is to secure perfect fifths, which can only be done by taking care that the four strings are in true proportion and uniform with each other. To string a violin correctly is a very difficult undertaking, and requires considerable patience. The first consideration should be the constitution of the Violin: the strings that please one instrument torture another. Neither Cremonese Violins nor old instruments in general require to be heavily strung: the mellowness of the wood and their delicate construction require the stringing to be such as will assist in bringing out that richness of tone which belongs to first-rate instruments. If the bridge and sound-board be heavily weighted with thick strings, vibration will surely be checked. In the case of modern instruments, heavy in wood, and needing constant use to wear down their freshness, strings of a larger size may be used with advantage, and particularly when such instruments are in use for orchestral purposes.

VIOLONCELLO BY ANTONIO STRADIVARI.
PRESENTED TO SIGNOR PIATTI BY GENERAL OLIVER.
(Herr Robert Mendelssohn.)

Plate III.

Vast improvements have been effected in the stringing of Violins within the last thirty years. Strings of immense size were used alike on Violins, Violoncellos, Tenors, and Double Basses. Robert Lindley, the king of English Violoncellists, used a string for his first very nearly equal in size to the second of the present time, and the same robust proportion was observed in his other strings. The Violoncello upon which he played was by Forster, and would bear much heavier stringing than an Italian instrument; and, again, he was a most forcible player, and his power of fingering quite exceptional.

Dragonetti, the famous Double-Bass player, and coadjutor of Lindley, possessed similar powers, and used similar strings as regards size. Their system of stringing was adopted indiscriminately. Instruments whether weakly or strongly built received uniform treatment, the result being in many cases an entire collapse, and the most disappointing effects in tone. It was vainly supposed that the ponderous strings of Dragonetti and Lindley were the talisman by use of which their tone would follow as a matter of course, whereas in point of fact it was scarcely possible to make the instruments utter a sound when deprived of the singular muscular power possessed by those famous players. After Lindley's death his system passed away gradually, and attention was directed to the better adaptation of strings to the instrument, and also to the production of perfect fifths.

We have now only to speak of covered strings, in which it is more difficult to obtain perfection than in the case of those of gut. There are several kinds of covered strings. There are those of silver wire, which are very durable, and have a soft quality of sound very suitable to old instruments, and are therefore much used by artistes; there are those of copper plated with silver, and also of copper without plating, which have a powerful sound; and, lastly, there are those which are made with mixed wire, an arrangement which prevents in a measure the tendency to rise in pitch, a disadvantage common to covered strings and caused by expansion of the metals; these strings also possess a tone which is a combination of that produced by silver and copper strings. Here again, however, great discrimination is needed, viz., before putting on the fourth string. The instrument must be understood. There are Violins which will take none but fourths of copper, there are others that would be simply crippled by their adoption. It cannot be too much impressed upon the mind of the player that the Violin requires deep and patient study with regard to every point connected with its regulation. So varied are these instruments in construction and constitution, that before their powers can be successfully developed they must be humoured, and treated as the child of a skilful educator, who watches to gain an insight into the character of his charge, and then adopts the best means for its advancement according to the circumstances ascertained.

The strain and pressure of the strings upon a Violin being an interesting subject of inquiry, I give the annexed particulars (*see* Table below) from experiments made in conjunction with a friend interested in the subject, and possessed of the necessary knowledge to arrive at accurate results.

The Violin being held in a frame in a nearly upright position, so that the string hung just clear of the nut to avoid friction, the note was obtained by pressing the string to the nut.

When the Violin was laid in a horizontal position, and the string passed over a small pulley, an additional weight of two or three pounds was required to overcome the friction on the nut and that of the pulley. Therefore it is probable that the difference in the results obtained by other experiments may have arisen from the different methods employed. But with a dead weight hung on the end of each string there could be no error.

TENSION OF VIOLIN STRINGS.
Ascertained by Hanging a Dead Weight on the End of the String.

Number of the String	SIZE.	Tension, in lbs Weight, hung on the end of the String to bring it to Concert Pitch.	Downward Pressure on the Bridge.	Downward Pressure on the Treble Foot of the Bridge.	Downward Pressure on the Bass Foot of the Bridge.
		lb.	lb. oz.	lb. oz.	lb. oz.
1st	Thick ...	23	10 3¼	10 3¼	—
,,	Medium	22	9 12	9 12	—
,,	Small ...	18	8 0	8 0	—
2nd	Thick ...	15½	6 14	4 9½	2 4½
,,	Medium	15¼	6 11¼	4 7¼	2 4
,,	Small ...	13½	6 0	4 0	2 0
3rd	Thick ...	13¼	5 14	1 15¼	3 14¾
,,	Medium	12¾	5 10½	1 13¾	3 12¾
,,	Small ...	11	4 14	1 10	3 4
4th	Thick ...	11	4 14	—	4 14
,,	Medium	10½	4 10½	—	4 10½
,,	Small ...	Say 10	4 7	—	4 7
The total of four thick strings is ...		62¾	27 13¼	16 12	11 1¼
The total of four small strings is ...		52½	23 5	13 10	9 11

B A C is the average angle formed by a string passing over the bridge of a Violin, and the tension acts equally in the direction A B, A C.

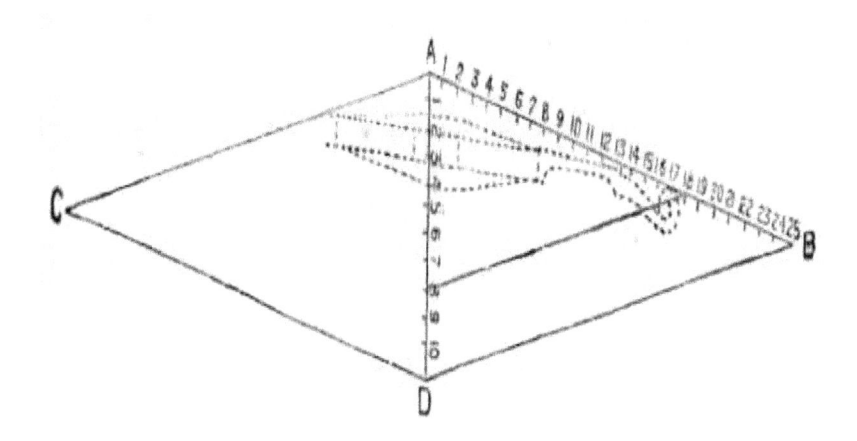

Take A C = A B.

From the point B draw B D parallel to A C. And from the point C draw C D parallel to A B, cutting B D at D.

Join A D.

Then, if a force acting on the point A, in the direction of A B, be represented in magnitude by the line A B, an equal force acting in the direction A C will be represented by the line A C, and the diagonal A D will represent the direction and magnitude of the force acting on the point A, to keep it at rest.

N.B.—The bridge of a Violin does not divide the angle B A C quite equally, but so nearly that A D may be taken as the position of the bridge.

Also, the plane passing through the string of a Violin, on both sides of the bridge, is not quite perpendicular to the belly. To introduce this variation into the calculation would render that less simple, and it will be sufficient to state that about the 150th part must be deducted from the downward pressures given in the above table from the first and fourth strings, and about the 300th part for the second and third strings. The total to be deducted for the four strings will not exceed three ounces.

On the line A B or A C set off a scale of equal parts, beginning at A, and on A D a similar scale beginning at A.

Mark off on the scale A B as many divisions as there are lbs. in the tension of a string, for example 18, and from that point draw a line parallel to B D, cutting A D at the point 8 in that scale. Then, if the tension of a string be 18 lb., the downward pressure on the bridge will be 8 lb.; and therefore for the above angle the downward pressure of any string on the bridge will be 8/18=4/9 of the tension of that string.

The whole of the downward pressure of the first string falls upon the Treble Foot of the Bridge.

The downward pressure of the second string is about 2/3 the Treble Foot of the Bridge, and 1/3 on the Bass Foot.

The downward pressure of the third string is about 1/3 on the Treble Foot, and 2/3 on the Bass Foot.

The whole of the downward pressure of the fourth string falls upon the Bass Foot of the Bridge.

SECTION IV

The Italian School

The fifteenth century may be considered as the period when the art of making instruments of the Viol class took root in Italy, a period rich in men labouring in the cause of Art. The long list of honoured names connected with Art in Italy during the fifteenth, sixteenth, and seventeenth centuries is a mighty roll-call indeed! The memory dwells upon the number of richly-stored minds that have, within the limits of these three centuries, bequeathed their art treasures to all time; and if here we cannot suppress a comparison of the art world of the present Italy with that of the periods named, still less can we fail to be astonished as we discover the abyss into which Italy must be judged to have sunk in point of merit, when measured by the high standard which in former days she set herself. But perhaps the greatest marvel of all is the rapidity of the decadence when it once set in, as it did immediately after the culminating point of artistic fame had been reached.

To reflect for a moment upon the many famous men in Italy engaged in artistic vocations contemporary with the great Viol and Violin makers cannot fail to be interesting to the lovers of our instrument, for it has the effect of surrounding their favourite with an interest extending beyond its own path. It also serves to make prominent the curious fact that the art of Italian Violin-making emerged from its chrysalis state when the painters of Italy displayed their greatest strength of genius, and perfected itself when the Fine Arts of Italy were cast in comparative darkness. It is both interesting and remarkable that the art of Italian Violin-making—which in its infancy shared with all the arts the advantage attending the revival of art and learning—should have been the last to mature and die.

Whilst the artist, scientist, and musician, Leonardo da Vinci, was painting, inventing, and singing his sonnets to the accompaniment of his Lute; whilst Raphael was executing the commands of Leo X., and Giorgio was superintending the manufacture of his inimitable majolica ware, the Viol-makers of Bologna were designing their instruments and assimilating them to the registers of the human voice, in order that the parts of Church and chamber madrigals might be played instead of sung, or that the voices might be sustained by the instruments.[1]

> 1 The importance of this epoch in its bearings upon instrumental music generally, and stringed instrument music in particular, can hardly be over-estimated. It may be said that in the Middle Ages no written music for

instruments existed. The melodies and accompaniments produced from instruments were either extemporaneous or parrot-like imitations of vocal music. Madrigals and a few dances constituted the food upon which instruments were nursed until towards the close of the sixteenth century, when Gabrielli, or a contemporary musician, prepared a special and distinct aliment, the outcome of which is found in the symphonies of Haydn, Mozart, and Beethoven.

If we turn to the days of Gasparo da Salò, Maggini, and Andrea Amati, we find that while they were sending forth their Fiddles, Titian was painting his immortal works, and Benvenuto Cellini, the greatest goldsmith of his own or any age, was setting the jewels of popes and princes, and enamelling the bindings of their books. Whilst the master-minds of Antonio Stradivari and Giuseppe Guarneri del Gesù were occupied with those instruments which have caused their names to be known throughout the civilised world (and *un*civilised too, for many thousands of Violins are yearly made into which their cherished names are thrust, after which they are despatched for the negro's use), Canaletto was painting his Venetian squares and canals, Venetians whose names are unrecorded were blowing glass of wondrous form and beauty. At the same time, in the musical world, Corelli was writing his jigs and sarabands, Geminiani penning one of the first instruction books for the Violin, and Tartini dreaming his "Sonata del Diavolo"; and while Guadagnini and the stars of lesser magnitude were exercising their calling, Viotti, the originator of a school of Violin-playing, was writing his concertos, and Boccherini laying the foundation of classical chamber-music of a light and pleasing character. It would be easy to continue this vein of thought, were it not likely to become irksome to the reader; enough has been said to refresh the memory as to the flourishing state of Italian art during these times. What a mine of wealth was then opened up for succeeding generations! and how curious is the fact that not only the Violin, but its music, has been the creature of the most luxurious age of art; for in that golden age musicians contemporary with the great Violin-makers were writing music destined to be better understood and appreciated when the Violins then made should have reached their maturity.

That Italy's greatest Violin-makers lived in times favourable to the production of works possessing a high degree of merit, cannot be doubted. They were surrounded by composers of rare powers, and also by numerous orchestras. These orchestras, composed mainly of stringed instruments, were scattered all over Italy, Germany, and France, in churches, convents, and palaces, and must have created a great demand for bow instruments of a high class.

The bare mention of a few of the names of composers then existing will be sufficient to bring to the mind of the reader well versed in musical matters the compositions to which they owe their fame. In the sixteenth century, Orlando di Lasso, Isaac, and Palestrina were engaged in writing Church music, in which stringed instruments were heard; in the seventeenth, lived Stradella, Lotti, Bononcini, Lully, and Corelli. In the eighteenth century, the period when the art of Violin-making was at its zenith, the list is indeed a glorious one. At this point is the constellation of Veracini, Geminiani, Vivaldi, Locatelli, Boccherini, Tartini, Viotti, Nardini, among the Italians; while in France it is the epoch of Leclair and Gaviniès, composers of Violin music of the highest excellence. Surrounded by these men of rare genius, who lived but to disseminate a taste for the king of instruments, the makers of Violins must certainly have enjoyed considerable patronage, and doubtless those of tried ability readily obtained highly remunerative prices for their instruments, and were encouraged in their march towards perfection both in design and workmanship. Besides the many writers for the Violin, and executants, there were numbers of ardent patrons of the Cremonese and Brescian makers. Among these may be mentioned the Duke of Ferrara, Charles IX., Cardinal Ottoboni (with whom Corelli was in high favour), Cardinal Orsini (afterwards Pope Benedict XIII.), Victor Amadeus Duke of Savoy, the Duke of Modena, the Marquis Ariberti, Charles III. (afterwards Charles VI., Emperor of Germany), and the Elector of Bavaria, all of whom gave encouragement to the art by ordering complete sets of stringed instruments for their chapels and for other purposes. By the aid of such valuable patronage the makers were enabled to centre their attention on their work, and received reward commensurate with the amount of skill displayed. This had the effect of raising them above the status of the ordinary workman, and permitted them as a body to pass their lives amid comparative plenty. There are, without doubt, instances of great results obtained under trying circumstances, but the genius required to combine a successful battle with adversity with high proficiency in art is indeed a rare phenomenon. Carlyle says of such minds: "In a word, they willed one thing, to which all other things were subordinate, and made subservient, and therefore they accomplished it. The wedge will rend rocks, but its edge must be sharp and single; if it be double, the wedge is bruised in pieces, and will rend nothing." It may, therefore, be affirmed that the greatest luminaries of the art world have shone most brightly under circumstances in keeping with their peaceful labours, it not being essential to success that men highly gifted for a particular art should have this strength of will unless there were immediate call for its exercise.

Judging from the large number of bow-instrument makers in Italy, more particularly during the seventeenth century, we should conclude that the Italians must have been considered as far in advance of the makers of other nations, and that they monopolised, in consequence, the chief part of the manufacture. The city of Cremona became the seat of the trade, and the centre whence, as the manufacture developed itself, other less famous places maintained their industry. In this way there arose several distinct schools of a character marked and thoroughly Italian, but not attaining the high standard reached by the parent city. Notwithstanding the inferiority of the makers of Naples, Florence, and other homes of the art as compared with the Cremonese, they seem to have received a fair amount of patronage, the number of instruments manufactured in these places of lesser fame being considerable.

To enable the reader to understand more readily the various types of Italian Violins, they may be classed as the outcome of five different schools. The first is that of Brescia, dating from about 1520 to 1620, which includes Gasparo da Salò, Maggini, and a few others of less note. The next, and most important school, was that of Cremona, dating from 1550 to 1760, or even later, and including the following makers: Andrea Amati, Girolamo Amati, Antonio Amati, Niccolò Amati, Girolamo Amati, son of Niccolò; Andrea Guarneri, Pietro Guarneri, Giuseppe Guarneri, the son of Andrea; Giuseppe Guarneri ("del Gesù"), the nephew of Andrea; Antonio Stradivari, and Carlo Bergonzi. Several well-known makers have been omitted in the foregoing list simply because they were followers of those mentioned, and therefore cannot be credited with originality of design. The makers of Milan and Naples may be braced together as one school, under the name of *Neapolitan*, dating from 1680 to 1800. This school contains makers of good repute, viz., the members of the Grancino family, Carlo Testore, Paolo Testore, the Gagliano family, and Ferdinando Landolfi. The makers of Florence, Bologna, and Rome may likewise be classed together in a school that dates from 1680 to 1760, and includes the following names: Gabrielli, Anselmo, Tecchler, and Tononi. The Venetian school, dating from 1690 to 1764, has two very prominent members in Domenico Montagnana and Santo Seraphino; but the former maker may, not inappropriately, be numbered with those of Cremona, for he passed his early years in that city, and imbibed all the characteristics belonging to its chief makers.

Upon glancing at this imposing list of makers, it is easy to understand that it must have been a lucrative trade which in those days gave support to so many; and, further, that Italy, as compared with Germany, France, or England at that period, must have possessed, at least, more makers by two-thirds than either of those three countries. And this goes far to prove, moreover, that the Italian makers received extensive foreign patronage, their number being far in excess of that required to supply their own country's wants in the manufacture of Violins. Roger North, in his "Memoirs of Musick," evidences the demand for Italian Violins in the days of James II.

He remarks: "Most of the young nobility and gentry that have travelled into Italy affected to learn of Corelli, and brought home with them such favour for the Italian music, as hath given it possession of our Parnassus. And the best utensil of Apollo, *the Violin*, is so universally courted and sought after, to be had of the best sort, that some say England hath dispeopled Italy of Violins." We also read of William Corbett, a member of the King's band, having formed about the year 1710 a "gallery of Cremonys and Stainers" during his residence in Rome.

Brescia was the cradle of Italian Violin-making, for the few makers of bowed instruments (among whom were Gaspard Duiffoprugcar, who established himself at Bologna; Dardelli, of Mantua; Linarolli and Maller, of Venice) cannot be counted among Violin-makers. The only maker, therefore, of the Violin of the earliest date, it remains to be said, was Gasparo da Salò, to whom belongs the credit of raising the manufacture of bowed instruments from a rude state to an art. There may be something in common between the early works of Gasparo da Salò and Gaspard Duiffoprugcar, but the link that connects these two makers is very slight, and in the absence of further information respecting the latter as an actual maker of Violins, the credit of authorship must certainly belong to Gasparo da Salò.

We are indebted to Brescia for the many grand Double-basses and Tenors that were made there by Gasparo da Salò and Maggini. These instruments formed the stepping-stones to Italian Violin-making, for it is evident that they were in use long before the first era of the Violin. The Brescian Violins have not the appearance of antiquity that is noticeable in the Double-basses or Tenors, and for one Brescian Violin there are ten Double-basses, a fact which goes far to prove that the latter was the principal instrument at that time.

ANTONIO STRADIVARI.
Date 1734.
(LATE LORD AMHERST OF HACKNEY.)

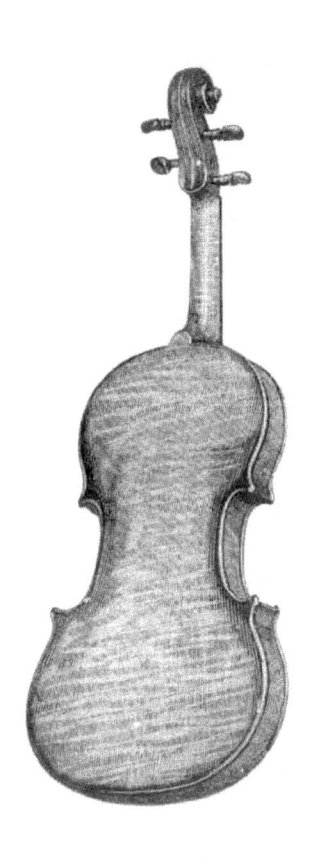

THE EMPEROR "STRAD."
Date 1715.
(LATE GEO. HADDOCK, ESQ.)

GUARNERI DEL GESÙ.
Date 1734.
(LATE LORD AMHERST OF HACKNEY.)

Plate IV.

From Brescia came the masters who established the School of Cremona. The Amatis took the lead, their founder being Andrea Amati, after whom each one of the clan appears to have gained a march on his predecessor, until the grand masters of their art, Antonio Stradivari and Giuseppe Guarneri del Gesù, advanced far beyond the reach of their fellow-makers or followers. The pupils of the Amati, Stradivari, and Guarneri settled in Milan, Florence, and other cities previously mentioned as centres of Violin-making, and thus formed the distinct character or School belonging to each city. A close study of the various Schools shows that there is much in common among them. A visible individuality is found throughout the works of the Italian makers, which is not to be met with in anything approaching the same degree in the similar productions of other nations. Among the Italians, each artist appears to have at first implicitly obeyed the teaching of his master, afterwards, as his knowledge increased, striking out a path for himself. To such important acts of self-reliance may be traced the absolute perfection to which the Italians at last attained. Not content with the production of instruments capable of producing the best tone, they strove to give them the highest finish, and were rewarded, possibly beyond their expectation. The individuality noticed as belonging in a high degree to Italian work is in many instances very remarkable. How characteristic the scroll and the sound-hole of each several maker! The work of master and pupil differs here in about the same degree as the handwriting of father and son, and often more. Although Stradivari was a pupil of Niccolò Amati, yet how marked is the difference between the scrolls and sound-holes of these two makers; Carlo Bergonzi worked with Stradivari, yet the productions of these two are more easily known apart. A similarly well-defined originality is found, in a more or less degree, to pervade the entire series of Italian Violins, and forms a feature of much interest to the connoisseur.

In closing my remarks upon the Italian School of Violin-making, I cannot withhold from the reader the concluding sentences of the Cremonese biographer, Vincenzo Lancetti, as contained in his manuscript relative to the makers of Cremona. He says: "I cannot help but deeply deplore the loss to my native city (where for two centuries the manufacture of stringed instruments formed an active and profitable trade) of the masterpieces of its renowned Violin-makers, together with the drawings, moulds, and patterns, the value of which would be inestimable to those practising the art. Is it not possible to find a citizen to do honour to himself and his city by securing the collection of instruments, models, and forms brought together by Count Cozio di Salabue, before the treasure be lost to Italy? I have the authority of Count Cozio to grant to such a patron every facility for the purchase and transfer of the collection, conditionally that the object be to resuscitate the art of Violin-making in Cremona, which desire alone prompted the Count in forming the collection." These interesting remarks were written in the year 1823, with a view to their publication at the end of the account of Italian Violin-makers which Lancetti purposed publishing. As the work did not see the light, the appeal of the first writer on the subject of Italian Violins was never heard. Had it been, in all probability Cremona would at this moment have been in possession of the most remarkable collection of instruments and models ever brought together, and be maintaining in at least some measure the prestige belonging to its past in Violin-making.

SECTION V

The Italian Varnish

A word or two must be said upon the famous varnish of the Italians, which has hitherto baffled all attempts to solve the mystery of its formation. Every instrument belonging to the school of Cremona has it, more or less, in all its marvellous beauty, and to these instruments the resolute investigator turns, promising himself the discovery of its constituent parts. The more its lustre penetrates his soul, the more determined become his efforts. As yet, however, all such praiseworthy researches have been futile, and the composition of the Cremonese varnish remains a secret lost to the world—as much so as the glorious ruby lustre of Maestro Giorgio, and the blue so coveted by connoisseurs of china. Mr. Charles Reade truly says: "No wonder, then, that many Violin-makers have tried hard to discover the secret of this varnish: many chemists have given anxious days and nights to it. More than once, even in my time, hopes have run high, but only to fall again. Some have even cried 'Eureka' to the public; but the moment others looked at their discovery and compared it with the real thing,

> 'Inextinguishable laughter shook the skies.'

At last despair has succeeded to all that energetic study, and the varnish of Cremona is sullenly given up as a lost art."

Declining, therefore, all speculation as to what the varnish is or what it is not, or any nostrums for its re-discovery, we will pass on at once to the description of the different Italian varnishes, which may be divided into four distinct classes, viz., the Brescian, Cremonese, Neapolitan, and Venetian. These varnishes are quite separable in one particular, which is, the depth of their colouring; and yet three of them, the Brescian, Cremonese, and Venetian, have to all appearance a common basis. This agreement may be accounted for with some show of reason by the supposition that there must have been a depot in each city where the varnish was sold in an incomplete form, and that the depth of colour used, or even the means adopted for colouring, rested with the maker of the instrument. If we examine the Brescian varnish, we find an almost complete resemblance between the material of Gasparo da Salò and that of his coadjutors, the colouring only being different. Upon turning to the Cremonese, we find that Guarneri, Stradivari, Carlo Bergonzi, and a few others, used varnish having the same characteristics, but, again, different in shade; possibly the method of laying it upon the instrument was peculiar to each maker. Similar facts are observable in the Venetian specimens. The varnish of Naples, again, is of a totally different composition, and as it was chiefly in vogue after the Cremonese was lost, we may conclude that it was probably produced by the Neapolitan makers for their own need.

If we reflect for a moment upon the extensive use which these makers made of the Cremonese varnish, it is reasonable to suppose that it was an ordinary commodity in their days, and that there was then no secret in the matter at all. To account for its sudden disappearance and total loss is, indeed, not easy. After 1760, or even at an earlier date, all trace of it is obliterated. The demand for it was certainly not so great as it had been, but quite sufficient to prevent the supply from dying out had it been possible. The problem of its sudden disappearance may, perhaps, be accounted for without overstepping the bounds of possibility, if we suppose that the varnish was composed of a particular gum quite common in those days, extensively used for other purposes besides the varnishing of Violins, and thereby caused to be a marketable article. Suddenly, we will suppose, the demand for its supply ceased, and the commercial world troubled no further about the matter. The natural consequence would be non-production. It is well known that there are numerous instances of commodities once in frequent supply and use, but now entirely obsolete and extinct.

While, however, our attention has been mainly directed to the basis of the celebrated varnish, it must not be supposed that its colouring is of no importance. In this particular each maker had the opportunity of displaying his skill and judgment, and probably it was here, if anywhere, that the secret rested. The gist of the matter, then, is simply that the varnish was common to all, but the colouring and mode of application belonged solely to the maker, and hence the varied and independent appearance of each separate instrument. With regard, however, to the general question as to what the exact composition of the gum was or was not, I shall hazard no further speculation, and am profoundly conscious of the fact that my present guesses have gained no nearer approaches to the re-discovery of the buried treasure.

A description, however, of the various Italian varnishes may not be inappropriate. The Brescian is mostly of a rich brown colour and soft texture, but not so clear as the Cremonese. The Cremonese is of various shades, the early instruments of the school being chiefly amber-coloured, afterwards deepening into a light red of charming appearance, later still into a rich brown of the Brescian type, though more transparent, and frequently broken up, while the earlier kinds are velvet-like. The Venetian is also of various shades, chiefly light red, and exceedingly transparent. The Neapolitan varnish (a generic term including that of Milan and a few other places) is very clear, and chiefly yellow in colour, but wanting the dainty softness of the Cremonese. It is quite impossible to give such a description of these varnishes as will enable the reader at once to recognise them; the eye must undergo considerable exercise before it can discriminate the various qualities; practice, however, makes it so sharp that often from a piece of varnishing the size of a shilling it will obtain evidence sufficient to decide upon the rank of the Violin.

And here, before we dismiss the subject of the varnish, another interesting question occurs: What is its effect, apart from the beauty of its appearance, upon the efficiency of the instrument? The idea that the varnish of a Violin has some influence upon its tone has often been ridiculed, and we can quite understand that it must appear absurd to those who have not viewed the question in all its bearings. Much misconception has arisen from pushing this theory about the varnish either too far or not far enough. What seems sometimes to be implied by enthusiasts is, that the form of the instrument is of little importance provided the varnish is good, which amounts to saying that a common Violin may be made good by means of varnishing it. The absurdity of such a doctrine is self-evident. On the other hand, there are rival authorities who attach no importance to varnish in relation to tone. That the varnish does influence the tone there is strong proof, and to make this plain to the reader should not be difficult. The finest varnishes are those of oil, and they require the utmost skill and patience in their use. They dry very slowly, and may be described as of a soft and yielding nature. The common varnish is known as spirit varnish; it is easily used and dries rapidly, in consideration of which qualities it is generally adopted in these days of high pressure. It may be described as precisely the reverse of the oil varnish; it is hard and unyielding. Now a Violin varnished with fine oil varnish, like all good things, takes time to mature, and will not bear forcing in any way. At first the instrument is somewhat muffled, as the pores of the wood have become impregnated with oil. This makes the instrument heavy both in weight and sound; but as time rolls on the oil dries, leaving the wood mellowed and wrapped in an elastic covering which yields to the tone of the instrument and imparts to it much of its own softness. We will now turn to spirit varnish. When this is used a diametrically opposite effect is produced. The Violin is, as it were, wrapped in glass, through which the sound passes, imbued with the characteristics of the varnish. The result is, that the resonance produced is metallic and piercing, and well calculated for common purposes; if, however, richness of tone be required, spirit-varnished instruments cannot supply it. From these remarks the reader may gather some notion of the vexed question of varnish in relation to tone, and be left to form his own opinion.

The chief features of the Italian School of Violin-makers having been noticed, it only remains to be said that the following list of makers is necessarily incomplete. This defect arises chiefly from old forgeries. Labels used as the trade marks of many deserving makers have from time to time been removed from their lawful instruments in order that others bearing a higher marketable value might be substituted. In the subjoined list will be found all the great names, and every care has been taken to render it as complete as possible. Several names given are evidently German, most of which belong to an early period, and are chiefly those in connection with the manufacture of Lutes and Viols in Italy. These are included in the Italian list, in order to show that many Germans were engaged in making stringed instruments in Italy, about the period when Tenor and Contralto Viols with four strings were manufactured there—a circumstance worthy of note in connection with the history of Viol and Violin making in Italy, bearing in mind that four-string Viols were used in Germany when Italy used those having six strings.

SECTION VI

Italian Makers

ABATI, Giambattista, Modena, about 1775 to 1793.

ACEVO, Saluzzo. Reference is made in the "Biographie Universelle des Musiciens" to this maker having been a pupil of Gioffredo Cappa, and M. Fétis mentions his having seen a Viol da Gamba dated 1693 of this make, which belonged to Marin Marais, the famous performer on the Viol.[1]

> 1 There seems good reason to question the existence of such a person, at all events as a maker of Violins.— EDITORS.

ALBANESI, Sebastiano, Cremona, 1720-1744. The pattern is bold and the model flat. Although made at Cremona, they do not properly belong to the school of that place, having the characteristics of Milanese work. The varnish is quite unlike that of Cremona.

ALBANI, Paolo, Palermo, 1650-80. Is said to have been a pupil of Niccolò Amati. The pattern is broad and the work carefully executed.

ALESSANDRO, named "Il Veneziano," 16th century.

ALETZIE, Paolo, Munich, 1720-36. He made chiefly Tenors and Violoncellos, some of which are well-finished instruments. The varnish is inferior, both as regards quality and colour. The characteristics of this maker are German, and might be classed with that school.

ALVANI, Cremona. Is said to have made instruments in imitation of those of Giuseppe Guarneri.

AMATI, Andrea, Cremona. The date of birth is unknown. It is supposed to have occurred about 1520. M. Fétis gave this date from evidence furnished by the list of instruments found in the possession of the banker Carlo Carli, which belonged to Count Cozio di Salabue. Mention is made of a Rebec, attributed to Andrea Amati, dated 1546. Upon reference to the MSS. of Lancetti, I find the following account of the Rebec: "In the collection of the said Count there exists also a Violin believed to be by Andrea Amati, with the label bearing the date 1546, which must have been strung with only three strings, and which at that epoch was called Rebec by the French. The father of Mantegazza altered the instrument into one of four strings, by changing the neck and scroll." From these remarks we gather that the authorship of this interesting Violin is doubtful. There is, however, some show of evidence to connect Andrea Amati with Rebecs and Geigen, in the notable fact that most of his Violins are small, their size being that known as three-quarter, which was, I am inclined to believe, about the size of the instruments which the four-stringed Violin succeeded. As to the time when Andrea Amati worked, I am of opinion that it was a little later than has hitherto been stated. We have evidence of his being alive in the year 1611, from an entry recently discovered in the register of the parish in which Andrea Amati lived, to the effect that his second wife died on April 10, 1611, and that Andrea was then living. The discovery of this entry (together with many important and interesting ones to which I shall have occasion to refer) we owe to the patience and industry of Monsignor Gaetano Bazzi, Canon of the Cathedral of Cremona.[2] Andrea Amati claims attention not so much on account of his instruments, as from his being regarded as the founder of the school of Cremona. There is no direct evidence as to the name of the master from whom he learnt the art of making stringed instruments. If his work be carefully examined, it will appear that the only maker to whose style it can be said to bear any resemblance is Gasparo da Salò, and it is possible that the great Brescian may have instructed him in his art. It is unfortunate that there are no data for our guidance in the matter. These men often, like their brothers in Art, the painters of olden times, began to live when they were dead, and their history thus passed without record. Andrea Amati may possibly have been self-taught, but there is much in favour of the view given above on this point. His early works are so Brescian in character as to cause them to be numbered with the productions of that school. For a general designation of the instruments of this maker the following notes may suffice. The work is carefully executed. The model is high, and, in consequence, lacks power of tone; but the Violins possess a charming sweetness. The soundhole is inelegant, has not the decision of Gasparo da Salò, although belonging to his style, and is usually broad. His varnish may be described as deep golden, of good quality. His method of cutting his material was not uniform, but he seems to have had a preference for cutting his backs in slab form, according to the example set for the most part by the Brescian makers. The sides were also made in a similar manner, the wood used being both sycamore and that known to makers as pear-tree. The instruments of Andrea Amati are now very scarce. Among the famous instruments of this maker were twenty-four Violins (twelve large and twelve small pattern), six Tenors, and eight Basses, made for Charles IX., which were kept in the Chapel Royal, Versailles, until October, 1790, when they disappeared. These were probably the finest instruments by Andrea Amati. On the backs were painted the arms of France and other devices, with the motto, *Pietate et Justitia*. In the "Archives Curieuses de l'Histoire de France," one Nicolas Delinet, a member of the French King's band, appears to have purchased in 1572 a Cremona Violin for his Majesty, for which he paid about ten pounds—a large sum, it must be confessed, when we think of its purchasing power in the sixteenth century.

Mr. Sandys, who cites this curious entry, rightly conjectures it may have included incidental expenses. No mention is made of the maker of the Violin in question; we find, however, that in the collection of instruments which belonged to Sir William Curtis there was a Violoncello having the arms of France painted on the back, together with the motto above noticed. The date of the instrument was 1572. We may therefore assume that the Violin purchased by Nicolas Delinet in the same year was the work of Andrea Amati, and belonged to the famous Charles IX. set.

2 The extracts were published by Signor Piccolellis at Florence in 1886.

AMATI, Niccolò, Cremona, brother of Andrea. Very little is known of this maker or of his instruments.

Antonius et Hieronymus Fr. Amati
Cremonen Andræ fil. F.

AMATI, Antonio and Girolamo, sons of Andrea Amati, Cremona. There does not exist certain evidence as to the date of the birth and death of Antonio Amati. We have information of the dates on which his brother Girolamo died in extracts from parish registers; also the date of his marriages, which took place in the year 1576, and on May 24, 1584. By his second wife, Girolamo had a family of nine children; the fifth child was Niccolò, who became the famous Violin-maker. The mother of Niccolò died of the plague on October 27, 1630, and her husband, Girolamo, died of the same disease six days later, viz., November 2, 1630, and was buried on the same day. Girolamo is described in the register as "Misser Hieronimo Amati detto il leutaro della vic di S. Faustino" (viz., maker to the Church). Vincenzo Lancetti states that "Count Cozio kept a register of all the instruments seen by him, from which it appeared that the earliest reliable date of the brothers Amati is 1577, and that they worked together until 1628; that Antonio survived Jerome and made instruments until after the year 1648—a fine Violin bearing the last-named date having been recently seen with the name of Antonio alone." This information serves in some measure to set at rest much of the uncertainty relative to the period when these makers lived. These skilful makers produced some of the most charming specimens of artistic work. To them we are indebted for the first form of the instrument known as "Amatese." The early efforts of the brothers Amati have many of the characteristics belonging to the work of their father Andrea; their sound-hole is similar to his, and in keeping with the Brescian form, and the model which they at first adopted is higher than that of their later and better instruments.

Although these makers placed their joint names in their Violins, it must not be supposed that each bore a proportionate part of the manufacture in every case; on the contrary, there are but few instances where such association is made manifest. The style of each was distinct, and one was immeasurably superior to the other. Antonio deviated but little from the teaching of his father. The sound-holes even of his latest instruments partake of the Brescian type, and the model is the only particular in which it may be said that a step in advance is traceable; here he wisely adopted a flatter form. His work throughout, as regards finish, is excellent.

Girolamo Amati possessed in a high degree the attributes of an artist. He was richly endowed with that rare power—*originality*. It is in his instruments that we discover the form of sound-hole which Niccolò Amati improved, and, after him, the inimitable Stradivari perfected. Girolamo Amati ignored the pointed sound-hole and width in the middle portions observable in his predecessor's Violins, and designed a model of extremely elegant proportions. How graceful is the turn of the sound-hole at both the upper and lower sections! With what nicety and daintiness are the outer lines made to point to the shapely curve! Niccolò Amati certainly improved even upon Girolamo's achievements, but he did not add more grace; and the essential difference between the instruments of the two is, that there is more vigour in the sound-hole of Niccolò than that of his father Girolamo.

The purfling of the brothers Amati is very beautifully executed. The scrolls differ very much, and in the earlier instruments of these makers are of a type anterior to that of the bodies. Further, the varnish on the earlier specimens is deeper in colour than that found on the later ones, which have varnish of a beautiful orange tint, sparingly laid on, and throwing up the markings of the wood with much distinctness. The material used by these makers and the mode of cutting it also varies considerably. In some specimens we find that they used backs of the slab form; in others, backs worked whole; in others, backs divided into two segments. The belly-wood is in every case of the finest description. The tone is far more powerful than that of the instruments of Andrea, and this increase of sound is obtained without any sacrifice of the richness of the quality.

CARLO BERGONZI.
Grand Pattern.
(GEO. GUDGEON, ESQ.)

Plate V.

Nicolaus Amatus Cremonen, Hieronymi
Fil. ac Antonij Nepos Fecit. 16—

AMATI, Niccolò, Cremona, born December 3, 1596, died April 12, 1684. Son of Girolamo Amati. It is gratifying in the notice of this famous Violin-maker to be able to supply dates of his birth, marriage, and death. Niccolò was christened on December 6, 1596. His marriage took place on May 23, 1645, and it is interesting to record that his pupil Andrea Guarneri witnessed the ceremony, and signed the register. The information recently supplied by Canon Bazzi of Cremona, relative to the pupils and workmen of Niccolò Amati, who were duly registered in the books of the parish of SS. Faustino and Giovita, is fraught with interest. It seems to carry us within the precincts, if not into the workshop, of the master. Andrea Guarneri heads the list in the year 1653, age twenty-seven, and married; next comes Leopoldo Todesca, age twenty-eight; and Francesco Mola, age twelve. In the following year Leopoldo Todesca appears to have been the only name registered as working with Amati. In the year 1666 we have the name Giorgio Fraiser, age eighteen. In 1668 no names of workmen seem to have been registered. In 1680 the name of Girolamo Segher appears, age thirty-four, and Bartolommeo Cristofori, age thirteen. In 1681 another name occurs, namely Giuseppe Stanza, a Venetian, age eighteen. In the following year the only name entered was that of Girolamo Segher, age thirty-six. Niccolò Amati was the greatest maker in his illustrious family, and the finest of his instruments are second only to those of his great pupil, Antonio Stradivari. His early efforts have all the marks of genius upon them, and clearly show that he had imbibed much of the taste of his father Girolamo. He continued for some time to follow the traditional pattern of the instruments, with the label of Antonius and Hieronymus Amati, and produced many Violins of small size, of which a large number are still extant. He appears to have laboured assiduously during these early years, with the view of making himself thoroughly acquainted with every portion of his art. We find several instances in which he has changed the chief principles in construction (particularly such as relate to the arching and thicknesses), and thereby shown the intention which he had from the first of framing a new model entirely according to the dictates of his own fancy. The experienced eye may trace the successive steps taken in this direction by carefully examining the instruments dating from about 1645 downwards. Prior to this period, there is a peculiarly striking similarity in his work and model to that of his father, but after this date we can watch the gradual change of form and outline which culminated in the production of those exquisite works of the art of Violin-making known as "grand Amatis"—a name which designates the grand proportions of the instruments of this later date. It may be said that the maker gained his great reputation from these famous productions. They may be described as having an outline of extreme elegance, in the details of which the most artistic treatment is visible. The corners are drawn out to points of singular fineness, and this gives them an appearance of prominence which serves to throw beauty into the entire work. The model is raised somewhat towards the centre, dipping rather suddenly from the feet of the bridge towards the outer edge, and forming a slight groove where the purfling is reached, but not the exaggerated scoop which is commonly seen in the instruments of the many copyists. This portion of the design has formed the subject of considerable discussion among the learned in the Violin world, the debatable points being the appearance of this peculiarity and its acoustic effect. As regards the former question, the writer of these pages feels convinced that the apparent irregularity is in perfect harmony with the general outline of the great Amati's instrument; and it pleases the eye. From the acoustical point of view, it may be conceded that it does not tend to increase of power; but, on the other hand, probably, the sweetness of tone so common to the instruments of Niccolò Amati must be set to its credit; for, in proportion as the form is departed from, the sweetness is found to decrease. The sound-hole has all the character of those of the preceding Amati, together with increased boldness; in fact, it is a repetition of that of Girolamo, with this exception. The sides are a shade deeper than those of the brothers Amati. The scroll is exquisitely cut. Its outline is perhaps a trifle contracted, and thus is robbed of the vigour which it would otherwise possess. From this circumstance it differs from the general tenor of the body, which is certainly of broad conception. The maker would seem to have been aware of this defect, if we may judge from the difference of form given to his earlier scrolls, as compared with those of a later date, in which he seems to have attempted to secure increased boldness, as more in keeping with the character of the body of the instrument. It must be acknowledged, however, that these efforts did not carry him far enough. The surface of the scroll is usually inclined to flatness. The wood used by Niccolò Amati for his grand instruments is of splendid quality, both as regards acoustical requirements and beauty of appearance. The grain of some of his backs has a wave-like form of much beauty, others have markings of great regularity, giving to the instrument a highly finished appearance. The bellies are of a soft silken nature, and usually of even grain. A few of them are of singular beauty, their grain being of a mottled character, which, within its transparent coat of varnish, flashes light here and there with singular force. The colour of the varnish varies in point of depth; sometimes it is of a rich amber colour, at others reddish-brown, and in a few instances light golden-red.

These, then, are the instruments which are so highly esteemed, and which form one of the chief links in the Violin family. The highest praise must be conceded to the originator of a design which combines extreme elegance with utility; and, simple as the result may appear, the successful construction of so graceful a whole must have been attended with rare ingenuity and persevering labour.

Here, again, is evidence of the master mind, never resting, ever seeking to improve—evidence, too, that mere elaboration of work was not the sole aim of the Cremonese makers. They designed and created as they worked, and their success, which no succeeding age has aspired to rival, entitles them to rank with the chief artists of the world.

On the form of the instrument known as the "grand Amati" Stradivari exerted all the power of his early years; and the fruits of his labours are, in point of finish, unsurpassed by any of his later works. Where Niccolò Amati failed, Stradivari conquered; and particularly is this victory to be seen in the scrolls of his instruments during the first period, which are masterpieces in themselves. How bold is the conception, how delicate the workmanship, what a marvel of perfection the sound-hole! But as these Violins are noticed under the head of "Stradivari," it is unnecessary to enter into details here. Beside Stradivari, many makers of less importance followed the "grand Amati" pattern, among whom may be mentioned Jacobs, of Amsterdam, who takes a prominent place as a copyist. The truthfulness of these copies, as regards the chief portions of the instrument, is singularly striking, so much so, indeed, as to cause them to be frequently mistaken for originals by those who are not deeply versed in the matter. The points of failure in these imitations may be cited as the scroll and sound-hole. The former lacks ease, and seems to defy its author to hide his nationality. The scroll has ever proved the most troublesome portion of the Violin to the imitator. It is here, if anywhere, that he must drop the mask and show his individuality, and this is remarkably the case in the instance above mentioned. A further difference between Amati and Jacobs lies in the circumstance that the latter invariably used a purfling of whalebone. Another copyist of Amati was Grancino. As the varnish which he used was of a different nature from that of his original, his power of imitation must be considered to be inferior to that of some others. Numerous German makers, whose names will be found under the "German School," were also liege subjects of Amati, and copied him with much exactness; so also, last, but not least, our own countrymen, Forster, Banks, and Samuel Gilkes.

Lancetti, writing of Niccolò Amati in 1823, says: "Some masterpieces by him still remain in Italy, among which is the Violin dated 1668, in the collection of Count Cozio. It is in perfect preservation, and for workmanship, quality, and power of tone far surpasses the instruments of his predecessors." The same writer remarks that "Niccolò Amati put his own name to his instruments about 1640." It was upon a Violoncello of this make that Signor Piatti played when he first appeared at the concert of the Philharmonic Society, on June 24, 1844. The instrument had been presented to him by Liszt, and is now in the possession of the Rev. Canon Hudson. In an entry in the Cathedral Register at Cremona, the name of the wife of Niccolò Amati is given as Lucrezia Paliari. The meagreness of accounts of a documentary character in relation to the famous makers of Cremona naturally renders every contribution of the kind of some value. The following extract, taken from the State documents in connection with the Court of Modena, serves to indicate the degree of esteem in which the instruments of Niccolò Amati were held during his lifetime, in comparison with those of his contemporary and pupil, Francesco Ruggieri. Tomaso Antonio Vitali, the famous Violinist, who was the director of the Duke of Modena's Orchestra, addressed his patron to this effect: "Please your most Serene Highness, Tomaso Antonio Vitali, your highness's most humble servant, bought of Francesco Capilupi, through the agency of the Rev. Ignazio Paltrineri, for the price of twelve doublons, a Violin, and paid such price on account of its having the name inside of Niccolò Amati, a maker of great repute in his profession. The petitioner has since found that this Violin has been wrongly named, as underneath the label is the signature of Francesco Ruggieri detto il Pero, a maker of less credit, whose Violins do not scarcely attain the price of three doublons."[3] Vitali closes his letter with an appeal to the Duke for assistance to obtain redress.

    3 "Luigi F. Valdrighi Nomocheliurgografia," Modena, 1884.

AMATI, Girolamo, Cremona, born 1649, third son of Niccolò. The labels which I have seen in a Violin and a Tenor bear the name "Hieronymus Amati," and describe the maker as the son of Niccolò. He was born on February 26, 1649, married in 1678. In 1736 he, together with his family, removed to another parish, as shown by the original extract from the books of the Cathedral at Cremona, sent by Canon Manfredini to Lancetti. Girolamo Amati died in the year 1740. There appears to have been some doubt as to whether Girolamo Amati, the son of Niccolò, made Violins, according to Lancetti. He says, "Those seen with his label, dated between 1703 and 1723, were ascribed by some to Sneider, of Pavia, and by others to J. B. Rogeri, of Brescia." In a letter of Count Cozio di Salabue to Lancetti, dated January 3, 1823, he states that "in May, 1806, Signor Carlo Cozzoni gave an old Amati Violin for repair to the Brothers Mantegazza, dealers and restorers of musical instruments, in Milan, and upon their removing the belly they were pleased to discover, written at the base of the neck, 'Revisto e coretto da me Girolamo figlio di Niccolò Amati, Cremona, 1710.'"

In some instances the instruments of this maker do not resemble those of Niccolò Amati, or indeed those of the Amati family. The sound-holes are straight, and the space between them is somewhat narrow. In others there is merit of a high order—the pattern is large, broad between the sound-holes, and very flat in model, and resembling the form of Stradivari rather than that of Amati. These differences are accounted for by the fact made known by Lancetti, that the tools and patterns of Niccolò Amati passed into the possession of Stradivari, and are therefore included with those now in the keeping of Count Cozio's descendant, the Marquis Dalla Valle. The varnish of Girolamo Amati shows signs of decadence; in some instances, however, we find it soft and transparent. The few which have this quality of varnish I am inclined to think were made in the time of Niccolò, since the instruments of a later date have a coating of varnish of an inferior kind. This maker—as with the Bergonzis—seems, therefore, to have been either ignorant of his parent's mode of making superior varnish, or was unable to obtain the same kind or quality of ingredients. With Girolamo closes the history of the family of the Amati as Violin-makers. Girolamo had a son, Niccolò Giuseppe, born in 1684, who removed with his father to another parish in 1736, as mentioned above, but he was not a maker of Violins.

   Petrus Ambrosi fecit Brixiæ, 17—

AMBROSI, Pietro, Rome and Brescia, about 1730. Average merit. The workmanship resembles that of Balestrieri, as seen in the inferior instruments of that maker.

ANSELMO, Pietro, Cremona, 1701. The instruments of this maker partake of the Ruggeri character. The varnish is rich in colour and of considerable body. Scarce. I have met with two excellent Violoncellos by this maker. Anselmo is said to have worked also in Venice.

ANTONIAZZI, Gaetano, Cremona, 1860. The work is passable, but the form faulty. The sound-holes are not properly placed.

ANTONIO OF BOLOGNA (Antonius Bononiensis). There is a Viol da Gamba by this maker at the Academy of Music, Bologna.

ANTONIO, Ciciliano, an Italian maker of Viols. A specimen exists at the Academy of Bologna, without date.

ASSALONE, Gasparo, Rome, 18th century. The model is high and the workmanship rough. Thin yellow varnish.

BAGONI, Luigi (or Bajoni), Milan, from about 1840. Was living in 1876.

BAGATELLA, Antonio, Padua, made both Violins and Violoncellos, a few of which have points of merit. He wrote a pamphlet in 1782 on a method of constructing Violins by means of a graduated perpendicular line similar to Wettengel's; but no benefit has been derived from it.

BAGATELLA, Pietro, Padua, is mentioned as a maker who worked about 1760.

   Thomas Balestrieri Cremonensis
      Fecit Mantuæ. Anno 17—

BALESTRIERI, Tommaso, middle of the 18th century. Said to have been a pupil of Stradivari, which is probable. The instruments of Balestrieri may be likened to those of Stradivari which were made during the last few years of his life, 1730-37. The form of both is similar, and the ruggedness observable in the latter instruments is found, but in a more marked degree, in those of Balestrieri. These remarks, however, must not be considered to suggest that comparison can fairly be made between these two makers in point of merit, but merely to point out a general rough resemblance in the character of their works. The absence of finish in the instruments of Tommaso Balestrieri is in a measure compensated by the presence of a style full of vigour. The wood which he used varies very much. A few Violins are handsome, but the majority are decidedly plain. The bellies were evidently selected with judgment, and have the necessary qualities for the production of good tone. The varnish seems to have been of two kinds, one resembling that of Guadagnini, the other softer and richer in colour. The tone may be described as large and very telling, and when the instrument has had much use there is a richness by no means common. It is singular that these instruments are more valued in Italy than they are either in England or France.

BALESTRIERI, Pietro, Cremona, about 1725.

BASSIANO, Rome. Lute-maker. 1666.

BENEDETTI. *See* Rinaldi.

BELLOSIO, Anselmo, Venice, 18th century. About 1788. Similar to Santo Serafino in pattern, but the workmanship is inferior; neat purfling; rather opaque varnish.

BENTE, Matteo, Brescia, latter part of the 16th century. M. Fétis mentions, in his "Biographie Universelle des Musiciens," a Lute by this maker, richly ornamented.

> Anno 17— Carlo Bergonzi, fece
> in Cremona.

BERGONZI, Carlo, Cremona, 1716-47. Pupil of Antonio Stradivari. That he was educated in Violin-making by the greatest master of his art is evidenced beyond doubt. In his instruments may be clearly traced the teachings of Stradivari. The model, the thicknesses, and the scroll, together with the general treatment, all agree in betokening that master's influence. Giuseppe Guarneri del Gesù here stands in strong contrast with Bergonzi. All writers on the subject of Violins assume that Guarneri was instructed by Stradivari, a statement based upon no reasons (for none have ever been adduced), and apparently a mere repetition of some one's first guess or error. As before remarked, Carlo Bergonzi, in his work, and in the way in which he carries out his ideas, satisfactorily shows the source whence his early instructions were derived, and may be said to have inscribed the name of his great master, not in print, but in the entire body of every instrument which he made. This cannot be said of Giuseppe Guarneri. On the contrary, there is not a point throughout his work that can be said to bear any resemblance to the sign manual of Stradivari. As this interesting subject is considered at length in the notice of Giuseppe Guarneri, it is unnecessary to make further comment in this place.

The instruments of Carlo Bergonzi are justly celebrated both for beauty of form and tone, and are rapidly gaining the appreciation of artistes and amateurs. Commercially, no instruments have risen more rapidly than those of this maker; their value has continuously increased within recent years, more particularly in England, where their merits were earliest acknowledged—a fact which certainly reflects much credit upon our connoisseurs. In France they had a good character years ago, and have been gaining rapidly upon their old reputation, and now our neighbours regard them with as much favour as we do.

They possess tone of rare quality, are for the most part extremely handsome, and, last and most important of all, their massive construction has helped them, by fair usage and age, to become instruments of the first order. The model of Bergonzi's Violins is generally flat, and the outline of his early efforts is of the Stradivari type; but later in life, he, in common with other great Italian makers, marked out a pattern for himself from which to construct. The essential difference between these two forms lies in the angularity of the latter. It would be very difficult to describe accurately the several points of deviation unless the reader could handle the specimens for himself and have ocular demonstration; the upper portion from the curve of the centre bouts is increased, and, in consequence, the sound-holes are placed slightly lower than in the Stradivari model. Bergonzi was peculiar in this arrangement, and he seldom deviated from it. Again, increased breadth is given to the lower portion of the instrument, and in consequence the centre bouts are set at a greater angle than is customary. The sound-hole may be described as an adaptation of the characteristics of both Stradivari and Guarneri, inclining certainly more to those of the former. As a further peculiarity, it is to be noticed that the sound-holes are set nearer the edge than is the case in the instruments of either of the makers named. Taken as a whole, Bergonzi's design is rich in artistic feeling, and one which he succeeded in treating with the utmost skill.

Carlo Bergonzi furnishes us with another example of the extensive research with which the great Cremonese makers pursued their art, and a refutation of the common assertion that these men worked and formed by accident rather than by judgment. The differences of the two makers mentioned above, as regards form, are certainly too wide to be explained away as a mere accident. It is further necessary to take into consideration the kind of tone belonging to these instruments respectively. If Bergonzi's instruments be compared with those of his master, Stradivari, or of Guarneri del Gesù, the appreciable difference to be found will amount to this, that in Bergonzi's instruments there is a just and exact combination of the qualities of both the other two makers named. Is it not, therefore, reasonable to conclude that Carlo Bergonzi was fully alive to the merits of both Stradivari and Guarneri, and deliberately set himself to construct a model that should embrace in a measure the chief characteristics of both of them?

The scroll is deserving of particular attention. It is quite in keeping with the body of the instrument, and has been cut with a decision of purpose that could only have been possessed by a master. It is flatter than usual, if we trace it from the cheek towards the turn, and is strikingly bold. Here, again, is the portrait of the character of the maker. Although by a pupil of Antonio Stradivari, the scroll is thoroughly distinct from any known production of that maker—it lacks his fine finish and exact proportion; but, on the other hand, it has an originality about it which is quite refreshing. The prominent feature is the ear of the scroll, which being made to stand forth in bold relief, gives it a broad appearance when looked at from the front.

The work of Bergonzi, as has been the case with many of his class, has been attributed to others. Many of his instruments are dubbed "Joseph Guarneri," a mistake in identification which arises chiefly from the form of the sound-hole at the upper and lower portions. There is little else that can be considered as bearing any resemblance whatever to the work of Guarneri, and even in this case the resemblance is very slight. Bergonzi's outline is totally different from that of Guarneri, and is so distinct and telling that it is sure to impress the eye of the experienced connoisseur when first seen.

The varnish of Bergonzi is often fully as resplendent as that of Giuseppe Guarneri or Stradivari, and shows him to have been initiated in the mysteries of its manufacture. It is sometimes seen to be extremely thick, at other times but sparingly laid on; often of a deep, rich red colour, sometimes of a pale red, and again, of rich amber, so that the variation of colour to be met with in Bergonzi's Violins is considerable. We must concede that his method of varnishing was scarcely so painstaking as that of his fellow-workers, if we judge from the clots here and there, particularly on the deep-coloured instruments; but, nevertheless, now that age has toned down the varnish, the effect is good.

Carlo Bergonzi lived next door to Stradivari, and I believe the house remained in the family until a few years since, when it was disposed of.

Lancetti remarks: "From want of information, we have forgotten in the second volume"—referring to his "Biographical Dictionary," part of which was printed in 1820—"to include an estimable maker named Carlo Bergonzi, who was pupil of Stradivari, and fellow-workman with his sons. From the list of names and dates collected by Count Cozio, it appears that Carlo Bergonzi worked by himself from 1719 to 1746. He used generally very fine foreign wood, and a varnish the quality of that of his master." In the collection of Count Cozio di Salabue, there were two Violins by Bergonzi, dated 1731 and 1733, and a Violoncello, 1746. We have in this country two remarkable Violoncellos of this maker. The perfect and unique Double Bass which Vuillaume purchased of the executors of Luigi Tarisio is now in the possession of the family of the late Mr. J. M. Sears, of Boston, U.S.

> Michael Angelo Bergonzi Figlio di
> Carlo fece in Cremona l'Anno 17—

BERGONZI, Michel Angelo, Cremona, 1730-60. Son of Carlo. The pattern of his instruments is somewhat varied. Many are large, and others undersized. The varnish is hard, and distinct from that associated with Cremonese instruments.

J. B. GUADAGNINI.

STORIONI.
1797.

Plate VI.

Nicolaus Bergonzi Cremonensis
faciebat Anno 17—

BERGONZI, Niccolò, Cremona. Son of the above. He made a great number of Violins of similar form to those of his father. The wood which he selected was of a close nature and hard appearance. The varnish is not equal to that of Carlo; it is thin and cold-looking. The workmanship is very good, being often highly finished, but yet wanting in character. The scroll is cramped, and scarcely of the Cremonese type. Lancetti mentions a Tenor by this maker, dated 1781.

In the correspondence which passed between the grandson of Antonio Stradivari and the agents of Count Cozio (which is given in these pages), reference is made to some of the moulds of the great maker being in the keeping of —— Bergonzi, they having been lent to him, the writer saying that he would obtain them and put them with the other patterns, which appears to have been done. These moulds were doubtless lent to Michel Angelo Bergonzi, and were used by Niccolò as well as his father, which accounts for the form of their instruments being varied.

BERGONZI, Zosimo, Cremona. Brother of Niccolò.

BERGONZI, Carlo, Cremona, about 1780-1820. Son of Michel Angelo. He made a few Violins, large Stradivarius form, sound-holes straight and inelegant.

BERGONZI, Benedetto, Cremona, died in 1840. Tarisio learned little points of interest concerning Stradivari and his contemporaries from Benedetto Bergonzi.

BERTASSI, Ambrogio, Piadena (near Cremona), about 1730.

BERTOLOTTI, Gaspar di. *See* [Gaspar da Salò]().

BIANCHI, Niccolò, Genoa and Nice. Worked until about 1875.

BIMBI, Bartolommeo, Siena, 1753-69. High-built, small pattern, orange-yellow varnish.

BODIO, G. B., Venice, about 1832. Good workmanship; oil varnish, wide purfling.

BORELLI, Andrea, Parma, about 1735. His instruments are little known; they resemble those of Giuseppe Guadagnini.

BRENSIO, Girolamo (BRENSIUS, Hieronymus), Bologna. Reference has been made to the Viols of this maker in the first section of this work.

BRESCIA, Da, Battista. A Pochette or Kit of this maker is at the Academy of Music, Bologna, signed "Baptista Bressano"; the period assigned to it is the end of the 15th century.

BROSCHI, Carlo, Parma.

>Carlo Broschi in Parma, fecit 1732.

BUSSETO, Giovanni M., Cremona, 1540-80. Maker of Viols. M. Fétis mentions, in his "Biographie des Musiciens," that Busseto derived his name from *Busseto*, a borough in the Duchy of Parma, where he was born. He also mentions a Viol of this maker, dated 1580, which was found at Milan in 1792.

>Bernardus Calcanius fecit Genuæ
>anno 17—

CALCAGNI, Bernardo, Genoa, about 1740. Neat workmanship, small scroll, flat model, well-cut sound-holes, Stradivari pattern, orange-red varnish.

CALVAROLA, Bartolommeo, Bergamo, about 1753. The work is neatly executed. These instruments are somewhat like those of Ruggeri in form. The scroll is weak, and ill-proportioned.

>Camillus Camilli Fecit Mantua 17—

CAMILLI, Camillo, Mantua, 17—. The form partakes of that of Stradivari; wood usually of excellent quality. The sound-hole is rather wide and short. The varnish resembles that of Landolfi, but is less brilliant.

>IOFREDVS CAPPA FECIT
>SALVTIIS ANNO 16—

CAPPA, Gioffredo, Cremona, 1644-1717. The dates of birth and death were ascertained by Dr. Orazio Roggiero, a lawyer of Saluzzo, whose researches set at rest many doubts and speculations as to this excellent maker and his period of activity. He was formerly held to be a pupil of the brothers Amati, but the assumption, having regard to the date of birth, is untenable.

The greater number of his productions consist of works of high merit. Their likeness to the instruments of the Amati is in some instances peculiarly striking, but in others there is a marked dissimilarity. Particularly is this the case in the form of the sound-hole and scroll. The sound-hole is sometimes large, and quite out of keeping with the elegant outline of Amati. The points of difference may be summed up as follows: the sound-hole is larger, and more obliquely set in the instrument; the upper portion of the body has a more contracted appearance; the head, as is the case with most makers, differs most, and, in this instance, in no way resembles Amati.

There are few specimens of Cappa that bear their original labels; most of them are counterfeit "Amatis," and hence the great confusion which has arisen concerning their parentage. Lancetti says: "Foreign professors and amateurs, and particularly the English—though connoisseurs of the good and the beautiful—in buying the instruments of Cappa thought they had acquired those of Amati, the outline and character of the varnish and the quality of the tone resembling in some measure the instruments of the Brothers Amati. It is, however, reserved to a few Italian connoisseurs to distinguish them. Those of large pattern, and even of medium size, that have not been injured by unskilful restorers, are scarce, and realise high prices." These remarks, suggested many years since, by so able a connoisseur as Count Cozio, possess a peculiar interest, and cannot fail to interest the reader. As Lancetti remarks, they are of two patterns, one larger than the other. The large one is, of course, the more valuable; it is flatter, and altogether better finished. The Violoncellos of Cappa are among the best of the second-class Italian instruments, and are well worthy the attention of the professor and amateur. The varnish is frequently of very rich quality, its colour resembling that of Amati in many instances.

CARCASSI, Francesco, Florence, about 1758.

CARCASSI, Lorenzo, about 1738.

CARCASSI, Tomaso, worked in partnership with Lorenzo, but also alone, according to labels. There were several makers of this name.

CASINI, Antonio, Modena.

Antonius Casini, fecit Mutine anno 1680.

Andrea Castagneri, nell Palazzo
   di Sæssone, Pariggi, 17—

CASTAGNERI, Andrea, Paris, about 1735. This Italian maker appears to have settled in Paris. I have seen a Violin by Castagneri, date 1735; flat model, bold outline, and varnish of good quality.

CASTELLANI, Pietro, Florence, died about 1820.

CASTELLANI, Luigi, Florence, died 1884.

CASTRO, Venice, 1680-1720. The wood is of good figure generally. The outline is defective; the middle bouts are too long to be proportionate. Sound-hole roughly worked. Varnish red, the quality of which is scarcely up to the Venetian standard.

CATENAR, Enrico, Turin, about 1671.

Henricus Catenar, fecit Taurini anno 167—

Joannes Franciscus Celoniatus,
   fecit Taurini, anno 17—

CELIONIATI, Gian Francesco, Turin, about 1734. Appears to have copied the form of Amati. Yellow varnish, good workmanship.

CERIN, Marco Antonio, Venice, end of the eighteenth century. Signed himself as a pupil of Belosio.

Marcus Antonius Cerin, alumnus Anselmi Belosii, fecit Venetiæ, 17—

Jo. Baptista Ceruti Cremonensis
   fecit Cremonæ an 18—

CERUTI, Giovanni Battista, Cremona, 1755-1817. Ceruti made a large number of Violins and Violoncellos of the Pattern of Amati. He appears to have been a prolific workman, his instruments numbering, it is said, about five hundred. His favourite model was the large Amati. Giovanni Ceruti succeeded to the business of Lorenzo Storioni in 1790, in the Via dei Coltellai, near the Piazza St. Domenico.

CERUTI, Giuseppe, son of Giovanni, Cremona, 1787-1860. Was a maker and restorer of instruments. He is said to have exhibited, at the Paris and other exhibitions, Violins of good quality. He died at Mantua, in 1860.

CERUTI, Enrico, son of Giuseppe, Cremona, born in 1808, died on October 30, 1883. Enrico Ceruti is the last of the long line of Cremonese Violin-makers; there is, in consequence, a peculiar interest attached to him. Independent of this, however, he is deserving of special notice from his having been the recipient of the traditional history attending the makers of Cremona, from Amati to Stradivari and Bergonzi, and from Bergonzi to Storioni and Ceruti. He was acquainted with Luigi Tarisio and with Vuillaume, to whom he gave many interesting particulars relative to the great makers of his native city. The instruments of Enrico Ceruti are much valued by Italian orchestral players. They are said to number about three hundred and sixty-five, among which are several Violoncellos. He exhibited at the London Exhibition of 1862, and at other exhibitions. The last Violin he made was shown at the Milan Exhibition, 1881.

CRISTOFORI, Bartolommeo, Padua and Florence, 1667-1731. Apprenticed to Niccolò Amati. Is best known as the inventor of the "hammer system," and, therefore, the father of the modern pianoforte. Bow instruments of his make are rare, but authentic examples are in every way excellent. A fine Double Bass, dated 1715, is in the museum of the Musical Academy in Florence. Violoncellos and other instruments are known, and it is to be regretted that so few specimens are to be met with.

CIRCAPA, Tommaso, Naples, about 1730.

COCCO, Cristoforo, Venice, 1654. A Lute-maker. The Museum of the Paris Conservatoire Nationale de Musique contains a specimen of this make, which is described in M. Gustave Chouquet's catalogue of the collection.

CONTRERAS, Joseph, Madrid, 1745-80. This being one of the few Spanish makers, his name is placed with the Italian, the number of the Spanish being insufficient for a separate list. The model of this maker is very good and the workmanship superior. He probably lived In Italy during his early life, the style being Italian. He was born in Granada, and was called the Spanish Stradivarius. He died about 1780, and is said to have been seventy years of age.

CORDANO, Jacopo Filippo, Genoa, about 1774.

> Jacobus Philipus Cordanus, fecit Genuæ anno sal. 1774.

CORNA, Dalla, Brescia, early maker of Viols, about 1530.

> Petrus Antonius a Costa, fecit
> ad similitudinem illorum quos
> fecerunt Antonius & Hieronymus
> Fratres Amati Cremonenses Filii
> Andræ. Tarvisii, 1757.

COSTA, Pietro Antonio dalla, Venice and Treviso. The label he used is curious. He copied the Brothers Amati with much skilfulness. The sound-holes are like those of the early instruments of the Amati; the varnish is golden in colour and excellent in quality; the scroll, as usual with all imitations, is a weak feature, but does not lack originality.

DARDELLI, Pietro, Mantua, about 1500. Is described as a maker of Lutes and Viols. M. Fétis relates, in his "Biographie des Musiciens," that the painter Richard, of Lyons, possessed about the year 1807 a beautiful Lute by this maker, which was made for the Duchess of Mantua. The instrument is described as richly inlaid with ebony, ivory, and silver, dated 1497, and having the name "Padre Dardelli." On the belly the Mantuan arms are represented. M. Fétis was unable to discover any tidings of this interesting instrument after the death of Richard. Dardelli was a Franciscan monk at Mantua, and occupied himself with making musical instruments and inlaying them. Work of any kind executed under such circumstances is rarely found to be other than artistic.

DESPINE, Alexander, Turin, nineteenth century. A very good maker; worked with Pressenda, whose labels his instruments sometimes bear.

DIEFFOPRUCHAR, Magno, Venice, 1612. Lute-maker. An instrument of this make is at the Academy of Music, Bologna. M. Engel remarks,[4] "There can be no doubt that we have here the Italianised name of the German Magnus Tieffenbrucker, who lived in Italy." There appears to be a connection between these Venetian Lute-makers of this name and Duiffoprugcar of the sixteenth century.

    [4] "Musical Myths and Facts," 1876.

DOMINICELLI, Ferrara, said to have worked about 1700.

DUIFFOPRUGCAR, Gaspar, Bologna. This famous maker of Viols is said to have settled in Bologna in the early part of the sixteenth century. He appears to have obtained much renown as an inlayer of musical instruments, and it is stated that Francis I., upon the occasion of his visit to Italy in 1515, prevailed upon the Viol-maker to settle in France. The name of Duiffoprugcar has been made familiar to us, not so much on account of his merits as a Viol-maker, but almost wholly on account of his having been represented as the first maker of the Violin tuned in fifths, and the representation having been supported by the production of three Violins signed and dated 1511, 1517, 1519. I saw, about the year 1877, one of these, and was informed by the owner that the others were almost identical. The instrument bore distinct evidence of its being a modern French imitation, or rather an ingenious creation evolved from a myth, which in all probability had its origin in France. Duiffoprugcar was unquestionably an artist of a high order, but his abilities appear to have been chiefly directed to the art of wood-inlaying, rather than to the making of stringed instruments. He made Viols da Gamba, and he may have made smaller Viols, though I am not aware of any being in existence; but there is no evidence whatever to show that he made Violins.

FARINATO, Paolo, Venice, 1695-1725.

FICKER, Johann Christian, Cremona, middle of the 18th century. Although dating from Cremona, has nothing in common with Cremonese work.

FICKER, Johann Gottlieb, Cremona, 1788.

FIORILLO, Giovanni, Ferrara, 1780. The style is a mixture of German and Italian, the former preponderating. The sound-hole is an imitation of that of Stainer. His Violoncellos are among his best instruments.

FIORINO, Fiorenzi, Bologna, about 1685.

FREI, Hans, Bologna, 1597. Lute and Viol-maker. There is an instrument of this make at the Bologna Academy of Music. It is probable there was a family connection between Hans Frey, of Nuremberg, and this maker.

> Gio Battista Gabrielli, fece in
> Firenze, 17—

> Johanes Baptista de Gabriellis,
> Florentinus fecit 1742.

GABRIELLI, Giovanni Battista, Florence, about the middle of the 18th century. The instruments of Gabrielli are now becoming better known and appreciated. They bear evident marks of having been made with extreme care. The model, unfortunately, is often not all that could be desired, being too rounded. When this is not the case, the tone is excellent. The wood is mostly very handsome, and the sides and backs evenly marked. The varnish is wanting in mellowness, but is very transparent; its colour is chiefly yellow. The Tenors and Violoncellos are superior to the Violins. The scroll is neatly cut, but weak in design. The letters G. B. G. were often branded on the instruments of Gabrielli.

GABRIELLI. Other makers of this name (Antonio, Bartolommeo, Cristoforo) appear to have dated from Florence.

GAFFINO, Giuseppe, Paris, about 1755. Pupil of Castagneri.

> Alexandrus Gagliano Alumnus
> Stradivari fecit Neapoli anno 1725.

GAGLIANO, Alessandro, Naples, 1695-1730. A pupil of Antonio Stradivari. The Gagliano family played no unimportant part in the art of Italian Violin-making. It commences with Alessandro, who imitated his master as regards the form which he gave to his instruments. Alessandro

Gagliano, upon leaving the workshop of Stradivari, removed to Naples, a city which afforded him greater scope for the exercise of his talents than Cremona. With others, he felt that his chance of success was very small if he remained on ground occupied by the greatest luminaries of his art. His labours at Naples seem to have been so well rewarded that he caused his sons to follow his calling. There is evidence of their having enjoyed what may be termed a monopoly of the Violin manufacture in and around Naples, there being no record of another maker of importance in that locality at the same period. To these makers we are indebted for the Neapolitan School. Although in its productions we miss the lustrous varnish and handsome wood of Cremona, Naples has furnished us with many excellent instruments.

The works of Alessandro Gagliano are mostly of large pattern and flat model. If we compare them with those of his master, the resemblance is not so great as might be expected, if it be remembered that they are copies, and not original works. The sound-holes are broader and more perpendicular than those of Stradivari. The scroll is diminutive, and the turn much contracted and of a somewhat mean appearance. The workmanship of the scroll is roughly executed, and points to the conclusion that Alessandro Gagliano was not gifted with the power of head-cutting. The character of Gagliano's Violins frequently reminds us of those by Stradivari made between 1725 and 1730.[5]

    5 Some of his Basses are of exceptionally fine workmanship.

The wood used for the backs was generally of a tough nature; the back and sides are often marked with a broad curl. The bellies are of wide and even grain, and very resonant. The varnish is quite distinct from that of Cremona; it is very transparent, and of various shades, chiefly yellow.

  Januarius Gagliano, filius Alexandri
        fecit Neap, 1732—

GAGLIANO, Gennaro, Naples, 1720 to about 1758; finely finished. Well-chosen wood, and excellent form. He sometimes wrote his name in pencil on the inside of the belly.

  Nicolaus Gagliano filius Alexandri
        fecit Neap 17—

GAGLIANO, Niccolò, Naples, son of Alessandro. His Violins and Violoncellos were made with care, and show that he possessed some amount of originality. They are not after the pattern of his father's instruments. They are narrower, and similar to those earlier works of Stradivari which come between the true "Amatese" and the long form. The varnish is of a deeper colour than that of Alessandro, and its quality is not inferior. The scroll is, in some cases, well formed, in others somewhat grotesque. The model is high. They are sometimes seen ornamented round the purfling with ebony, diamond and lozenge shape.

GAGLIANO, Giovanni Battista, about 1730.

> Ferdinandus Gagliano filius Nicolai
> fecit Neap 17—

GAGLIANO, Ferdinando, Naples, son of Niccolò. His instruments are usually excellently made, and have a varnish of a warmer tint than is met with on the instruments of the Gagliano family.

GAGLIANO, Giuseppe, Naples, 1780. Son of Ferdinando.

GAGLIANO, Giovanni,
GAGLIANO, Antonio,
GAGLIANO, Raffaele, Naples. These makers bring the family down to a very recent date as residents in Naples. The merit belonging to them is of the slightest kind. Some of our English provincial makers have shown themselves superior.

GALBUSERA, C. A., Milan, 1832-47. This maker appears to have attracted attention in Italy. In a little volume entitled "L'Italie Économique," 1847, he is mentioned as a maker who rivals Vuillaume. I am not acquainted with his instruments. Mention is made of his having made Violins without corners, and that he applied to the wood a preparation for the purpose of extracting the resinous particles from it. The adoption of such means of forcing on maturity makes it unlikely that he made instruments worthy of notice.

GARANI, Michel Angelo, Bologna, 1681-1720. His Tenors in particular are well-made instruments.

GARANI, Niccolò, Naples. Gagliano type of instrument, usually plain wood.

GASPARO DA SALÒ (*see* Salò).

GATINARI, Francesco, Turin, about 1700.

GENNARO, Giacomo. Worked at Cremona, in the shop of Niccolò Amati, about 1641. His name is mentioned in the parish registers in Cremona as being employed by Amati.

GERONI, Domenico, Ostiano (Province of Brescia), dated 1817.

GHIDINI, Carlo, Parma, about 1746.

GIBERTINI, Antonio, Parma, about 1830. Stradivari model, excellent work, deep rose-coloured varnish. This maker was at times employed by Paganini to repair or regulate his Violins.

GIORGI, Niccolò, Turin, about 1760.

>Franciscus Gobetti fecit
>   Venetiis 1705.

GOBETTI, Francesco (sometimes called *Gobit*), Venice, 1690-1715. This is one of the little-known makers, a fact which may be attributed to the practice, common some years ago, of removing the original label of an instrument and substituting another, bearing a name more likely from its familiarity to command attention.

When we see such Violins bearing the stamp of genius upon them, and reflecting much credit on the maker, the lovers of the instrument cannot but regret that the author should have been eclipsed, and deprived of his just praise.

Had the name of Gobetti been permitted to associate itself with the instruments into which it was originally placed, they would have been as highly valued as any belonging to the Venetian school, with the single exception of Domenico Montagnana. The admirers of that finished maker, Santo Serafino, may perhaps dispute the justice of this observation; but, having carefully weighed the merits of both Serafino and Gobetti, I have no hesitation in awarding to the latter the foremost place. Gobetti's style is superior, being more Cremonese than Venetian; and further, his model is preferable.

Gobetti has been considered to have been a pupil of Antonio Stradivari, possibly with some reason, for his instruments bear a similarity to the early works of the great master. The instruments of this maker, like those of many others of his class, have passed for the works of Ruggeri, and sometimes of Amati. There is a slight likeness about the sound-hole to the work of Francesco Ruggeri; but to the skilled in such matters, no feature interchangeable with Amati can be detected.

The workmanship is uniformly neat in execution; the scroll is the least successful part, being weak in character as compared with the body. The varnish is equal to any belonging to the Venetian school, and its beauty is second only to that of Cremona; its colour is generally a pale red, of considerable transparency. The wood is most handsome. These Venetians were not a little happy in selecting beautiful wood; in fact, it is scarcely possible to discover a single Venetian instrument the wood of which is plain.

The tone of Gobetti's work is round, without great power; but the quality is singularly sweet.

GOFRILLER, Matteo, Venice, about 1700-1735. The workmanship is often good, and the wood of fine quality. The style is somewhat different from that we are accustomed to associate with Italy. The tone and character of the varnish are generally excellent.

GOFRILLER, Francesco, Venice. Brother of the above, with whom he worked.

   Antonius Gragnani, fecit
     Liburni, anno 1780.

GRAGNANI, Antonio, Leghorn. Usually branded his initials below the tail-pin. Varnish somewhat hard; ordinary wood. The tone is often of good quality.

| STRADIVARI. 1716. (LE MESSIE.) | STRADIVARI. 1709. (LA PUCELLE.) | STRADIVARI. 1686. | STRADIVARI. 1710. |

| GIUSEPPE GUARNERI. 1735. | GIUSEPPE GUARNERI. Violon du Diable. | NICCOLÒ AMATI. |

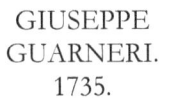

Plate VII.

GRANCINO, Paolo, Milan, 1665-92. Pupil of Niccolò Amati. The Grancino family, as makers of Violins, commence with this maker, and occupy a similar position, as followers of the Amati pattern, to that of the Gagliani as imitators of Stradivari. Paolo Grancino was pupil of Niccolò Amati. His early works bear the stamp of the mere copyist; later on the borrowed plumes are less apparent, the dictates of his own fancy are discoverable, but never to such an extent as to permit him to be classed with Stradivari, Bergonzi, and Guarneri, as striking out into entirely untrodden paths.

His Violoncellos are particularly fine instruments; his Tenors also are worthy of notice. The wood he used was varied, but is, for the most part, plain. It is curious to observe how various centres of Violin-making ran upon different qualities of wood. In Venice the handsomest wood was used, in Milan and Naples the plainest. The commercial importance of Venice would, of course, draw to it the largest selection of wood, and thus permit the second and third rate maker to use it, and at the same rate, probably, as a less handsome material would cost in cities farther removed. The scroll of Paolo Grancino has a very decisive character; it is quite distinct from that of the Amati. From the ear of the scroll the turn is rapidly made, and has an elongated appearance.

>   Giovan Grancino in Contrada
>   larga di Milano al segno
>   della Corona 16—

GRANCINO, Giovanni, Milan, 1694-1720. Son of Paolo. The workmanship is smooth, and the form good. The material of his instruments is of a better nature than that used by his father. The model is slightly flatter. The tone is powerful. Varnish mostly yellow.

GRANCINO, Giovanni Battista, Milan, 1690. Son of Giovanni mentioned above. Similar characteristics.

GRANCINO, Francesco. Son of Giovanni Battista. Here we have the same falling off as in the case of the Gagliani, a family beginning with artists, and ending with common workmen.

GRULLI, Pietro, Cremona. Contemporary.

>   Laurentius Guadagnini
>   Cremonæ Alumnus Stradivari
>   fecit Anno Domini 17—

GUADAGNINI, Lorenzo, Cremona, 1695 to about 1740. No matter to which of the Guadagnini the instrument may owe its origin, if it bears the name, importance is attached to it, often without due regard to the merits of the particular specimen. The later members of the family have thus received attention measured by the excellence of the work of their forefathers. That this should be so, to a certain extent, can scarcely excite surprise, nor is it singular in the Italian branch of the art. The great makers of the Guadagnini family were Lorenzo and Giovanni Battista. The former has been considered the chief maker; but if the merits of each be duly weighed, they will be found to be nearly equal. It is probable that Lorenzo has been looked upon as the principal maker from the association of his name with that of Antonio Stradivari, a fact which, it must be granted, lends to it a certain degree of importance.

The instruments of Lorenzo are exceedingly bold in design, and differ in this respect from those of Giovanni Battista, which retain much of the delicate form of Stradivari. Lorenzo frequently changed the form of his sound-hole, giving it the pointed character of Giuseppe Guarneri in some instances, and in others retaining the type of sound-hole perfected by his master. The model is inclined to flatness, the declivity being of the gentlest kind: the breadth of the design commands admiration. The scroll is certainly not an imitation of that of Stradivari; it has considerable originality, and is more attractive on that account than for its beauty. The varnish is not so brilliant as that of Giovanni Battista, but possesses a mellowness foreign to the other members of the family. The tone is powerful, tempered with a rich quality.

Lorenzo Guadagnini was born at Piacenza, and upon leaving the workshop of his master returned to his native town, where he remained until about the year 1695, at which period he is said to have removed to Milan. In the last mentioned city he continued to work until about the year 1740.[6]

> 6 This and other information relative to the Guadagnini family I have obtained from its descendants at Turin.

Joannes Baptista Guadagnini
Placentinus fecit Mediolani 17—

Joannes Baptista Guadagnini
Cremonensis fecit Taurini 1776.

GUADAGNINI, Giovanni Battista, Piacenza, 1711-86. Son of Lorenzo Guadagnini. He was born, according to Count Cozio di Salabue, at Cremona, and Lancetti states that he worked with his father in Milan. Later he worked at Piacenza, then at Parma, where he became instrument-maker to the Duke. Upon the pensions to the artists of the Duke's Court being discontinued in 1772, he went to Turin, where he died.[7] Count Cozio di Salabue communicated to Lancetti the following particulars relative to Giovanni Battista Guadagnini. He says: "He imitated Stradivari, but avoided close imitation of all detail, and prided himself on not being a mere copyist." He is said to have excited the jealousy of other makers, which caused him to move so frequently, but most likely he offended chiefly with his hasty temper. Many of his instruments made in Turin between 1773 and 1776 have wood of the handsomest kind. Count Cozio ordered from him several instruments which he added to his collection, among them two Tenors and two Violoncellos. The interest Count Cozio manifested with regard to this maker is shown in his having obtained from the parish registers the date of his birth and death. He states that he was born in Cremona in 1711, and died in Turin, September 18, 1786. This last-named date is in conformity with that of 1785, given to me by the representatives of the family at Turin, as the last year in which he made instruments. Lorenzo has been regarded as the only pupil of Stradivari in the Guadagnini family; but if their respective works be closely examined, it will be found that those of Giovanni Battista more closely resemble the instruments of Stradivari than even those of Lorenzo, which is suggestive of his having, in some way, been brought early under the great master's influence.[8] It is singular that his early labels contain no reference to Cremona, whilst on the late ones there is mention of the famous town, which evidences the correctness of the statement of Count Cozio relative to his birthplace. It is quite evident that he considered the model of Stradivari as that to be followed, and he does not appear to have changed his views on this point at any time, all his works being in accordance with the teachings of the great master.

> 7 The present representative of the family mentions Piacenza as the place of birth.

> 8 The labels in many of the later instruments dating from Turin contain the words "alumnus Antoni Stradivari."

Giovanni Battista was particularly happy in the selection of his wood, it being generally of the handsomest kind. The backs of his instruments are mostly found to be divided, the markings of the wood being very regular; the bellies are of wood well chosen for tone, the varnish very transparent and of a brilliant colour. The scroll may be described as a rough imitation of that of Stradivari, and to partake generally of the character of the Stradivarian scroll from the date of 1728. The English possess some of the finest specimens of this maker, and were probably the first to recognise their sterling merits. In the correspondence which passed between Count Cozio di Salabue and Vincenzo Lancetti, in the year 1823, the Count says: "The instruments of G. B. Guadagnini are highly esteemed by connoisseurs and professional men in Holland and Germany."

GUADAGNINI, Gaetano, Turin. Son of Giovanni Battista. Was both a maker and a repairer of Violins; it was, however, in the latter capacity that his abilities were mainly exercised.

GUADAGNINI, Giuseppe. Second son of Giovanni Battista. Worked with his father for some time at Turin. He ultimately went to Lombardy, and settled in Pavia, where he made a great number of instruments. The work and character belonging to these instruments are varied. The model is that of Stradivari. In some instances the sound-holes partake of the character of Giuseppe Guarneri. The varnish is inferior to that of his predecessors, and the wood often hard and plain. Some of his Violins bear the labels of his father, and were doubtless made when they were living together.

GUADAGNINI, Carlo, Turin. Son of Gaetano Guadagnini. This maker is chiefly known as a maker of Guitars. Carlo left three sons, Gaetano, Giuseppe, and Felice. These are said to have been all makers of Violins, though they appear to have accomplished but little in that direction, with the exception of Felice.

GUADAGNINI, Felice (or Felix), about 1835, Turin. Son of Carlo. Excellent work, varnish rather hard, well-cut scroll.

GUADAGNINI, Antonio. Son of Gaetano and grandson of Carlo, born 1831, died 1881. Worked with much diligence, and produced a great number of instruments. His sons Francesco and Giuseppe, the representatives of a long line of Italian Violin-makers, learned at Turin the art so long associated with the family name, with a view to their following in the footsteps of their father Antonio.

> Andreas Guarnerius fecit Cremonæ
> sub titulo Sanctæ Teresiæ 16—

GUARNERI, Andrea, Cremona, born about 1626, died 1698. The name of "Guarnerius" is probably known to every possessor of a Violin throughout the world. The familiar style is attached to scores of copies and non-copies every week, and despatched to the four quarters of the globe. Little did Andrea imagine that he was destined to be the means of lifting his patronymic of Guarneri to such a giddy height!

Andrea Guarneri, like Andrea Amati, was the pioneer of the family: but for his influence we might never have had the extraordinary works of his nephew, Giuseppe. How full of interest would the smallest events of Andrea's workshop life prove if we could only ascertain them! We know that in early years he was working in the shop of Niccolò Amati. With what delight would any record, or even anecdote, of those golden days in the history of the Violin be received by the lovers of the instrument! The bare idea that these men were living in daily close converse is sufficient to awaken interest of a lively nature in the mind of a lover of Fiddles. Unhappily, however, no Boswell was at hand to dot down events, of small value when passing, but of great consequence to after-time. The want of that direct biographical information which is handed down to us from recorded personal knowledge leads to the opening of many a mouldy, worm-eaten, and half-forgotten parish register, wherein we read, in language stiff and statutory, accounts of departed parishioners having duly performed and executed divers acts and deeds. These entries often shed much unexpected light on subjects previously dark or obscured. The pages of the Cremonese parish register, to which allusion has been made in the notices of the members of the Amati family, have served this purpose in some measure. From the same source we have a few interesting facts concerning Andrea Guarneri. It appears that Niccolò Amati entered, in the year 1641, the age of his pupil Andrea Guarneri in the parish rate-book as being fifteen years, thus supplying the hitherto unknown date of his birth. Again we learn that Andrea Guarneri does not appear to have been with Niccolò Amati in 1646, but was so in the year 1653, the register showing that he was at that date married. There is no further reference to his connection with Niccolò Amati after the year 1653. Andrea was married, December 31, 1652, and had seven children. Two of his sons, namely Pietro Giovanni and Giuseppe Giovan Battista, became Violin-makers. Andrea died on December 7, 1698, and we learn from the register that he was buried on the following day near the remains of his wife, in the Church of St. Domenico, in the same chapel where the body of Antonio Stradivari was laid forty years later.

Andrea Guarneri for some years worked upon the model of his master, though he afterwards changed the character of the sound-hole.[9] At the same time the form of the instrument became flatter, and the scroll showed signs of originality. The varnish is much varied, but is generally of a light orange colour of beautiful hue; it sometimes has considerable body, but when so, lacks the transparency of light-coloured varnishes. The Violoncellos are of two sizes. The wood in the Violoncellos is often very plain, but possesses singular tone-producing qualities. The Violins of this maker are among his finest efforts; the workmanship is excellent, but has not the fine finish of Amati.

> 9 Lancetti, in his MS., mentions 1670 as about the period of his change of style.

Joseph Guarnerius filius Andreæ fecit
Cremonæ sub titulo S. Teresiæ 16—

GUARNERI, Giuseppe Giovan Battista, second son of Andrea, born November 25, 1666. This maker possessed a greater amount of originality than Andrea. His earliest works evidence that power of thinking for himself which, later, led him to construct instruments entirely distinct from those produced by his father. The outline is particularly striking. The waist of the instrument is narrowed, rapidly widening, however, from the centre. The result is a curve of much elegance, one of the points which Giuseppe Guarneri del Gesù appears to have admired, as he adopted and perfected it. It is here, more particularly, that a resemblance between this maker and his famous kinsman is to be traced. There are also other features which will furnish matter for comment in their proper place. To return to the form given to the instruments of Guarneri, the son of Andrea: the sound-hole has a singular combination of the Amati and the Guarneri in its conception. We have here a reappearance of the pointed form which originated with the grand old Brescian master, Gasparo da Salò, and which was left by him to be revived and perfected by his followers. Andrea's son, in adopting this long-neglected form, showed much judgment. It must be admitted that he improved upon it, and left his cousin an easy task in completing and perfecting it.

The method of this maker with regard to the setting of the sound-holes in his instruments is peculiar. In his plan they are set in a lower position than is customary. Carlo Bergonzi followed him in this particular, and also in placing the hole a trifle nearer the edge of the instrument than is seen in most instruments. How interesting is it to observe the salient points wherein each maker seems to have adopted some isolated feature from a predecessor!

The varnish is of the richest description, and in some instances has been so plentifully used as to cause it to clot in some places; nevertheless, its rare qualities are never deadened.

He made Violins, Tenors, and Violoncellos, the latter being very scarce. The wood used in his Violins and Tenors varies, but may be pronounced as generally handsome; that of his Violoncellos is, on the contrary, chiefly plain, and the workmanship somewhat careless, but the tone is always fine in quality. Guarneri, Joseph, son of Andrea, according to the parish register, was married on January 4, 1690, and had six children.

> Petrus Guarnerius Cremonensis fecit
> Mantuæ sub-tit. Sanctæ Teresiæ 16—

GUARNERI, Pietro Giovanni, Cremona and Mantua, son of Andrea, born February 18, 1655. In this maker, again, there is much originality, his work, together with his model, differing entirely from that of his brother, and in outline from that of his father Andrea. There is increased breadth between the sound-holes; the sound-hole is rounded and more perpendicular; the middle bouts are more contracted, and the model is more raised. The scroll abounds in individuality of design. The ear is brought out with much effect; the purfling is splendidly executed, the corners being worked up to that extreme point of delicacy which is characteristic of the works of Niccolò Amati. The purfling is embedded after the manner of Amati in his "grand" instruments, but to a greater extent. The varnish is superb; its quality is of the richest description, and its transparency unsurpassed. Its colour varies; it is sometimes of a golden tint, sometimes of a pale red, on which the light plays with delightful variety. Pietro Guarneri used some of the finest wood. The bellies are invariably wide in grain and very even.

The parish register supplies the information that Pietro was married in the year 1677. He appears to have left Cremona for Mantua soon after the year 1698. He visited Cremona about the period when his father died; in which year he appears to have acted as god-father at the christening of his brother Joseph's son Bartolommeo. Pietro returned to Mantua, and later went to Venice, where he is said to have died at an advanced age.

GUARNERI, Pietro, Mantua, born 1695. Son of Giuseppe filius Andrea. He followed to some extent the form of the instruments of his uncle Pietro, from whom, while in Mantua, he probably learnt his art. The work is very good, and his productions are well worthy of the Guarnerian name. The varnish is rich, but not so transparent nor so well laid on as to come up to the full standard. The scroll is rather weak.

    Joseph Guarnerius fecit ✠
      Cremone Anno 17—   IHS

GUARNERI, Giuseppe, Cremona. Better known as Giuseppe del Gesù, his labels having the cypher ✠IHS upon them. It is not known why he adopted this monogram, which is that of the Jesuits. It is possible that he belonged to a fraternity in Cremona, common at that period among Italian tradesmen, who banded themselves together in various societies bearing religious titles.

This famous maker of Violins was born at Cremona in the year 1687, and died in or about 1745. The house of Giuseppe Guarneri is said to have been No. 5, Piazza S. Domenico, now called Piazza Roma.

An extract from the register proves that Giuseppe Antonio Guarneri, legitimate son of Giovanni Battista Guarneri and Angela Maria Locadelli, was born at Cremona on June 8, 1683, and was baptized on the 11th of the same month, in the parish of San Donato, at the chapel-of-ease of the cathedral.

This extract which was supposed to refer to the subject of this notice relates to a child who died in infancy, and it is now satisfactorily settled that Joseph del Gesù first saw the light on October 16, 1687. The date of death is merely conjectural, and unsupported by definite evidence.

The father of Guarneri del Gesù, namely Gio. Battista, was the son of Bernardo, a cousin of Andrea Guarneri. He does not appear to have had any knowledge of the manufacture of stringed instruments, and was thus an exception to the majority of a family which numbered many prominent makers within it. It has been asserted on all sides that Giuseppe Guarneri del Gesù was a pupil of Antonio Stradivari, but in every case this statement has been made without a shadow of proof, either from recorded fact or analogy. That this bare assertion should have so long remained unchallenged is a matter of some surprise to the writer of these pages, who fails to see anything in common between the two makers, with the exception of the varnish, and perhaps the high finish, as apparent in the works of the second epoch of Guarneri. The following remarks on this point are the result of the most careful consideration of the subject, and may serve to assist the reader in forming an opinion.

Had Giuseppe Guarneri received his early instructions from Stradivari, should we not expect his instruments to bear the character of the master in some slight degree? The most diligent student will, however, fail to discover an early work of Guarneri bearing any likeness whatever to the work of Stradivari. Among the instruments of the second epoch may be found a few that show some gleam of the desired similarity in respect of high finish; but it would be to the earliest efforts of Guarneri that we should turn in our endeavour to discover the source of his first instructions. The faint gleam of similarity, then, attaching to the instruments of the second epoch, be it understood, is in no way sufficient to demonstrate that Guarneri was a pupil of Stradivari. Upon turning to other makers, what will be the result if we judge them by the criterion above mentioned? Bergonzi, Guadagnini, Gagliano, and others, whose names it is unnecessary to mention, leave upon their earliest efforts the indelible stamp of the master who first instructed them. To suppose that Guarneri del Gesù formed the single exception to the likeness between the work of master and pupil, is scarcely sufficient to satisfy the inquiry.

There are three essential points of difference between Guarneri and Stradivari. The first is the outline of the work, which, as the mere tyro must at once observe, is totally different in their respective instruments. The second is the sound-hole, in which, again, the two do not approach one another; that of Guarneri is long, and a modified form of that of Gasparo da Salò. The third is the scroll, in which Guarneri is as distinct from Stradivari as it is possible to be.

It may be asked, then, if not from Stradivari, from whom did Guarneri receive instruction?[10] To disagree with what is popularly accepted, and yet to withhold one's own counter-theory, may perhaps tend to weaken one's case. There can be but one method to be pursued if, in the absence of any historical data, we set about the investigation of the question, viz., that of analogy. Starting upon this ground, the first step to be taken is to endeavour to discover the maker whose work and style bear some degree of similarity to those of Giuseppe del Gesù. If we carefully review the works of the Cremonese makers, it will be found that Giuseppe Guarneri, son of Andrea, and a relative of Guarneri del Gesù, is the only maker in whose productions we can find the strong similarity needed. Analogy, therefore, would point to him as the instructor of his kinsman. Giuseppe Guarneri, son of Andrea, was del Gesù's senior by many years, and it is far more reasonable to conclude that it was in his workshop that del Gesù was first instructed, than that he was the pupil of a maker whose work he never copied, and whose style has nothing in common with his own. Enough has been said on this question to enable the reader to judge for himself, and this may the more readily be conceded when it is also admitted that, after all, it is of little importance to determine where the early training of this kingly maker was passed, as he so soon displayed that rare originality which separated him from his brethren for ever.

> 10 The *evidence*—if indeed it is to be characterised as such—upon which it has been recently asserted that del Gesù was a pupil of Andreas Gisalberti is so trivial and altogether unconvincing that it seems unsuitable for discussion or analysis in a serious work of reference.—EDITORS.

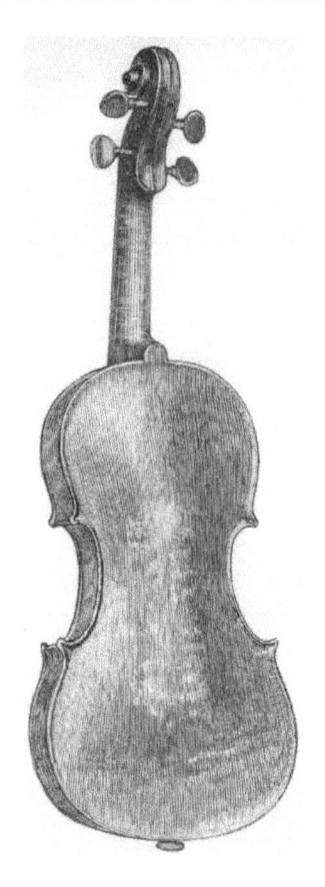

GIUSEPPE GUARNERI.
Date 1742.
(LATE H. B. HEATH, ESQ.)

ANTONIO STRADIVARI.
Date 1711.
(LATE R. D. HAWLEY, ESQ.)

ANTONIO STRADIVARI.
Date 1703.
(J. S. COOKE, ESQ.)

Plate VIII.

We will now inquire into the character of Guarneri del Gesù's model. In forming this, he seems to have turned to Gasparo da Salò as the maker whose lead he wished to follow; and if each point be critically considered, an impression is left that, after well weighing the merits and demerits of Gasparo's model, he resolved to commence where Gasparo ceased, and carry out the plan left incomplete by the great Brescian maker. To commence with that all-important element the sound-hole, it will be seen that Guarneri del Gesù retained its pointed form. Next comes the outline of the body, where, again, there is much affinity to the type of Gasparo da Salò, particularly in the middle bouts. Lastly, the quality of wood selected for the bellies is in both makers similar. In continuing the path trodden by Gasparo, Guarneri proved himself an artist possessed of no little discernment. His chief desire was evidently to make instruments capable of producing a quality of tone hitherto unknown, and that he succeeded is universally acknowledged. Workmanship, as evidenced by the instruments of his first and last epoch, was with him a purely secondary consideration. In the second epoch, his work shows him to have been not unmindful of it. That he brought much judgment to bear upon his work, the vast number of instruments that he has left and the great variety of their construction are sufficient to prove. The extent of his researches is surprising, and there is no ground for the assertion frequently made that he worked without plan or reason. The idea that such a maker as Guarneri groped in the dark savours of the ridiculous; moreover, there is direct evidence, on the contrary, of his marvellous fertility of design. At one period his instruments are extremely flat, without any perceptible rise; at another, the form is raised in a marked manner and the purfling sunk into a groove; a parallel of this type of instrument is to be found in the works of Pietro Guarneri and Montagnana. At one time his sound-holes were cut nearly perpendicularly (a freak which, by the way, has some show of reason, for though it sacrifices beauty, it also prevents the breaking up of the fibres), at another shortened and slanting, and some, again, are occasionally seen immoderately long. These hastily-marshalled instances are quite sufficient to show the extent of his experiments, and the many resources which he adopted in order to produce exceptional qualities of tone.

In order that the reader may better understand the subject, before going farther into the peculiar features belonging to the instruments of Guarneri, we will classify his work. M. Fétis, doubtless under the guidance of M. Vuillaume, has divided the career of Guarneri into three periods—an excellent arrangement, and one that cannot be improved upon. It only remains to point out certain peculiarities omitted in the description of these three stages which M. Fétis gives us. In the first epoch we find instruments of various patterns, the character of the sound-holes being very changeable. At one time there is a strange mixture of grace and boldness; at another the whole is singularly deformed, and the purfling roughly executed, as though the maker had no time to finish his work properly. It seems as if he had hastily finished off a set of Violins that he had already tested, eager to lay the stocks for another fresh venture. The second epoch has given us some of the finest specimens of the art of Violin-making. In these culminate the most exquisite finish, a thoroughly artistic and original form, and the most handsome material. In some cases the lustre of the wood of the backs, set in its casing of deep amber, that unrivalled varnish, may be likened to the effect produced by the setting summer sun on cloud and wave. The reader may pardon a somewhat novel application of the loveliest description of the glow of evening to be found in the compass of the English language, which paints the heavens' colours as—

"Melted to one vast iris of the west,
　　Where the day joins the past eternity.
　　　　　　　　... All its hues,
　From the rich sunset to the rising star,
　Their magical variety diffuse.

　And now they change; a paler shadow strews
　　Its mantle o'er the mountains; parting day
　Dies like the dolphin, whom each pang imbues
　　With a new colour as it gasps away,
The last still loveliest, till—'tis gone—and all is grey."

The effect of this beautiful coruscation upon the backs of Violins is obtained by cutting the wood upon the cross, or, as the French term it, *sur maille*. It is seen, though rarely, on backs divided, when the wood is particularly handsome in curl. The varnish on such instruments is of a rich golden hue, highly transparent; it is lightly laid on. The size of these works varies; they are sometimes a trifle smaller than the other specimens of Guarneri. In the last epoch we find Violins of an altogether bolder conception, dating from about 1740 and a little later. They are massively constructed, and have in them material of the finest acoustic properties. The sound-hole loses the pointed form so much associated with Guarneri: the purfling is embedded, the edges heavy, the corners somewhat grotesque, the scroll has a mixture of vigour, comicality, and majesty, which may force a smile and then a frown from the connoisseur. The comparison may seem a little forced, but the head of a thoroughbred English mastiff, if carved, might give some idea of the appearance sought to be described. Mr. Reade says of these instruments with much truth, "Such is the force of genius, that I believe in our secret hearts we love these impudent Fiddles best, they are so full of *chic*." Among the Violins of this period may be mentioned Paganini's, and M. Alard's, both rare specimens. These splendid *chefs-d'oeuvre* are strangely mixed with those commonly known as the "*prison Fiddles*"—a sorry title. The name arose from the story current in Italy that Guarneri made some Fiddles whilst undergoing imprisonment, and that the gaoler's daughter procured him the necessary materials, which were of the coarsest kind. M. Fétis refers to the story, and mentions that Benedetto Bergonzi, who died in 1840, used to relate it. Allusion is also made to it by Vincenzo Lancetti, to whom it was doubtless communicated by Count Cozio di Salabue. These references lead to the belief that the tradition has some foundation in fact, though not to the extent that he ended his days *in durance vile*. Lancetti refers to the offence as an encounter with some person in which his antagonist lost his life.[11] A deplorable circumstance of this kind may have occurred without the accused having been criminally at fault, though he may have suffered the penalty of being so.

His reported love of wine and pleasure, his idleness and irregularity, in all probability were statements added by successive narrators of the prison story. A recent search made by Canon Bazzi in the obituary registers of the cathedral at Cremona, discovers the fact that one Giacomo Guarneri died in prison on October 8, 1715. Bearing in mind how frequently we find fact and fiction jumbled together in historical pursuits, the prison story in connection with the name of Giuseppe Guarneri may have no other foundation than a story, long current, that a person named Guarneri was imprisoned, and wholly regardless of identity.

11 Alexander Gagliano is the subject of a similar story.

I have referred to the three periods of this remarkable man's life in relation to his art, and it remains to point out some other features in his work and material. His selection of wood, when he had the opportunity of exercising his own judgment, was all that could be desired, and the belly wood in particular was of the choicest description. He seems to have obtained a piece of pine, of considerable size, possessing extraordinary acoustic properties, from which he made nearly the whole of his bellies. The bellies made from this wood have a singular stain, running parallel with the finger-board on either side, and unmistakable, though frequently seen but faintly. If we may judge from the constant use he made of this material, it would seem that he regarded it as a mine of wealth. The care he bestowed, when working it, that none should be lost, affords clear evidence of the value that he set upon this precious piece of wood. I have met with three Violins by Carlo Bergonzi, having bellies evidently cut from the same piece of pine, and these instruments passed as the work of Guarneri for a long period. The sycamore that he used was varied both in appearance and quality; it is chiefly of a broad description of grain, the whole-backs being impressively marked like a tiger's skin. There are a few instances where, in his jointed-backs, the markings of the wood are turned upwards.

Upon examining the works of Guarneri with respect to their graduation, it is found that he varied very much as to the quantity of wood left in the several instruments. Notwithstanding these differences, however, it will be found, upon closer comparison of the thickness, that there is every reason to be sure that he had a guiding principle in their management. They vary with the quality of the wood; and hard material was treated as needing a slighter solidity than wood of a softer nature.

His workmanship in numerous instances is, without doubt, careless; but, even in the instruments where this negligence is most observed, there is an appearance which at once excites the admiration of the beholder, and forces from the most exacting the admission that, after every deduction on account of want of finish, there remains a style defying all imitation. Who can fail to recognise the quaint head, into which he seems to have thrown such singular character by the mere turn of his chisel, and which, when imitated, always partakes of the ludicrous, and betrays the unhappy copyist who is unable to compass that necessary turn! In matters of the highest art it is always so; the possessor of genius is constantly showing some last resort, as it were, impregnable to imitation.

The sound-hole, also, of Guarneri always preserves its distinctive character, and a grotesque humour which at once pleases the eye, though it is found to vary considerably with the three periods of his life. Again, the button—that portion of the back against which the heel of the neck rests, which forms a prominent mark in all Violins, and an evidence of style, has a remarkably pronounced development in the Violins of Guarneri, and, in fact, may be said to give a vitality to the whole work. There are many instances where excellent and original specimens of workmanship have been, speaking artistically, ruined for want of skill in handling that simple factor of the Violin.

Having endeavoured to point out the chief features in the work and style of this remarkable maker, I have only to add that his imitators would far exceed in number all the Violin-makers that the city of Cremona ever sheltered. There has ever been a diversity of purpose with these Guarneri imitators, distinct from those of Stradivari and others. They may be divided into three orders, viz., the *bonâ fide* copyist, the subtle copyist, and the wholesale copyist. The first sets about making his instrument resemble the original as closely as possible, and when completed, sends it forth as a copy, and nothing else. Among these legitimate imitators were Lupot, Gand, Vuillaume, and others. The subtle copyist takes advantage of the disturbed styles belonging to Guarneri, coupled with his misfortunes, manufactures and translates at will. He "spots" a back on an old fiddle, in which he sees Guarneri in embryo; he secures it. In his possession is a belly which, with a little skilful manoeuvring of sound-holes and corners, may be accommodated to the back. The sides need well matching in point of colour; workmanship is purely secondary. The scroll he sets *himself* to carve, giving it a hideous, burglar-like appearance. The inevitable label is inserted, and the Violin leaves the translator's hand a "Prison Joseph." Now comes the difficulty. How is this "Joseph," unaccustomed to elbow his legitimate namesakes in the world of Fiddles, to maintain the character he has assumed? The subtle copyist puzzles his brain without arriving at anything very satisfactory. He resolves to slip it into a sale of household effects. It is described in the catalogue, in glowing terms, as having been in the possession of Geminiani (he not being alive to dispute the assertion). Previous to the sale the instrument is viewed. The knowing ones pass it by with contempt. The *half*-informed turn it over and over, puzzled, and replace it in its case disconsolate. The thoroughly ignorant looks inside; "Joseph Guarnerius Cremonensis faciebat 1724," in old type, stares him in the face; he puts the bow on the strings and demands the maker's name—his thoughts are echoed back in gentle sounds: "Joseph Guarnerius." He returns it to its case, shuts the lid, and exultingly sallies forth, congratulating himself again upon his good fortune in having at last the opportunity of securing the real thing at the price of "a mere song." The time of sale arrives. The beauties of the instrument are dwelt upon by the auctioneer; he begs to be permitted to say two hundred guineas to commence with. Silence around. "Well, gentlemen, shall I say one hundred and fifty guineas?" Dogged silence. "Come, come, gentlemen, this is mere trifling. A 'Joseph Guarnerius' for one hundred and fifty guineas! Shall I say one hundred guineas?" The customary witty frequenter of sale-rooms, unable to restrain himself longer, cries out, "I'll give yer a pound!" The auctioneer sees the whole thing; it is a copy that he is selling, and not the original. The pound bid is capped by another from our friend, who fondly fancies himself behind the scenes. The subtle copyist, seeing his eagerness, bids on his bid, and the "Joseph Guarnerius del Gesù" falls with the hammer to the anxious buyer for ten pounds. He demands possession of it at once, in case another may be substituted, and retires, perfectly satisfied with his day's work. The wholesale copyists are those who manufacture Violins in Bavaria and France in large factories, where the Violins undergo all kinds of processes to make them modern antiques. The wood is put into ovens and baked until it assumes the required brownness, or steeped in strong acids until it becomes more like a piece of charred wood than anything else; the sharp edges are removed by the file; the wear of years is effected in a few moments by rubbing down those parts subject to friction; it is ticketed and dated, regardless alike of orthography and chronology, the date being generally before or after the original's existence. These imitations are so barefaced as to render them comparatively harmless.

GUIDANTI, Giovanni, Bologna, about 1740. High model; sound-hole long; purfling badly let in; the outer form inelegant, particularly the middle bouts. At the Exhibition at Milan, 1881, a Viola d'Amore was exhibited, signed "Joannes Guidantus, fecit Bononiæ, anno 1715," ornamented with a beautiful head artistically carved, representing a blindfolded Cupid.

GUILLAMI, Spanish family of Violin-makers, about 1680-1780.

HARTON, Michael, Padua, 1600. Lute-maker.

KERLINO, Joan, 1449. Maker of Viols. Numerous instruments of the Violin shape have been attributed to this maker, particularly those of quaint appearance, but it is doubtful whether he made any instruments but those of the Viol type.

LAGETTO, Luigi, Paris, about 1753.

> Carolus Ferdinandus Landulphus,
> fecit Mediolani in Via S. Margaritæ
> anno 17—

LANDOLFI, Carlo Ferdinando, Milan, 1750. Though he belonged to the latest of the Italian makers, his merits were of no ordinary kind. His instruments vary very much, and hence, probably, a confusion has arisen as to there being two makers of this name, which is not the case. Those instruments which have the bright red varnish are certainly the best. The varnish is very transparent, and, the wood being strikingly handsome, the effect is most pleasing. The pattern is not a copy of Guarneri, as often stated, but thoroughly original. His sound-hole cannot be considered an effective one, and is not in keeping with the work. The outer edge is generally grooved. The scroll is weak. His Violoncellos are mostly of small size. Some of this maker's instruments are very unfinished, many not being purfled, and having only a single coat of varnish.

LANZA, Antonio Maria, 1674. Copied the Brescian makers.

LAVAZZA, Santino, Milan, about 1700.

> Santino Lavazza fece in Milano in Contrada larga 17—

LAVAZZA, Antonio, Milan.

> Lavazza Antonio Maria fece in Milano in Contrada larga 17—

LINAROLLI, Venturo, Venice, 1520. A maker of Viols.

LOLY, Jacopo, Naples, 17th century. Of the Grancino type. Scroll diminutive. Yellow varnish. Material very hard. Flat model. He made a few large tenors.

> Gio Paolo Maggini in Brescia.

MAGGINI, Giovanni Paolo, Brescia, 1590. This famous maker followed Gasparo da Salò, and was his pupil. It is surmised that he may have died of the plague in or about the year 1632. No Italian maker is more frequently mistaken than Maggini. Any instrument having ornamentations on the back in the shape of purfled scroll-work is at once said to be by Paolo Maggini. Barak Norman, the old English maker, thus comes in for a large share of Maggini's patronage, as also a vast number of early German makers, who adopted similar devices; to the real connoisseur, however, there is no difficulty in distinguishing the work. A more pardonable error is the confusion of Gasparo da Salò and Maggini, which is of frequent occurrence.

The Double Basses of these two makers have much in common to the eye of the not deeply versed examiner. Maggini, however, was not so successful as his compeer in the selection of the *form* of his instruments. In them we miss the harmony of outline belonging to those of Gasparo, particularly as relates to his Double Basses. Gasparo's Violins are less harmonious in design, and evince his unsettled views as to the form they should take; a perfectly natural circumstance when the infantile state of the Violin in his day is considered. The outline of Maggini is broad, but lacks the classic symmetry of the rare old Brescian maker. The form is flat, and the means which he adopted in order to obtain a full and telling tone were very complete. The sides are frequently shallow, and in accordance with the outline. With others who followed him, he evidently recognised the necessity of reducing the height of the sides in proportion to the dimensions of the instrument. The sound-hole is long and pointed, and admirably set in the instrument. The scroll is primitive, but boldly cut, and clearly marks an onward step from the somewhat crude production of Gasparo, the back of which is not grooved, or but slightly. Maggini's varnish is of brown or yellow colour, and of good quality. The instruments covered with the brown varnish are often without any device on their backs, and seldom have two rows of purfling. De Bériot, the famous Belgian Violinist, used one of Maggini's Violins, and, in consequence, their value was much increased.[12]

> 12 The genuine labels are undated, as in the case of his master, Gasparo da Salò.

MALER, Laux, Bologna, about 1450. Maker of Lutes. Maler appears to have been regarded by Lutinists as the Stradivari of Lutes. Thomas Mace informs us in his "Musick's Monument," 1676, they were sold for as much as one hundred pounds each, though often "pittiful, old, batter'd, crack'd things." He tells us he has "often seen Lutes of three or four pounds price far more illustrious and taking to a common eye." History repeats itself at every turn. The uneducated eye of to-day is equally apt to regard a Mirecourt or Bavarian copy with as much favour as a genuine Cremona. Mace proceeds to instruct the "common eye." "First, know that an old Lute is better than a new one." Thus also with Viols: "We chiefly value old instruments before new; for by experience they are found to be far the best." "The pores of the wood have a more and free liberty to move, stir, or secretly vibrate, by which means the air—which is the life of all things, both animate and inanimate—has a more free and easie recourse to pass and repass." This explanation accounts, in part at least, for the superiority of old over new instruments, and in language delightfully quaint and simple.

Pietro Giov Fratelli Mantegazza nella
Contrada di Santa Margarita in
Milano al Segno dell' Angelo 17—

Petrus Jo[es.] Fratresq Mantegatia
Mediolani in Via S. Margarite
anno 1760.

Petrus Joannes Mantegatia, fecit
Mediolani in Via S. Margaritæ 1784.

MANTEGAZZA, Pietro Giovanni, Milan. Vincenzo Lancetti states that "about 1800 the Brothers Mantegazza were restorers of instruments, and were often entrusted by French and Italian artistes to lengthen the necks of their Violins after the Paris fashion, an example which was followed by amateurs and professors all over North Italy." This extract shows that the short necks were dispensed with in Paris towards the close of the last century, and doubtless Viotti was the chief instigator with regard to the change. The family of Mantegazza, as Violin-makers, date back to about the middle of the eighteenth century. They appear to have made many Tenors. The workmanship is good, and also the modelling of the later-dated instruments. The older ones are rather high, but the varnish is brilliant. The wood is somewhat hard. Count Cozio was a patron of the Brothers Mantegazza, and he appears to have increased his knowledge of Italian Violins from information acquired from them.

MARATTI, Verona, about 1700.

MARCHETTI, Enrico, Turin, contemporary.

MARIANI, Antonio, Pesaro, from about 1580 to 1619. Long middle bouts and corners; style and work very primitive, mostly double purfled.

MEIBERI, Francesco, Leghorn, 1750.

MESSEGUER, Spanish, about 1646.

MEZADRI, Alessandro, Ferrara, 1690-1722. The pattern is inelegant, and the sound-holes too close.

MEZADRI, Francesco, Milan, about 1712.

MIALFI, Joannes, 1769. The label is in Spanish. Ordinary character of work.

GIUSEPPE GUARNERI DEL GESÙ.
1737.
(LATE H. O. HAVEMEYER, ESQ.)

Plate IX.

Dominicus Montagnana Sub Signo
    Cremonæ Venetiis 17—

MONTAGNANA, Domenico, Cremona and Venice, 1700-1740. Pupil of Antonio Stradivari. After leaving the workshop of his famous master, he followed his art in Cremona. He afterwards removed to Venice, where Violin manufacture was in the most flourishing condition, and adopted the name of "Cremona" as the sign of his house. In days when houses were unnumbered, tradesmen were found by their sign, and they were often puzzled to select one both distinctive and effective. The Violin-makers of Italy, having exhausted the calendar of its Saints emblematic of Harmony, left it to the Venetian to honour the name of himself and the city which was the seat of the greatest Violin manufacture the world had witnessed. In Venice he soon attained great popularity, and made the splendid specimens of his art with which we are familiar. The instructions which he had received at Cremona enabled him to surpass all in Venice. He gained great knowledge of the qualities of material, and of the thicknesses to be observed; and, moreover, he carried with him the superior form of the Cremonese school, and the glorious varnish. Mr. Reade names him "the mighty Venetian," an appellation not a whit too high-sounding, though it may appear so to those not acquainted with his finest works. The truth is, that Montagnana is less known than any of the great makers. For years his works have been roaming about, bearing the magic labels of "Guarnerius filius Andreæ," "Carlo Bergonzi," and sometimes of "Pietro Guarneri," although there is barely a particle of resemblance between the works of our author and the makers named, whose labels have been used as floats.

Montagnana was in every way original, but the fraud that has foisted his works upon makers who were better known has prevented his name from being associated with many of his choicest instruments, and deprived him of the place which he would long since have held in the estimation of the true connoisseur. This injustice, however, is fast passing away; as ever, genius comes forth triumphant.

The time is near when the "mighty Venetian" and Carlo Bergonzi will occupy positions little less considerable than that of the two great masters. Already the merits of these makers are daily more appreciated, and when the scarcity of their genuine works is considered, it becomes a matter of certainty that their rank must be raised to the point indicated.

It is much to be regretted that both Montagnana and Bergonzi did not leave more numerous specimens behind them. Would that each had been as prolific as their common master! We should then have inherited a store from which our coming Violinists and Violoncellists could have possessed themselves of splendid instruments, when those of Guarneri and Stradivari were placed far beyond reach.

In these times, when the love of music is rapidly developing itself among all classes, the question of supply must attract notice. The prime question with respect to Violins of the highest character is not now as to price, but as to the supply of limited and daily decreasing material; and the doubtful point is, not whether purchasers are to be found who may not be unwilling to pay the increased cost consequent upon scarcity, but whether the instruments required will be available in sufficient numbers to satisfy the demands of those quite prepared to gratify their wishes for the possession of an instrument of the first rank. A single glance is sufficient to remind us that the list of makers of the highest class, and particularly of original artists, is scanty indeed. There are a few copyists, it is true, notably Lupot and Panormo, whose instruments must take a considerable position, but on the whole the demand will far exceed the supply. The difficulty here noticed is intensified from the fact of the Violin being sought after as it is, unlike any other musical instrument, for the cabinets of the collector as well as for actual use—a state of things perfectly natural when its artistic beauties are considered. Violinists possibly consider they smart under a sense of wrong at the hands of collectors who thus indulge their taste; but, on the other hand, we have reason to be grateful to the lovers of art for having stayed the hand of Time in demolishing these treasures.

To return to the subject of this present notice: it is evident that when Montagnana left the workshop of Stradivari, he gave full scope to his creative powers. He at once began to construct upon principles of his own, and thus followed the example of his fellow-worker, Carlo Bergonzi. If comparison be made between the work of Stradivari and that of Domenico Montagnana, with regard to detail, the two makers will not be found to have much in common. It is when Montagnana's instrument is viewed as a whole that the teaching of Stradivari is evidenced. A similar assertion may, in a lesser degree, be made in the case of Carlo Bergonzi. To dissect the several points of difference is a simple matter. If we begin with the outline, that of Montagnana has not the smoothness and grace of the Stradivarian type; the upper and lower curves are flattened, while those of the centre are extended. The sound-hole partakes more of the character of Guarneri; the scroll is larger, and the turns bolder than in the Stradivari form. These, then, may be considered to be the chief points wherein, if viewed as separate items, Montagnana seems to have varied from his master: and hence we may obtain some idea of the amount of originality belonging to this maker—an amount, indeed, not inferior to that of any Cremonese artist that can be cited. The increasing popularity of Montagnana's instruments is sufficient proof that his design was fraught with much that is valuable. In departing from the form of Antonio Stradivari, Carlo Bergonzi and Montagnana doubtless intended to bring out in a stronger degree certain particular qualities of tone: at the same time we may be sure that they had no idea of attempting to improve upon Stradivari in his own field of work, for they must have well known the Herculean character of such a task. On the other hand, had these remarkable makers been mere copyists, they would certainly have handed down to us more instruments moulded in exact accord with the style of their great teacher; while, at the same time, we should have lost many variations, which are at present not only an evidence of their fertility of resource, but also in themselves most pleasing objects. If, in the sister art, Tintoretto had made it his sole business to copy Titian, the world would have been rich in copies of Titian, but poor in Tintorettos.

The varnish of Montagnana has long excited the admiration of connoisseurs throughout Europe. The extreme richness and velvet-like softness which are its characteristics constitute it a fitting countersign of the workmanship of this great maker, an artist of the first magnitude. He made Violins, Tenors, and Violoncellos. His Violins are of two sizes.

MONTALDI, Gregorio, Cremona, 1730. Copied Stradivari.

MORELLA, ——, Mantua, about 1550. M. Fétis, in his "Biographie Universelle des Musiciens," states that he was famous for his Viols and Lutes. S. Ang. Maffei, in his "Annali di Mantova" (fol. 147), highly praises the instruments made by Morella.

NADOTTI, Giuseppe, Piacenza. A Violin by this maker was in 1881 exhibited at the Milan Exhibition, dated 1767.

NELLA, Raffaele, Brescia, copied Maggini.

ORTEGA, ——, Madrid, about 1840. Maker and restorer of instruments.

PANDOLFI, Antonio, Venice. A Violin of this make, dated 1719, was among the instruments exhibited at the Milan Exhibition in 1881.

PANORMO, Vincenzo, Palermo, born about 1740, died 1813. This maker was one of the most successful followers of Antonio Stradivari. Panormo and Lupot share the palm as copyists of the great Cremonese master. Neither appears to have attempted to create a model of his own; their sole aim was to imitate to the utmost the various patterns of Stradivari, Guarneri, and Amati, but they principally confined themselves to Stradivari.

Vincenzo Panormo left Italy in early life, and settled for a short time in Paris, from which city a few of his instruments are dated. From Paris he removed to London, where he remained many years. He also visited Ireland, where he made, it is said, several beautiful instruments from an old maple billiard-table, with which he was fortunate enough to meet. He was of a restless temperament, which showed itself in continual self-imposed changes. He would not, or could not, permit his reputation to grow steadily, by residing long in one place, but as soon as fame was within his grasp, he sacrificed the work of years by removing to an entirely new field of labour.

Panormo furnishes us with another example of the certain appreciation, sooner or later, of exceptional talents. No matter how trifling the circumstances under which gifted men have laboured, some time or other their genius is discovered, and acknowledged with its due award, if not of fortune, at least of fame. The peculiar circumstances under which Panormo lived would have been sufficient in the case of most men to dwarf all efforts. Unable to obtain readily that patronage to which his abilities justly entitled him, he removed from city to city, hoping to discover a resting-place, in which favour might attend his art. No doubt this was a mistaken course, and one which robbed his work of the attention which a mind undisturbed by the care of existence can bestow; nevertheless his natural gifts had a vitality that could not entirely be suppressed. He worked and toiled for his art and for bare sustenance alternately. His life, like that of many others in the paths of literature and science, was a continued battle with adversity. Such persons are forced to satisfy daily wants by slaving at work which brings them but little credit in after time, and becomes a standard by which they are too often erroneously judged.

Vincenzo Panormo was the slave of many, manufacturing Double Basses and other instruments from the material selected and purchased by his temporary employer, ofttimes compelled to carry out some crotchet of the patron much against his own wishes. The wood thus forced upon him was often of the worst description; and, in addition, he was frequently obliged to complete his work within a given time. Instruments manufactured under such conditions can scarcely, it may be supposed, add to their maker's reputation. We cannot but regret that he should have been obliged to waste himself on such poor materials. Fortunately, however, in some cases he found time to exercise his skilful powers to their full extent, and has thus bequeathed to us some of the finest specimens of the copyist's art.

His workmanship is of a lighter description than that of Lupot, and is therefore more graceful. The sound-hole is admirably cut, and the scroll also well carved.

PANSANI, Antonio, Rome, 1735.

PASTA, Antonio, Brescia, 1700-1730. Good work. Model a little high; varnish of soft quality.

PASTA, Domenico, Brescia, about 1700.

PAZZINI, Gaetano, Florence, about 1630, pupil of Maggini.

PICINO, Padua, 1712. High model; dark varnish.

PLATNER, Michel, Rome, about 1750. The instruments of this maker resemble those of Tecchler, both in workmanship and varnish.

<blockquote>Michael Platner fecit Romæ anno 17—</blockquote>

POLLUSCA, Antonio, Rome, about 1751.

POSTIGLIONE, Vincenzo, Naples, contemporary.

Joannes Franciscus Pressenda
q. Raphael fecit Taurini
Anno Domini 1826.

PRESSENDA, Giovanni Francesco, Turin. Born in the year 1777. The Violins bearing the label of Pressenda are excellently made, and in many instances the varnish is superior to that met with on any Violins dated from Italy in the present century. Pressenda appears to have interested himself to some extent in the matter of varnish. In a little book published in Italy[13] there is the following passage: "A pale reflection of the old art (Violin-making) is found in Piedmont, with Guadagnini." The writer continues with the following reference to Pressenda of Turin, who, he remarks, was in his youth at Cremona, "where he collected the traditions of the school as regards modelling and the preparation of the varnish, which is the chief merit of his Violins." It is almost needless to remark that traditional information is frequently unsatisfactory, but particularly so in connection with Cremonese Violin-making and varnishing, near the middle of the last century. In short, the great makers left no other record of the steps they took both in manufacture and in the preparation of their varnish than can be discovered in their works. The instruments of Pressenda present a singular contrast with others of Italian make belonging to this century, most of which evidence what may be termed the throes of a dying manufacture. With Pressenda we appear to have a new departure, in which there is some show of attention having been paid to the work accomplished in the best workshops of Paris. The then condition of Violin-making in Italy made it necessary for any Italian maker—no matter how great his ability—to seek information elsewhere, if desirous of excelling in his art. Pressenda appears to have sought to emulate and even surpass many Parisian makers by associating his name for the most part with good and unsophisticated work. The results of his labours reflect no little credit on his skill and judgment. Pressenda may be styled a born maker of Violins. From an account published by Signor Rinaldi, of Turin, in 1873, we learn that Pressenda was the son of poor parents, who lived in Lequio-Berria, a hamlet in the vicinity of Alba, in Piedmont. His father Raffaele was a strolling fiddler, and gained his precarious livelihood by playing at village fairs and other rejoicings. On these occasions he was accompanied by his son Giovanni, who followed the occupation of his father, playing the Violin with some degree of skill. It was at this period that he appears to have manifested a desire to know something of Violin manufacture, and frequently asked for information from his parent, who, however, was rarely able to satisfy his curiosity. Learning that Cremona was in some way associated with good Violins, he resolved to fiddle his way to that city. There he found Storioni, from whom he obtained some rudimentary knowledge of the manufacture he was so much interested in. Later he removed to Piedmont, and established himself in Alba in 1814, as a maker of Violins. The patronage he gained was, however, insufficient to maintain him, and he combined the business of cabinet-making with his favourite pursuit. After removing to Carmagnola, he went in the year 1820 to Turin, where his abilities were recognised and rewarded. He was encouraged in his manufacture by Giovanni Battista Polledro, the famous Violinist, who, in 1824, became Musical Director of the Royal Orchestra at Turin. Pressenda died in the year 1854 at Turin. His Violins are chiefly of the model of Stradivari. The sound-holes are well cut. The thicknesses of his best instruments are well arranged, and the wood appears to have been selected with good judgment. The scrolls, whilst having much character, are somewhat roughly cut. The Violins belonging to his early period are chiefly of the Amatese character.

       13 "L'Italie économique," 1847.

RACCERIS,——, Mantua, about 1670.

RINALDI, Gioffredo, Turin. (Benedetti, Gioffredo.) Chiefly known as a dealer in Violins. He exhibited a few Violins by Giovanni F. Pressenda at the Vienna Exhibition, 1873, and published a short notice of that maker, which he inscribed to the Archduke Rannieri.

RIVOLTA, Giacomo, Milan, about 1822. Excellent work; scroll well cut. One of the best Italian makers of the nineteenth century.

ROCCA, Joseph Antonio, Piedmont, 1837-1863. Chiefly followed the pattern of Stradivarius. Neat workmanship, varnish rather thin, well-cut scroll. He worked for some time with Pressenda.

RODIANI, Giovita, sometimes called Budiani; Brescia, about 1580-1620. His instruments resemble those of Maggini. Dragonetti is said to have had a Double Bass of this make.

ROTA, Giovanni, Cremona. Yellow varnish, plain wood, heavy work, rough purfling.

       Joannes Rota fecit Cremonese Anno 1808.

ROVETTA, Bergamo, 1840-70.

  Io: Bapt. Rogerius Bon: Nicolai
    Amati de Cremona Alumnus
  Brixiæ fecit Anno Domini 1705.

ROGERI, Giovanni Battista, Cremona and Brescia. The word Bon after his name refers to his having been a citizen of Bologna. Vincenzo Lancetti speaks of its being certain that he called himself *Bononiensis*. The instruments of this maker are of a different pattern from those of Francesco Ruggeri. They are higher modelled, the sound-holes less elegant, and the scroll heavier. They possess, however, high merits, and command prices nearly equivalent to those of the instruments of Francesco. The labels of this maker are sometimes met with printed in red ink. The instruments he made of large Amati pattern are highly valued. He appears to have worked from about the close of the seventeenth century. Count Cozio di Salabue and Lancetti speak of G. B. Rogeri having worked down to 1723, and possibly later, and state that he lived for many years in Brescia. There are some instruments bearing original Amati labels of this make, made, doubtless, when he was in the shop of Amati.

ROGERI, Pietro Giacomo, Brescia, describes himself on his label as a pupil of Niccolò Amati. Lancetti refers to a Violoncello by Pietro Rogeri as having belonged to Count Cozio, and remarks that he was a "nearly unknown member of the Rogeri family." The date of the instrument is given as 1714. He cannot now be looked upon as almost unknown, since Signor Piatti played for many years upon a famous Violoncello of his make. The pattern is a little narrower than that of G. B. Rogeri. Varnish of beautiful quality; sound-hole resembles that of Francesco Ruggeri.

   Francesco Ruggeri detto
     il Per Cremona 16—

RUGGERI, Francesco, Cremona, 1668-1720. Surnamed "Il Per." The family of Ruggeri long occupied a foremost place in the city of Cremona as makers of Violins, Tenors, and Violoncellos. Their position must have been but little inferior to that of the Amati family. Francesco, in his earliest works, gives evidence of exceptional artistic feeling, and the sequel of his career, as evidenced by his productions, is a genuine development of the first impulses of his genius. His work belongs to the school of Amati, but though the list of instruments which he has bequeathed to us be a long one, there is no sign of his ever having been a mere copyist. He evidently thought for himself. His sound-hole is a beautiful piece of workmanship, and may be said to come between that of Niccolò Amati and Stradivari, being of the most delicate execution. The outline of his work is very graceful, and the arching admirable. The scroll has quite an equal merit with the body. He was very successful in selecting his material, much of which is handsome. His varnish, thoroughly Cremonese in character, and of a most beautiful hue, may be equalled, but never surpassed. This maker also knew how to use his varnish. There is no instance in which it has been laid on in clumsy patches; the surface is always true and even, and, in consequence, the brilliancy of its appearance is perfect. Lancetti remarks, "Francesco Ruggeri was a pupil of Niccolò Amati, and perhaps a more exact imitator of his instruments than G. B. Rogeri, and made several instruments, beautifully finished, and which are not easily distinguished from those of his master." Count Cozio possessed a fine Violin by Francesco, dated 1684, and the Marquis Castiglioni also possessed one made in the same year. Francesco Ruggeri died at the house No. 7, Contrada Coltellai, Cremona.

RUGGERI, Giacinto detto Il Per, Cremona. Son of Francesco Ruggeri. A Violoncello bearing this label is in the possession of Mr. G. Foster Cooke:

Giacinto filio di
Francesco Ruggeri detto il Per
1696.

RUGGERI, Vincenzo, Cremona, also uses the name "Il Per." Worked from about 1700 to 1730. He appears to have made many Violoncellos.

Vincenzo Ruger detto il Per
in Cremona 17—

RUGGERI, Giambattista, Cremona. About 1693. Also called himself Il Per. Lancetti suggests that this maker was a relative of Francesco. He made several Violoncellos of large size and deep sides, the wood of which is often plain. The varnish is of good quality and dark brown colour. He also made Violins and Tenors, the latter being excellent instruments.

SACCHINI, Sebastiano.

Sebastino Sacchni da Pesaro l'anno 1686.

Gasparo da Salò Brescia.

SALÒ, Gasparo da. His real name was Gasparo dei Bertolotti. The researches of Cavalliere Livi, keeper of the Brescian Archives, have brought to light much valuable information as to this famous maker. He was born in the town of Salò (Province of Brescia) in or about the year 1542, died there on the 14th of April, 1609, and was buried in the church of San Joseffo. A son (Francesco) appears to have worked with him and to have died in 1614. Several Viols of Gasparo's workmanship, of different sizes, are still extant. The Violins are very rare. A few large Violas exist, the tone of which is magnificent. His genuine labels bear no date. Gio Paolo Maggini was apprenticed to him, and is believed to have purchased the business, after Gasparo's death, from his son Francesco.

To Gasparo da Salò belongs the credit of having laid the foundation of the Italian style of Violin-making. In his works may be traced the gradual development of the system upon which his followers built their reputation, viz., a well-defined model, excellent materials, and choice varnish. It is to be regretted that his immediate followers, with the exception of Paolo Maggini, departed from the path so successfully trodden by this great pioneer. But for this deviation, the works of the early Amati and a few others would have occupied a higher position than that which they now command. They were men possessing great abilities, and might easily have carried out the designs of the great Brescian maker. They appear, however, to have arrived at a different conclusion, as regards the form of their instrument, from that shaped by Gasparo da Salò. Their works show an evident preference for the high model, and thus undid much that Gasparo had accomplished. It is clear that Gasparo only arrived at his conclusions after painstaking labour, for he commenced with the high form, and gradually, as experience taught, lowered it. It is, further, remarkable that the latter members of the Amati family pursued the same course as Andrea Amati (though in a less degree), after which they awoke, as it were, to the reasonableness of the example set by Gasparo, and gave us those instruments so highly thought of by the connoisseur, the form of which has much in common with that adopted by Niccolò Amati and perfected by Antonio Stradivari.

It has been before remarked that Gasparo da Salò did not arrive at his conclusions without mature consideration. In fact, a long and deliberate process of experiment may be traced in his instruments. We find that at times his Violins and Violas were treated differently from the Accordos and Violonos. The Violins are found to be high in model, while the above-named instruments, evidently of the same date, are flat. He would seem to have been desirous of testing the powers of either model, and it is possible that he fostered the idea of varying the construction of each of the four species in the family of stringed instruments according to the part which should be allotted to it. To treat each part of the stringed quartette in a different way is certainly an error, for they are to be looked upon as gradations of one and the same instrument; nevertheless, the attempt of Gasparo, although mistaken, offers but another instance of his prolific ingenuity and unwearied diligence. An praise is due to the great Brescian maker for having opened up, as a pioneer, so wide a field of research. The Cremonese artists followed up his clue, and brought the Violin to the highest state of excellence.

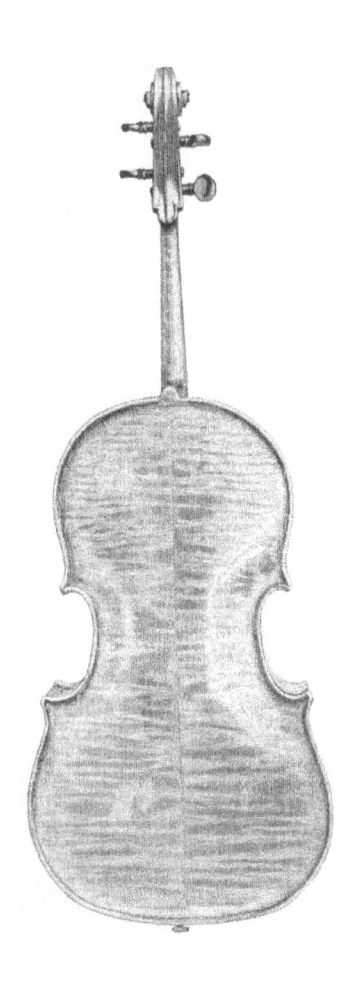

DOMENICO MONTAGNANA.
(GEO. GUDGEON, ESQ.)

Plate X.

The chief characteristics of the works of Gasparo da Salò are the sound-holes, shortened centre-bouts, scroll, and peculiar choice of material. The length of the sound-hole at first strikes one as somewhat crude, but as the eye becomes more acquainted with the general form of the instrument, it is seen to be in perfect harmony with the primitive outline. With this sound-hole commences the pointed form to which Giuseppe Guarneri, nearly a century and a half later, gave such perfection. The material used for the larger instruments is mostly pear-wood, or wood of that description, the quality of which is particularly fine. In the selection of this wood he showed a still minuter discrimination, using it generally for Accordos and Violonos, and not for Violins or Violas; few specimens of the latter have backs of pearwood. His work was bold, but not highly finished; no other result could be looked for at so early a date. The grain of the bellies is usually very even and well defined. Signor Dragonetti, the late eminent Double-Bass player, possessed three or four Double-Basses by this maker of various sizes. The most celebrated of these instruments was presented to him by the monks of the monastery of St. Mark's, Venice, about the year 1776, and was returned to the Canons of that Church (the monks and the monastery having been suppressed since the French occupation of Venice in 1805 or 1809) after Dragonetti's death, in 1846. Another was bequeathed by Dragonetti to the late Duke of Leinster. A third is in the possession of the Rev. George Leigh Blake. Among his chamber Double-Basses the one formerly belonging to Mr. Bennett is regarded as a singularly perfect example. It was numbered with the rarities of Luigi Tarisio's collection, and highly valued by him as a specimen of the maker. Among his Violins, the instrument formerly owned by Lord Amherst, of Hackney, is unique; the infancy of the Violin at this period is better seen here than any specimen with which I am acquainted. The Violin of this make which belonged to Ole Bull, and with which I am familiar, is another well-known example. This instrument is characteristic of its author. Its varnish is soft-looking and rich, though paler than usual. The finger-board is inlaid, and is made of a light description of wood. The head is carved and painted, and is a very choice piece of Italian work.

SANONI, Giovanni Battista, Verona. About 1740. His instruments are seldom met with in England. High model.

SANTO, Giovanni, Naples, 1700-30. Copied Amati. Varnish very hard, and workmanship indifferent.

SANZO, Milan. Middle and early eighteenth century. Similar to Grancino.

SARDI, ——, Venice, 1649. A broken Violin bearing this name was at the Milan Exhibition, 1881.

SEIGHER, Girolamo. Worked in the shop of Niccolò Amati from 1680 to 1682.

SELLAS, Matteo, Lute-maker. M. Chouquet, in his "Catalogue Raisonné" of the instruments at the Paris Conservatoire, mentions two Arch-Lutes made by this maker.

> Sanctus Seraphin
> utinensis Fecit
> Venetijs Ann. 17—

SERAFINO, Santo, Udine—Venice, 1710-48. This maker is chiefly famed for the exquisite finish of his workmanship. The modelling of his instruments varied. There are instances, particularly in the case of his Violins, where he has entirely set aside the Stainer form, and copied Amati. These Violins are wonderfully like the work of Francesco Ruggeri. The varnish upon them, of a rich red colour, is of so exceptional a quality, that one is compelled to look twice before being satisfied as to the author. The greater number, however, of his instruments are of the German character, the sound-hole, scroll, and outline all hinting of Stainer. These Venetians were wonderfully fortunate in obtaining handsome wood, and in this respect Santo Serafino was pre-eminent, for his sides and backs are simply beautiful to perfection. His method of cutting the wood was invariably to show the grain in even stripes. The scroll is well cut in point of workmanship, but the style is poor. Santo Serafino cannot be regarded as having displayed originality in any shape, and he thus forms an exception to the great majority of Italian makers. His instruments are either copies of Amati or of Stainer; there is, of course, a strong Italian flavour about his Stainer copies, which lifts them above the German school of imitators, and hence their higher value. Nearly all his instruments were branded with his name above the tail-pin. He used an ornamental label of large size. The Violoncello in the possession of Mr. M. J. Astle is a charming specimen of Serafino's work, I may say unequalled.

SNEIDER, Josefo, Pavia. Lancetti remarks that many of the Violins by Girolamo Amati, son of Niccolò, were attributed to this maker.

Joseph Sneider Papiæ
Alumnus Nicolai Amati Cremonae
fecit Anno 17—

SOCCHI, Vincenzo, 1661, Bologna. In the Catalogue of M. Chouquet mention is made of a Kit or Pochette by this maker in the Paris Conservatoire.

SORSANA, Giuseppe, 1700-1750. Said to have been a pupil of Stradivari. Highly finished work, varnish of beautiful quality.

Joseph Sorsana fecit
Cremone sub discip. Ant.
Stradivarii 1737.

STATLEE, Anderl, Genoa, about 1714. Signed himself as a pupil of Hieronymus Amati (son of Niccolò). Not unlike the work of Urquhart.

STREGNER, Magno, Venice, Lute-maker.

Laurentius Storioni Fecit
Cremonae 17—

STORIONI, Lorenzo, Cremona, about 1769 to 1799. The last of the old makers who evinced any marked degree of originality. Although there is an almost total absence of refinement in his works, there is much that is clever, which has gradually caused these instruments to be valued very highly. He appears to have made Giuseppe Guarneri del Gesù his idol. Although his instruments cannot be considered as copies, yet there is evidence of his having made use of the salient points belonging to Guarneri, which he fitted, as it were, to his own model. He had much of the disregard of mere appearance which Guarneri so often displayed, and seems to have been guided by similar fancies. His freak was to place his sound-holes in all sorts of ways, scarcely twice alike. His outline is always vigorous, but without thought of symmetrical appearance. There is not an instrument of his make that could have been made upon a mould—they were built from the blocks, and the result, as may be expected, is not graceful. M. Vieuxtemps, some years ago, possessed himself of a Storioni Violin, now belonging to Mr. Proctor, and, having carefully regulated it, succeeded in bringing forth its great powers. His hearers were so delighted that attention was speedily directed to this neglected maker. These instruments are highly thought of in Italy. The varnish is not of the Cremonese description, but partakes of the Neapolitan character. The purfling is unusually narrow, and roughly worked; the scroll is stiff, and the absence of finish is observable. The material he used was generally good in point of acoustical properties, though not handsome. Storioni does not appear to have made many Tenors or Violoncellos—the latter are rarely met with.

Storioni died in 1799. He lived at the house No. 3, Contrada Coltellai, which was afterwards occupied by G. B. Ceruti.

STRADIVARI, Antonio, Cremona.

"The instrument on which he played
Was in Cremona's workshops made,
By a great master of the past,
Ere yet was lost the art divine;
Fashioned of maple and of pine,
That in Tyrolian forests vast
Had rocked and wrestled with the blast;
Exquisite was it in design,
A marvel of the lutist's art,
Perfect in each minutest part;

And in its hollow chamber, thus,
The maker from whose hands it came
Had written his unrivalled name—
'Antonius Stradivarius.'"—LONGFELLOW.

> Antonius Stradiuarius Cremonensis
> Faciebat Anno 17—

The renown of this remarkable maker of Violins is beyond that of all others; his praise has been sung alike by poet, artist, and musician. His magic name is ever rising to the lips in the presence of the "king of instruments"; its sound is as familiar to the humble player as to the finished artist. He has received the undisputed homage of two centuries, and time seems but to add to the number and devotion of his liege subjects: to-day he is as little likely to be dethroned as Shakespeare.

Although many interesting particulars concerning Antonio Stradivari have been obtained from time to time, there is wanting that which alone can fully satisfy his admirers, viz., connected records of the chief events of his life. Every endeavour has been made to supply, in some way, this deficiency, by consulting documents relating to the city of Cremona during the 17th and 18th centuries. The results of these inquiries are of much value, and the reader will be made acquainted with them in the following pages.

With a patience worthy of reward, the late librarian at Cremona, Professor Peter Fécit, searched for the will of Stradivari, but as no proper register appears to have been kept until long after the famous maker died, his efforts were unsuccessful. Although the contents of the will might throw but a faint light upon the doings of the testator, there might be found particulars that would link together much of the information we already possess.

The date of birth of Antonio Stradivari was made known to M. Fétis in 1856,[14] upon evidence contained in an inventory of instruments which belonged to Count Cozio di Salabue. The inventory was made upon the occasion of the instruments being deposited with Carlo Carli, a Milanese banker. Among the Violins there appears to have been one by Antonio Stradivari, bearing a label upon which, in the handwriting of its maker, was stated his age, namely, ninety-two years, and the date 1736; thus making the year of birth 1644.

"That plain white-aproned man who stood at work,
  Patient and accurate, full *fourscore* years,
Cherished his sight and touch by temperance;

And, since keen sense is love of perfectness,
Made perfect Violins, the needed paths
For inspiration and high mastery."

Stradivari, by GEORGE ELIOT.

14 "Antoine Stradivari, luthier célèbre," par F. I. Fétis. Paris, 1856.

Previous to the publication of this evidence by M. Fétis, the date of birth was given as 1664, and it has been stated as 1644 or 1650. Don Paolo Lombardini, in his pamphlet on Stradivari published at Cremona in 1872, gives an interesting genealogical account of the great Cremonese maker and his family. The author follows the date of birth as stated by M. Fétis. This is succeeded by information of his own discovery, namely, the date of the marriage of Stradivari, July 4, 1667.

He appears to have married a widow named Capra, whose maiden name was Ferraboschi, her age being twenty-seven, and that of Stradivari twenty-three, according to the date given by Lombardini.

GENEALOGICAL TABLE OF THE FAMILY OF STRADIVARI.

EXTRACTED FROM THE PAMPHLET OF PAOLO LOMBARDINI.

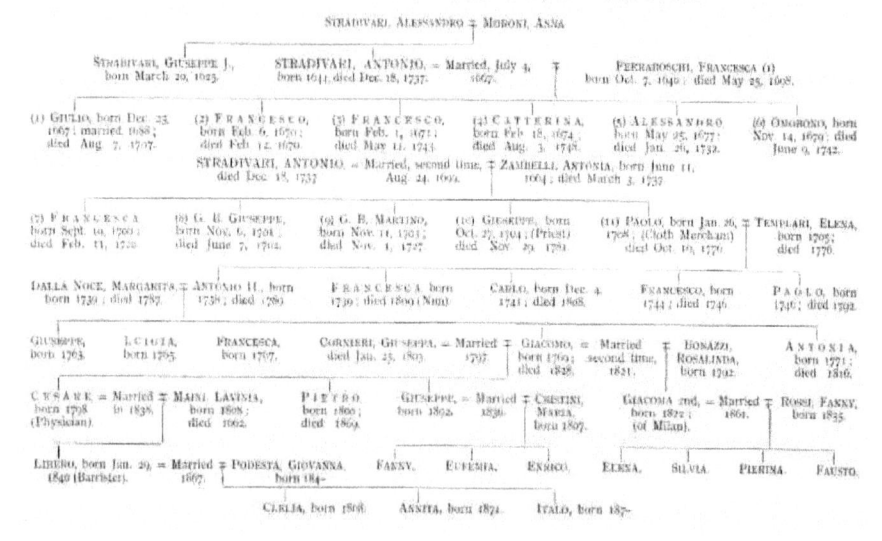

It is interesting to find evidence of some importance relative to the question of the age of Stradivari from the pen of Lancetti. He says, "Antonio having worked to the age of ninety-three years, died in Cremona in the year 1738, at the age of ninety-four years." Though this is obviously incorrect (the register showing that he died in 1737), the extract serves to support the date of birth, resting upon the evidence of the inventory, inasmuch as it satisfactorily shows the age Stradivari was considered to be by his own family, since Count Cozio communicated the information to Lancetti from correspondence with Paolo Stradivari, son of Antonio. In passing, it may be observed that Stradivari died December 18, 1737, and therefore the year mentioned by his son Paolo was only incorrect by thirteen days. He was equally as near the truth in saying his father was ninety-four when he should have said he was in his ninety-fourth year.

Having referred to the manuscript inventory, upon which rests the date of birth as given by Fétis—which document, taken by itself, it must be said is unsatisfactory—and having noticed the age of Stradivari as represented by his son, I will turn to other evidence in support of the inventory. The late Mr. Muntz, of Birmingham, possessed a Violin by Stradivari, dated 1736, and, in writing, the age of the maker is given as ninety-two. Another Violin by Stradivari, made in the same year, and similarly labelled, was bequeathed by the late Mrs. Lewis Hill to the Royal Academy of Music. This Violin has been regarded as one of the instruments found in the maker's shop when he died. It originally belonged to Habeneck, the well-known professor, and was taken to Paris between the years 1824 and 1830. Luigi Tarisio became possessed of some of the instruments mentioned in the inventory found among the papers of Carlo Carli, the banker, and one of these Violins in all probability furnished the evidence of the date of birth referred to by M. Fétis, and both instruments were probably purchased by Tarisio, together with the Violin dated 1716, named by Vuillaume "le Messie."[15] The last instrument necessary to notice in confirmation of the date, hitherto resting alone on the inventory, was in the possession of the late M. H. de St. Sennoch, of Paris. It is dated 1737, and in the handwriting of Stradivari is his age, ninety-three years, which decides the correctness of the statement made by Lancetti (upon the authority of Count Cozio di Salabue, who received the information from Paolo Stradivari in 1775) that "Antonio worked up to the age of ninety-three years."

> [15] The information which M. Fétis gives of this Violin was based on the inventory of Carlo Carli. It is also mentioned in the correspondence between Count Cozio and Lancetti.

In the absence of direct information concerning the life of Stradivari, we must turn to his instruments for such evidence as we require; and these, happily, give us a greater insight into his career than would be readily imagined. I am not aware that any Violin of Stradivari is known in which it is stated that he was a pupil of Niccolò Amati, or that the assumption has been maintained on any other grounds than the indisputable evidence furnished by the early instruments of this great maker.[16] Never has affinity in the art of Violin manufacture been more marked than that between Stradivari and Niccolò Amati during the early life of the former. I have, in another place, remarked upon the almost invariable similarity occurring between the works of master and pupil, and have used this canon in refutation of the doctrine that Giuseppe Guarneri del Gesù was ever a pupil of Antonio Stradivari. Lancetti states that the instruments of Stradivari made in 1665, and others in 1666, bear the label of Niccolò Amati, and instances one that was in the collection of Count Cozio, to which Stradivari made a new belly, many years later, in his best style. It is certain that instruments as described by Lancetti have been recognised by intelligent connoisseurs as wholly the work of Stradivari (in which case, as may be imagined, they have no longer been allowed to sail under false colours, but have had their proper certificate of birth attached to them). In other instances the beautiful scroll of Stradivari has been recognised on the body of an Amati, or the sound-hole has shown that it was cut by the hand of Stradivari.

> 16 Upon reference to Lancetti's MSS., I find that he states Stradivari used a label with the words "Nicolai Amati Alumnus," about 1666.

Having met with a Violin by Stradivari (since the publication of the first edition of this work) dated 1666, it would appear that he left the workshop of his master at that time, or not later than the year of his marriage in 1667. The extracts obtained by Canon Bazzi from the parish registers, relative to the pupils of Niccolò Amati, help to establish the correctness of this view. Stradivari must have been in the workshop of his master between the years 1658 and 1666. We have no information of the pupils of Amati from 1654 to 1665. In 1666 the name of Giorgio Fraiser is given; consequently Stradivari must have left previous to 1666 or early in that year, and prior to the registration. Between the years 1666 and 1672 there is observable a marked change in style, and the workmanship is better. The instruments he made about this period have wood for the most part singularly plain, and different in kind from what his master used. His use of this material I am disposed to attribute to the want of means rather than choice. The purfling of these early instruments is very narrow, and many of the backs are cut slab-form. Previous to about the year 1672, we find that his whole work is in accordance with the plans of Amati (not as seen in the latter's *grand* pattern, but in his ordinary full-sized instrument); the arching is identical, the corners are treated similarly, the sound-hole is quite Amati-like in form, yet easily distinguished by its extreme delicacy, the scroll a thorough imitation of Amati, and presenting a singular contrast to the vigorous individuality which Stradivari displayed in this portion of his work a few years later. Enough has been said to enable the reader to recognise the connection which must have existed between Amati and Stradivari, to admit of such marked resemblances.

Taking the instruments of Stradivari as beacons throwing light upon many curious and interesting points of the maker's manufacture, the number and character of his Violins and Violoncellos made during the decade following 1674 is indicative of his having increased both his reputation and his patronage. The last year of this period, namely 1684, was that in which his master, Niccolò Amati, died, at the age of eighty-eight. We have already seen, in the notice of Amati, that Niccolò was the last member of the family who maintained unbroken the long chain of associations connected with the house of Amati, extending over a period of a century and a half. The circumstance of all the tools, patterns, and models of Niccolò Amati having passed into the possession of his pupil Stradivari, and not into that of his son Girolamo (who was then thirty-five years of age), clearly shows that the son did not succeed to his father's business. We are thus led to believe that during the ten years above referred to, Niccolò Amati had been gradually lessening his activity, and that the patronage so long enjoyed by the Amati family fell for the most part to his gifted pupil, Antonio Stradivari. Among the interesting items of information supplied by the efforts of Paolo Lombardini, relative to Stradivari, is that of the purchase of the house, in 1680, of the Brothers Picenardi for seven thousand imperial lire, equivalent to above £800 in present English money. This purchase, made about fourteen years after Stradivari began to manufacture on his own account, well marks the progress he made. I have, however, further proof of his fame and prosperity at this period in the valuable extracts from the manuscript of Desiderio Arisi, at Cremona.

ANTONIO STRADIVARI. *Tenor.*
Date 1690.
(Made for the Grand Duke of
Florence.)

ANTONIO STRADIVARI.
1734.
(LATE GEO. AMES, ESQ.)

Plate XI.

The knowledge Arisi had of Stradivari is shown by the following remarks written by him in the year 1720. He says, "In Cremona is also living my intimate friend Antonio Stradivari, an excellent maker of all kinds of musical instruments.[17] It will not be out of place to make special mention of his merits. His fame is unequalled as a maker of instruments of the finest qualities, and he has made many of extraordinary beauty, which are richly ornamented with small figures, flowers, fruits, arabesques, and graceful interlaying of fanciful ornaments, all in perfect drawing, which he sometimes paints in black or inlays with ebony and ivory, all of which is executed with the greatest skill, rendering them worthy of the exalted personages to whom they are intended to be presented. I have thought proper, therefore, to mention some works of this great master, in testimony of the high esteem and universal admiration which he enjoys." These prefatory remarks of Arisi are followed by several important statements, which I have arranged in accordance with the different periods it will be necessary to refer to in the course of this notice.

> 17 Mention is made by Lancetti that in the year 1820 the Marquis Carlo dal Negro, of Genoa, possessed a Harp bearing the name of Stradivari. Mandolines and other stringed instruments have been seen with his name attached.

"In the year 1682, on the 8th of September, the banker Michele Monzi, of Venice, sent him an order for the whole set of Violins, Altos, and Violoncellos which that gentleman sent as a present to King James of England."[18] The interesting remarks of Arisi with regard to the inlaid instruments of Stradivari are those we should expect from an admirer of delicate artistic work, who possessed no special knowledge of Violins as instruments of music. The existence of some of the instruments to which he refers, together with the tracings of the actual designs and the tools with which the work was accomplished, render his observations, read at this distance of time, peculiarly pleasing. The possessor of the models, tools, labels, and drawings used by Stradivari is the Marquis Dalla Valle, of Casale, to whom they passed by inheritance from his great-uncle, Count Cozio, who purchased them in 1775.

> 18 These instruments were probably sent to England in 1685, or later.

THE HOUSE OF STRADIVARI, WEST SIDE, PIAZZA ROMA, CREMONA.

Vincenzo Lancetti, referring to the collection, after mention of Stradivari having been buried in the Church of S. Domenico, continues, "As appears from the correspondence held in 1775, by the said Count Cozio with Antonio's son Paolo Stradivari, cloth merchant, when the former bought of the latter all the remaining Violins, the forms, the patterns, moulds, and drawings of the said celebrated Antonio, as well as those of the Amati, with which he enriched his collection." In an article published in the "Gazzetta Piedmontese," October, 1881, upon the occasion of the exhibition, at Milan, of the relics of the shop of Stradivari, the writer gives the following account of the negotiations: "Count Cozio, a great patron, intimate with the greatest artists of the period, especially with Rolla, purchased, through the instrumentality of the firm of merchants, Anselmi di Briata, from Paolo and Antonio junior, respectively son and nephew of Antonio Stradivari, in 1776, all the tools, drawings, labels, &c., which had been used by the celebrated Violin-maker, and his heirs, who were desirous that nothing belonging to him should remain in his native town, as it is inferred, from a curious document, hastened to conclude the sale."[19] It is certain, however, that Lancetti received his information from the Count himself, and negotiations were certainly carried on between Paolo and the Count, either directly or through his agents, Anselmi di Briata.

> 19 Upon reference to the copy of this document (the correspondence is given in the fourth edition of this work), I find the words used by Paolo Stradivari to his correspondents Anselmi di Briata run, after commenting upon the price offered, "However, to show my desire to please you, and in order that not a single thing belonging to my father be left in Cremona, &c.," having reference, possibly, to some supposed feeling of indifference on the part of the municipal authorities towards the memory of Antonio Stradivari, they not having secured the moulds, patterns, &c.

The contents of the letters of Paolo and Antonio Stradivari junior, which the Marquis Dalla Valle has placed at my disposal, serve to explain the two different accounts above given. We find that the Count had two distinct transactions, directly or indirectly, with the family of Stradivari. In 1775 he purchased the ten instruments made by Antonio which remained out of ninety-one (complete and partly finished) left by the maker at the time of his death in 1737. The payment in connection with this transaction was arranged by the banker Carlo Carli, which gave rise to the inventory upon which M. Fétis based his statement as to the age of Stradivari. In the month of May, 1776, negotiations were entered upon with Paolo Stradivari, relative to the tools, which led to their being sold. During their progress Paolo died, October, 1776, and the business was left for his son Antonio to complete in December, 1776. The copies of the letters written by Paolo and Antonio Stradivari are given in the fourth edition of this work, and the chief part of the matter therein is referred to in the Section, "The Violin and its Votaries."

The next period to be noticed relative to the work of Stradivari is that dating from 1686 to 1694. We here observe a marked advance in every particular. The form is flatter, the arching differently treated. The sound-hole, which is a masterpiece of gracefulness, reclines more. The curves of the middle bouts are more extended than in this maker's later instruments. The corners are brought out, though not prominently so. Here, too, we notice the change in the formation of the scroll. He suddenly leaves the form that he had hitherto imitated, and follows the dictates of his own fancy. The result is bold and striking, and foreshadows much of the character belonging to the bodies of the instruments of his latter period, and though it may seem daring and presumptuous criticism, I have often been impressed with the idea that these scrolls would have been more in harmony with his later works than those to which they belong. The varnish on the instruments belonging to the period under consideration is very varied. Sometimes it is of a rich golden colour, deliciously soft and transparent; in other instances he has used varnish of a deeper hue, which might be described as light red, the quality of which is also very beautiful. The purfling is a trifle wider, but narrower than that afterwards used.

From the, Arisi MSS. we have the following interesting information relative to this period:—

"In the year 1685, on the 12th of March, Cardinal Orsini, Archbishop of Benevento,[20] ordered a Violoncello and two Violins, which were sent as a present to the Duke of Natalona, in Spain. The Cardinal, besides paying liberally for the work, wrote an appreciative acknowledgment of their merits, and appointed the artist to the place of one of his private attendants." It may be remarked that the honour conferred upon Stradivari was equivalent to appointing him maker to the Archbishop.

> 20 Vincenzo Maria Orsini (of the illustrious family of the Orsinis, Dukes of Gravina), born 1648, in the Neapolitan province of Bari, was a learned professor of theology, and visited, between 1668 and 1672, several cities and towns, among others Naples, Bologna, Venice, Brescia, and most likely Cremona, where he held conferences, which were largely attended. He was created a Cardinal by Clement X., in 1672, Archbishop in 1675 in Manfredonia, in 1680 to Cesena, in 1686 to Benevento and Porto. In 1724 he was elected Pope, under the name of Benedict XIII., and remained on the Pontifical throne until February, 1730, when he died, aged eighty-one.

"In the same year, on the 12th of September, Bartolomeo Grandi, called Il Fassina, leader of the Court Orchestra of His Royal Highness the Duke of Savoy,[21] ordered of Stradivari a whole set of instruments for the Court Orchestra."

> 21 Victor Amadeus II., Duke of Savoy and King of Sardinia, was the Prince for whom Bartolomeo Grandi ordered the concerto of instruments.

"In the year 1686, on the 5th of April, His Serene Highness the Duke of Modena (Francesco II. D'Este was then twenty-six years of age) ordered a Violoncello, which, by special invitation, Stradivari was requested to take to the Duke himself, who told him how pleased he was to make his personal acquaintance, praised greatly his work, and beyond the sum agreed paid him thirty pistoles (golden Spanish) as a present."

On the 22nd of August, 1686, Marquis Michele Rodeschini ordered a Viol da Gamba to be sent to King James II. of England.

In the year 1687 he made the set of instruments for the Spanish Court, inlaid with ivory, and having a beautiful scroll work running round the sides and scroll. Arisi evidently refers to this event in the following extract: "On the 19th of January, 1687, the Marquis Niccolò Rota ordered a Violoncello for the King of Spain." One of the Violins of this set was purchased in Madrid about thirty years since by Ole Bull. The Tenor belonging to this quatuor has lost its ivory work, a blemish which is to be regretted. He also made, about this period, some very small Violins with similar designs, instruments evidently made to order.

"On the 7th of August of the same year, 1687, the nobleman Don Agostino Daria, General-in-Chief of the Spanish Cavalry in Lombardy, while he was residing in Cremona, obtained from him a Violoncello."

We now reach the year 1690, in connection with which Arisi has supplied information of singular interest. He says: "On the 19th of September, 1690, Stradivari received the following letter from the Marquis Bartolommeo Ariberti,[22] a Cremonese nobleman—'The other day I made a present of the two Violins and the Violoncello which you made for me to His Highness the Prince of Tuscany;[23] and I assure you, to my great satisfaction, he has accepted them with such pleasure that more I could not expect. The members of his orchestra—and he possesses a select number—were unanimous in expressing their great appreciation, declaring the instruments quite perfect, and, above all, exclaiming with one voice that they had never heard a Violoncello with such an agreeable tone. For the highly flattering reception with which my present has been received by His Highness, and which I cannot sufficiently describe, I am principally indebted to the care which you have used in the manufacture of the instruments. At the same time I hope to have by this present shown you my appreciation, and of having acquired the merit of practically bringing to the knowledge of such a personage the truth of your great skill, which will procure you, undoubtedly, many orders from this exalted house. To prove this, I have now to request you to begin at once two Tenors, one *Tenor* and the other *Contralto*, which are wanted to complete the concerto.'"[24]

22 The Marquis of Ariberti was born in 1666, and died 1724. He was an elegant writer, and a member of several literary academies. He was for some time in Tuscany. Upon returning to Cremona, where he settled, he built in 1687, at his own expense, a theatre called after his own name, Ariberti. He, being a passionate lover of music, was anxious to have in his own establishment (the theatre adjoining his palace) a place of amusement for himself and his family. About the year 1710 he gave up the building to a religious brotherhood, and a church was built on the site, and used until 1798, when the brotherhood was suppressed, and, by a singular coincidence, the building was bought in 1801 by a society of dramatic authors, and again opened as a theatre, which still exists, and is called Teatro Filodrammatico. The Marquis Ariberti was appointed by Joseph I., Emperor of Austria, to the title of Lieutenant-Marshal; he was a member of the High Council of State in Milan. He was buried in the church, which, as above mentioned, was afterwards used as a theatre. (*See* Lancetti, "Biografia Cremonese," I vol., Milano, 1819.)

23 Cosimo III. de Medici.

24 A chest of Viols, Mace tells us, in his "Musick's Monument," 1676, consisted of two Basses, two Tenors, and two Trebles. A Concerto of Violins in Italy, according to the letter of Ariberti, consisted of one Bass, two Tenors (Contralto and Tenor) and two Violins. The term "Concerto" was introduced at the beginning of the 17th century, in connection with sacred music in parts. These compositions were called Church Concertos. Towards the end of the 17th century compositions were introduced for instruments called Chamber Concertos.

In the collection of relics of the great master, in the possession of the Marquis Dalla Valle, there are some items which appear to be connected with this most interesting letter: I refer to the designs for a case, or cases, for a concerto of instruments dated 1684, which Stradivari himself describes as being for the Grand Duke of Florence. The date upon these designs is indicative of the order for the Violins and the Violoncellos having been given in that year (1684) by the Marquis Ariberti, who at the same time gave certain instructions as to cases and armorial designs. The completion of the order, however, appears to have been delayed, and the instruments were not delivered until 1690. The instructions given in the above letter to Stradivari to complete the concerto by making the Tenors (the patterns of which are among those in the possession of the Marquis Dalla Valle, signed, and dated 1690), and the existence of the Violoncello and one of the Tenors at Florence, dated 1690, are confirmatory of the opinion that the order was executed in 1690. The following inscription, under the left shoulder or side, is in the Tenor: "Prima 20 Ottobre 1690 per S. A. Da Fiorenza." It is interesting to find that the Grand Duke also possessed a Stradivari Violin, dated 1716, which is in Florence, together with the instruments above referred to. It is therefore evident that the belief of the Marquis that Stradivari would receive further orders from the Grand Duke was realised.

Between the years 1690 and 1700 Stradivari made, together with the form of instrument just described, that known to connoisseurs as the "long Strad." We have here quite a differently constructed instrument; it is less graceful, although there is no absence of the masterly hand throughout the work. It has received the title of "long Strad" from its increased length, as the name would imply.[25]

> 25 The usual length measurements of the various patterns are as under:—
>
> > (1) "Amatisé," 13-7/8 inches.
> > (2) "Long Strad," 14-1/8 (occasionally 14-1/4) inches.
> > (3) "Grand pattern," 14 to 14-1/16 inches.—EDITORS.

Fortified with the experience which the variously constructed instruments referred to had enabled him to gather, he would seem to have marshalled all his forces in order to enter on an entirely new campaign, one that should be alike glorious to himself and his art. That he succeeded in achieving all that he could have desired, my readers will have an opportunity of judging by the evidence I propose to offer. It was about the year 1700 when Stradivari entered upon a new era in his art. All his past labours appear to have been only measures preliminary to that which he proposed afterwards to accomplish, and were made for the purpose of testing, to the minutest degree, the effect of particular modifications in the form and thickness of his works.

If we stay to consider for a moment the field of research traversed by Stradivari before entering upon what may be not inaptly named the golden period of his life, artistically considered, we shall be better enabled to appreciate his labours.

Starting from the days when he left the workshop of Niccolò Amati, we find him following implicitly in the footsteps of his master. About 1686 he makes use of the more commendable points belonging to the works of former years, adding others of great beauty and utility. At this period he begins to make his originality felt, continuing in this vein, with but little intermission, down to about the year 1690, when he again gives forth fresh evidence of his power to create, as shown in the "long Strad." In expending his powers on those instruments of varied proportions, it might occur to the mind of the observer that he was undoing much that he had accomplished; but I do not consider that such was the case. His project in making these instruments *together* with those of larger dimensions, evidences, in my opinion, a desire that he had of fairly testing the result of changed methods of construction. The marked variety of his work about this period of his life, I cannot but regard as sufficient proof of the tentative character of the steps he was taking in his art.

From this brief summary of the varied styles given to the works of this true artist, the reader may gather some idea of the solidity of the foundation which he laid, before trusting himself to raise those works which have become monuments to his memory.

That which I have termed the golden period of Stradivari, commenced about 1700, at which time he reached his 56th year: a time of life when it is a rare occurrence to find genius asserting itself with any degree of power—a time, if not of waning, at least of resting, when the mind usually stays from giving forth originality bearing the freshness of earlier years; but Stradivari, with a few other notable instances in the field of art, forms an exception to this rule, and he proves to us that his talent was then in its full vigour, and ripe for new achievements. George Eliot's fancy well contrasts the painter Naldo—

"Knowing all tricks of style at thirty-one,
And weary of them; while Antonio
At sixty-nine *wrought placidly his best.*"

From about 1700 his instruments show to us much of that which follows later. The outline is changed, but the curves, blending one with another, are beautiful in the extreme. The corners are treated differently. The wood used for the backs and sides is most handsome, having a broad curl. The scrolls are of bold conception, and finely executed. The varnish also is very rich, and leaves nothing to be desired.

It is not possible to convey to the reader, by means of mere description, anything approaching an adequate notion of the surpassing gracefulness of the entire work of this epoch. The eye must be made the channel to the mind. If the work is present, then, with the aid which these remarks will afford, the reader may gain, by careful study, much valuable insight into the beauties and genius of this famous artist, together with much useful information.

But during this period of his maturity, even, we find that Stradivari did not absolutely confine himself to making instruments as near as possible alike; on the contrary, it is easy to point out certain variations, the meaning of which he doubtless well understood. We find him guided throughout this period by his usual ideas as regards grandeur of outline and degrees of thickness; but the rotundity of the model, the shape that he gave to the sound-hole, the method of setting the sound-hole in the instrument, although, as before remarked, all executed with a breadth of purpose which his earlier efforts fail to show, may be cited as points in which he varied. I have no hesitation in hazarding an explanation of the reasons that prompted him to these differences of construction. It is my firm conviction that these great makers had certain guiding principles as regards the nature and qualities of the wood they used, and that Stradivari, in particular, made the subject a special study. If this be granted, I do not think there is any great difficulty in understanding the meaning of the differences pointed out. If Stradivari constructed his instruments upon philosophical principles, the chief element of variation in the treatment of any particular instrument must have been the difference of *quality* in the material; it is evident that a method eminently successful when applied to wood of a certain texture and character, would ensure as eminent a failure if applied indiscriminately in all cases. To obtain wood sufficient for two bellies that should be alike in every particular is impossible, though cuttings should be made from the same piece; and we find that the more the material varies in its nature, so much the greater the variations—a fact which helps the view advanced considerably. In another place I have stated that scarcity of sycamore in the days of these old makers is impossible to understand, but scarcity of a particular *kind* of sycamore is easy to comprehend. He might have had a cartload of wood handsome in appearance; but handsome wood combined with acoustical properties he deemed needful, was another matter. With what extraordinary care he permitted himself to use the lovely wood he did possess! There are several instances where he has used, during one year, four or five distinct cuttings of wood, more particularly as regards the sycamore. These several cuttings include often the handsomest and the plainest. A year or so later we find him again making use of wood from the same cuttings, which proves satisfactorily that he did not work up one piece before commencing with another. He would seem to have kept back the handsomest wood for certain important commissions. I have seen three Stradivari Violins of 1714, with backs having but little figure, yet this was the year in which he made the "Dolphin," which is regarded by the chief connoisseurs in Europe as a *chef-d'oeuvre* of Stradivari. From the days when it was in the possession of the Marquis de la Rosa to the present time, its beauty has excited the admiration of the Fiddle world. The splendour of the wood is unsurpassed in any Violin, ancient or modern, and it was named the "Dolphin" from the richness and variety of the tints it gives to the varnish. The model is perfection; its solidity of construction and glorious varnish all tend to make it unique. Its beauty is of a kind that does not require the eye of the skilled connoisseur to recognise it; it causes those to exclaim whose knowledge is limited to being aware that it is a Fiddle. His making this superb work of art in the same year in which he made instruments having wood quite opposite in figure, bears out, I consider, what I have before stated, viz., that Stradivari jealously guarded the material he possessed having both handsome figure and valuable acoustical properties. Mr. Charles Reade says of these "Strads": "When a red Stradivari Violin is made of soft, velvety wood, and the varnish is just half worn off the back in a rough triangular form, that produces a certain beauty of light and shade which is, in my opinion, the *ne plus ultra*. These Violins are rare; I never had but two in my life."

GIUSEPPE GUARNERI DEL GESÙ.
1738.
(B. SINSHEIMER, ESQ.)

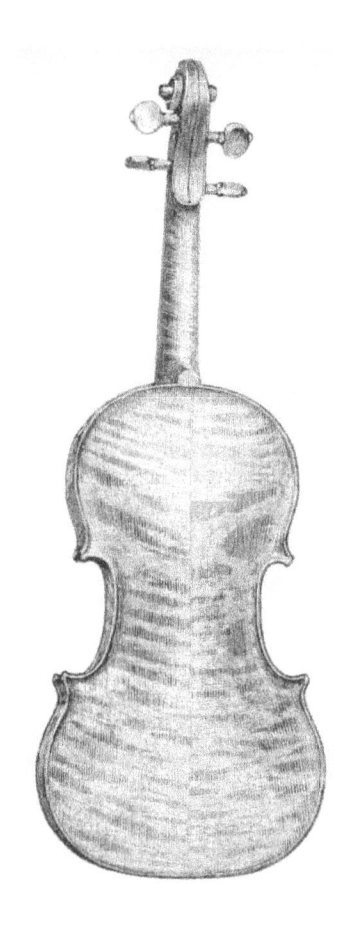

THE "DOLPHIN" STRAD.
Date 1714.

ANTONIO STRADIVARI.
1718.
(W. S. McMILLAN, ESQ.)

Plate XII.

It is conceivable that a manufacture so successful as Violin-making proves itself to have been in Italy during the seventeenth and part of the eighteenth centuries, should give rise to scientific inquiry, in order to discover the reason of the excellence of the best Italian instruments, and, if possible, the principles or laws which guided the makers in the exercise of their genius. That investigations of this character should be attended with important results in connection with the science of acoustics, is to be expected. As to laws or principles of a scientific character, I doubt whether such were recognised or understood when the excellence of the manufacture was greatest, believing that Violin makers of the order of Stradivari must be like poets, "born artificers, not made." The chief merits of Stradivari and his contemporary makers were intuitive. Their rules, having their origin in experience, were applied as dictated by their marvellous sense of touch and cunning, with results infinitely superior to any obtained with the aid of the most approved mechanical contrivances. When to these considerations we add that devotedness of purpose, without which nothing really great in art has been accomplished, we have a catalogue of excellences sufficient to account for the greatness of their achievements.

Turning again to the manuscript of Arisi, we find that "On the 12th of May, 1701, Don Antonio Cavezudo, leader of the private orchestra of King Charles II. of Spain, wrote a highly complimentary letter to Stradivari from Madrid, assuring him that though he had received bow instruments from several makers, for different courts, yet he had never been able to obtain them of such a refined and beautiful tone as those made by him." Arisi adds that Don Antonio Cavezudo was also in the service of the Duke of Anjou.

M. Fétis, in his notice of Stradivari,[26] remarks: "The life of Antonio Stradivari was as tranquil as his calling was peaceful. The year 1702, alone, must have caused him much disquiet, when, during the war concerning the succession, the city of Cremona was taken by Marshal Villeroy, retaken by Prince Eugene, and finally taken a third time by the French; but after that period Italy enjoyed a long tranquillity, in which the old age of the artist glided peacefully away."

> 26 "Notice of Anthony Stradivari," by F. J. Fétis, translated by John Bishop. 1864.

A campaign had taken place in Italy in 1701, when Prince Eugene, with thirty thousand troops, out-generalled Catinat, the able French commander, giving Louis XIV. the opportunity of placing the empty and presumptuous Villeroy in command. Prince Eugene had greatly harassed the French in Italy, when, in the night of February 1, 1702, he surprised the French garrison of Cremona, and, though momentarily successful, "missed the town," as Eugene said, "by a quarter of an hour," but carried off the Commander-in-Chief, Villeroy, which the popular song-writers of the day construed into "a double gain to France"—Cremona saved, and Villeroy lost.

It is conceivable that Stradivari, together with his fellow-citizens, witnessed during the year 1702 more of the pomp of war than was agreeable. The blowing of trumpets, the beating of drums, and other martial sounds, would be music not likely to touch pleasantly the ears of Stradivari, apart from the discomfort attendant on military occupation. He, however, appears to have practised his art with undiminished zeal, judging from the following interesting information given by Arisi. He says: "Stradivari made a complete set of bow instruments, which he intended to present to Philip V. of Spain, on the occasion of the passage of the King through Cremona; and he had prepared a memorial to that effect; but he was dissuaded, and the instruments are still in his possession."

No date is supplied with regard to the events above named; we are therefore left to assign the period when the presentation was to have taken place by reference to other sources of information. In an official diary of the journey of Philip V. to Italy[27] it appears that the King arrived in Lombardy on the 10th of June, 1702, and that from Milan he went to Lodi on the 1st of July, and made his entry into Cremona two days later, July the 3rd, at one o'clock in the afternoon. Philip remained several days in the town, receiving visits from the Dukes of Parma and of Mantua, and held there several councils of war with the generals of the allied armies (Spanish and French), and appears to have left Cremona on the 20th of July for the seat of war near Mantua. After the victories of Luzzara and Guastalla, the King passed again through Cremona, arriving there on the 3rd of October, staying one night, and leaving the following day for Milan. On this occasion there was much festivity on account of the victories, and the King distributed sums of money and presents for the wounded, the officers, and the generals. It would therefore appear that Stradivari purposed presenting the instruments to Philip either in July or October, 1702. The condition of affairs at Cremona at this period apparently serves to explain the cause of Stradivari having been dissuaded from presenting the instruments.

> [27] Contained in the work of Don A. de Ubilla y Medina, Marquis de Ribas, entitled, "Succession de el Rèy D. Philipe V.'; Diario de sus Viages, &c." Madrid, 1704, fol.

"On the 10th of November, 1702, the Marquis Giovanni Battista Toralba, General of Cavalry and Governor of Cremona, sent for Stradivari, and, after complimenting him on his peculiar genius, ordered two Violins and a Violoncello, which were afterwards sent as a present to the Duke of Alba.

"In the year 1707, the Marquis Desiderio Cleri wrote to Stradivari, by order of King Charles III. of Spain, from Barcelona, ordering for the royal orchestra six Violins, two Tenors, and one Violoncello."

This extract refers to the Archduke Charles of Austria, afterwards Emperor Charles VI. Charles III., aided by the British fleet, occupied Barcelona in 1706. We have, therefore, the interesting facts that Stradivari made a complete set of instruments which he intended to present to Philip V., and that he was afterwards commissioned to make another set for Philip's opponent, the Archduke.

Lorenzo Giustiniani, a Venetian nobleman, wrote to Stradivari the following letter, which he received July 7, 1716:—

> "Venice, Giustiniani Palace,
> "Campiello dei Squellini.

"It is generally known that there is not at the present time in the world a more skilled maker of musical instruments than yourself; and as I wish to preserve a record of such an illustrious man and famous artist, I trouble you with this letter, to ask whether you feel disposed to make me a Violin, of the highest quality and finish that you can bestow upon it."

The following extract from Arisi's manuscript brings us to the end of the interesting information therein contained in reference to the subject of this notice, and amply justifies the closing words of the author, who says: "From what I have written it may be seen how great is the excellence of Stradivari's art."

"In 1715, on the 10th of June, Giovanni Battista Volème, director of the private orchestra of the King of Poland, arrived in Cremona, by special order of the King, to await the completion of twelve Violins, which had been ordered of Stradivari, and he remained here three months; and when all the instruments were ready, he took them with him to Poland."

Arisi doubtless refers to the Belgian musician Jean Baptiste Volumier, who was musical director to Augustus, Elector of Saxony and King of Poland, famous as a patron of music and the arts. It was Augustus who appointed Francesco Maria Veracini as his solo Violinist in 1720, and on the title-page of the charming Sonatas of Veracini we read—

"Dedicata
a sua Altezza Reale,
il Serenissimo Principe Reale di Pollonia
et Elettorale di Sassonia.
Francesco Maria Veracini Fiorentino
Compositore di Camera di sua Maestà."

The blending of the names of Stradivari, Augustus, and Veracini, serves to carry our thoughts into channels overflowing with interesting musical records. Volème (Volumier) is said to have taken the instruments from Cremona to Poland. It would therefore appear that the Royal Orchestra was then stationed at Warsaw, the Court Musicians having to divide their time between that city and Dresden. In these capitals Jean Baptiste Volumier directed the music of the Elector Augustus from the year 1706 to 1728. Veracini was appointed solo Violinist in 1720 to Augustus, and the instruments which Stradivari made for the King were, therefore, only five years old. Though new, their tones were doubtless rich and beautiful. Veracini, it may be assumed, saw, heard, and played upon these comparatively new Stradivari Violins. He, however, whilst fully alive to their sterling merits, played, in all probability, upon his Stainers, which he named

"St. Peter" and "St. Paul," with more pleasure, from their being thoroughly matured. The order given by Augustus to Stradivari, and the King's determination to have it executed, throws a strong side-light on the lofty position held by Stradivari as a maker of Violins. It also appears to furnish, in some measure, an explanation of the length of time he took to execute the order given by the Marquis Ariberti. We have here an artist of European celebrity, who was incapable of executing indifferent work. Commissions flowed from the chief courts faster than they could be executed. The genius of Stradivari could not but be true to itself. He scorned to sacrifice quality at the shrine of quantity. His patrons had, therefore, to wait patiently for their instruments, though it might be for years. The Elector of Saxony was evidently resolved upon securing his Violins, and it cannot be denied that the measures he adopted to accomplish his purpose did credit to his perseverance, and reflected honour on the Raphael of Violin-making.

Passing to the last period of this great maker, we enter upon the consideration of a set of instruments very distinct from those of an earlier date, and which have given rise to a great divergence of opinion. Some have gone to the extent of denying the authenticity of these works, as far as they relate to Stradivari; others, again, admit that portions of these instruments are from his hand, and finished by his sons or Carlo Bergonzi. There are, doubtless, many exceedingly crude-looking instruments passing under his name, bearing dates ranging from 1730 to 1737, in the making of which he has taken no part; but, on the other hand, to deny that there are any works of Stradivari having these dates is to deny established facts. He must be an ill-informed judge of Violins who fails to recognise the hand of the master in several splendid specimens of this period. The rich oil varnish with which they are covered is precisely the same in quality as that found upon the instruments belonging to other periods, and which he used without exception throughout his career. It is, perhaps, laid on less carefully, and its colour is more varied. In some instances it is brown, and in others light red, the tone of colour varying according to the number of coats. He seems to have used, generally, more varnish upon these instruments than on his earlier ones. The thickness of the coats is seen in those parts (on the back in particular) where the varnish is worn and broken, caused, in all cases, by the shoulder of the player and the lining of the case upon which the back rests. It must be borne in mind that Stradivari had reached a great age when he made these instruments, and he evidently felt proud of his ability to continue his artistic labours after passing his ninetieth year, from the number of Violins wherein, in his own handwriting, he proclaimed himself a nonagenarian. It would not be reasonable to expect to find so high a finish as in the instruments made from 1700 to 1725, but even in these there is a finish distinct from that of either his sons or Bergonzi. But, beyond this, there is recognisable the splendid form, the masterly scroll, and the perfect sound-hole. To say that Omobono Stradivari, Francesco Stradivari, or Carlo Bergonzi had any share in these notable works, evidences hasty judgment, if not ignorance of the style of those makers to whom these instruments are attributed. The work of Carlo Bergonzi is now pretty well understood; in England, particularly, we have some glorious specimens. I need only ask the unbiassed connoisseur if he can reconcile one of these instruments with those of Stradivari of the period named. I have no hesitation in saying that there is not a single feature in common. The work of the sons of Stradivari is less known, but it is as characteristic as that of Bergonzi, and quite as distinct from that of their father, if not *more* so. The outline is rugged, the modelling distinct, the scroll a ponderous piece of carving, quite foreign to Stradivari the elder, and the varnish, though good, is totally different from the superb coats found on the father's works of late date.

The division of the work of Stradivari into periods makes the reader more acquainted with the maker's style. It must be remembered, however, that he did not strictly confine himself to making instruments wholly of one pattern at any time, although he certainly did so with but few exceptions until the last period, when, as Lancetti rightly observes, he used more frequently his earlier patterns.

The exact spot where Stradivari was buried was made known by the researches of Signor Sacchi, a Cremonese conversant with the annals of his native city.[28] This was an interesting addition to the meagre information previously handed down to us touching Stradivari. It had long been known that a family grave was purchased by Stradivari in the church of San Domenico, in the year 1729: but in the certificates from the Cathedral of Cremona it is stated that he was buried in the tomb of Francesco Villani, no mention being made of San Domenico. The exact words are, "*Buried in the Chapel of the Rosary, in the parish of St. Matthew.*" The omission of the name of the church wherein this chapel stood has led to the belief that the precise spot where the mortal remains of Stradivari rest was unknown. Signor Sacchi finds that the historians of Cremona (but especially Panni, in his "Report on the Churches of Cremona, 1762") mention that the Church of San Domenico was in the parish of St. Matthew, and that the only chapel known by the name of "The Rosary" was the third on the right, entering the Church of San Domenico.

> 28 "The Orchestra" of July 15, 1870, contains a notice relative to the circumstance, entitled "The Tomb of Stradivari."

An important point is mentioned by the historian above quoted, viz., that about the year 1720 the Parish Church of St. Matthew being judged too full to allow of further burials in its interior, the Church of San Domenico (its subsidiary church) was chosen as a place of burial for the parishioners, for which purpose it was used down to about 1780, and that Stradivari purchased there the grave mentioned. This statement is confirmed by the autograph letter of Count Cozio di Salabue, of Casale Monferato, Piedmont.

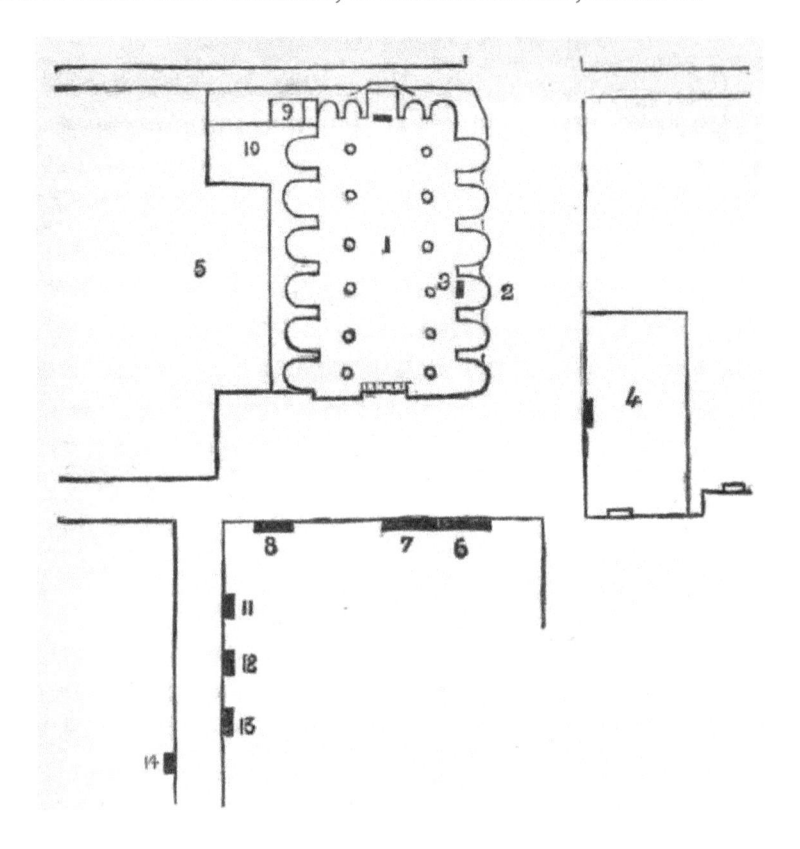

1. Church of S. Domenico. 2. Chapel of the Rosary. 3. Tomb of Stradivari. 4. Church of St. Matthew (since 1820 the Post Office, the church having been profaned in 1808 by the French). 5. Convent of the Dominican Friars. 6. House of Stradivari. 7. House of Bergonzi. 8. House of Guarneri. 9. Tower of the Church of S. Domenico. 10. The Sacristy. 11. Shop of Ruggeri (Via dei Coltellai). 12-13. Shop of Amati. 14. Shop of Storioni, and afterwards that of Ceruti.

The Church of San Domenico was, in consequence of its decayed condition, demolished about the year 1870. Becoming aware of what was taking place, I gave instructions that a photograph should be taken of the chapel in which the body of Stradivari was interred. This was accomplished whilst the workmen were in the act of levelling the structure, and it has been engraved on wood for the purpose of insertion in this volume. The stone with the inscription "Sepolcro di Antonio Stradivari E Svoi Eredi Anno 1729," which served to denote the spot where the body was buried, is now preserved in the Town Hall of Cremona. Signor Sacchi remembered it having been placed in the corner, close to the steps and iron railing inside the third chapel on the right, in the Church of San Domenico.

M. Fétis says of Stradivari, "We know but little respecting that uneventful existence. Polledro, late first Violin at the Chapel Royal of Turin, who died a few years ago, at a very advanced age, declared that his master had known Stradivari, and that he was fond of talking about him. He was, he said, tall and thin, habitually wore, in winter, a cap of white wool, and one of cotton in summer. He wore over his clothes an apron of white leather when he worked, and as he was always working, his costume scarcely ever varied. He had acquired more than competency by labour and economy, for the inhabitants of Cremona were accustomed to say, 'As rich as Stradivari!'"[29] The house he occupied stands in the Piazza Roma, formerly called the Square of San Domenico, in the centre of which was the church of the same name. The house is still in good condition, and is the principal place of interest in the old city of Cremona to the many admirers of Stradivari who visit the seat of Violin-making in olden times. After the death of Stradivari it was occupied by his sons Omobono and Francesco; and afterwards by the maker's youngest son, Paolo, who carried on there the business of a cloth merchant. Stradivari worked on the ground floor, and used the upper storey for varnishing.

    29 "Notice of Anthony Stradivari."

It is somewhat singular that the Cremonese take but little apparent interest in the matter, and have expressed themselves as being astonished at the demonstrations of respect which their French and English visitors pay to the hallowed spot. The better-informed Cremonese have some acquaintance with the name of Stradivari; but to create any enthusiasm among them from the fact of his having been a Cremonese, or from the historical associations which connect him with that city, would be difficult. After the exercise of considerable patience and determination, Signor Sacchi, in conjunction with a few Cremonese, managed to raise sufficient enthusiasm among the inhabitants to permit the authorities to name a street after Stradivari, and another after Amati. This worthy act was performed by the late librarian, Professor Pietro Fecit, who aided Signor Sacchi in his researches in connection with the past of Cremona's Violin-makers.

This street-naming was much opposed at the time. The citizens of Cremona are, however, not quite singular in this respect. It has been remarked that our American friends show far greater interest in Stratford-upon-Avon and its memories than we ourselves do. I must confess that I have great respect for the genuine enthusiast.

The Cremonese have scarcely an idea of the extent of veneration with which we admirers of the art regard their illustrious citizen. They will be astonished to hear that "Stradivari" forms the Christian name of some Englishmen. A well-known dealer, some years since, determined to commemorate his admiration for the great maker, and, accordingly, named his descendant "Stradivari Turner." We have stepped out of the ordinary path of house nomenclature, and have adopted the cherished name of "Stradivari" to the bewilderment of the passer-by, whose unmusical soul fails to be impressed by it. To crown our seeming eccentricities (in the eyes of our Italian friends), I may mention that the magic name has found its way into circles where little interest is taken in the subject of this notice, judging from the following announcement, which appeared in the profane pages of a newspaper: "*Waterloo Purse.*—E. Mr. *Goodlake's Gilderoy beat Earl of Stair's Stradivarius, and won the Purse;*" the result showing that Stradivari was evidently out of place in such company.

Franciscus Stradivarius Cremonensis
Filius Antonii faciebat Anno 1742

STRADIVARI, Francesco, Cremona, 1720-43. Son of Antonio Stradivari. Worked with his brother Omobono for several years. Many of the later works of Antonio Stradivari have been attributed to his sons. The character of the work is wholly distinct. I can well understand the error of attributing the instruments of Francesco Stradivari to Carlo Bergonzi, there being many points in common, but that so many marked specimens of the works of Antonio should be deemed apocryphal is beyond my comprehension. The work of Francesco is altogether less finished, but at the same time it shows the hand of the master. The design is bold and original. The tone of Francesco's instruments is invariably rich and telling.

Lancetti states—speaking of Francesco Stradivari—"After the death of his father, he made several Violins and Tenors, to which he put his own name. Although he did not succeed in perfectly imitating the works of his father, the instruments which he made in the years 1740 and 1742, and which remained after his death in the possession of his brother Paolo, were sold at the same price as those of his father, as mentioned in the correspondence between Count Cozio and Paolo. Francesco died at the end of 1742, the year Omobono died, and in which he made the Violins bought by Count Cozio." The date of death (as given by Lancetti), though incorrect by some months—he having died May 11, 1743, aged 72 years—shows the care and trouble taken to render the information as complete as possible, these dates having been given without reference to registers, but simply as stated by Paolo.

> Omobonus Stradivarius filius Antonii
> Cremone fecit, Anno 1740.

STRADIVARI, Omobono, Cremona, 1742. Brother of Francesco. Lancetti remarks, "Omobono chiefly restored instruments and arranged and regulated them." Francesco, it will be seen, survived his brother about thirteen months, and with him, as with Girolamo Amati, the son of Niccolò, we reach the end of the family's long and historical career of Violin-making. Upon the death of Francesco, the shop in the Piazza San Domenico (now named Piazza Roma) was closed, after having been occupied by the family of Stradivari as Violin-makers for upwards of sixty-three years. From here were sent into cathedral, church, and royal orchestras the largest number of Violins and kindred instruments ever made by one maker—instruments which bore the indelible stamp of genius and have gladdened the sight and hearing of untold thousands. The famous shop, as previously noticed, was next opened by Paolo Stradivari, who was a cloth merchant or warehouseman. Paolo died in 1776, a year after the date of the correspondence which passed between him and Count Cozio di Salabue. Antonio, son of Paolo, born in 1738 and married in 1762, had a son Giacomo, born in 1769 and married in 1797. Cesare, the son of Giacomo, became a physician in Cremona, married in 1838, and left, as the representative of the Cremonese branch of the family, Dr. Libero Stradivari, a barrister-at-law and an excellent performer on the flute.

SURSANO, Spirito, Coni, 1714-35.

TANEGIA, Carlo Antonio, Milan, early in the 18th century.

TANINGARD, Giorgio, Rome, 17—.

> David Tecchler Liutaro
> fecit Romæ 17—

TECCHLER, David, Rome, 1680-1743. A highly esteemed maker. He worked in Venice, Salzburg, and Rome, chiefly in the latter city. His instruments vary in form, some having a marked German style: they are high-modelled, and the sound-hole partakes of the Stainer character. These were probably made in Salzburg, to the order of his patrons. Those instruments which date from Rome are chiefly of the Italian type, and are so much superior to the others that it seems difficult to reconcile varieties so distinct as the work of the same man. They are finely formed, have splendid wood, and rich varnish of a yellow tint; the bellies are of a mottled character, similar to those so much used by Niccolò Amati. His Violoncellos are among the finest of his instruments. They are mostly of a large size.

TEDESCO, Leopoldo, pupil of Niccolò Amati. He went to Rome. I have seen a Violin of his make dated from there 1658. Workmanship a little rough, good varnish, Amati outline.

TESTORE, Carlo Giuseppe, Milan, about 1690 to 1720. The form resembles that of Guarneri. The wood is often plain in figure.

TESTORE, Carlo Antonio, Milan, about 1730 to 1764. Son of Giuseppe. Copied Guarneri and Amati. These instruments are bold and well made; their tone is excellent; wood often plain in figure.

TESTORE, Giovanni, son of Carlo Antonio.

TESTORE, Paolo Antonio, Milan, about 1740. Brother of Carlo Antonio. Copied Guarneri. The varnish is mostly yellow; frequently unpurfled.

TIEFFENBRUCKER, Leonardo, Padua, 1587. Lute-maker.

TODINI, Michele, seventeenth century, a native of Saluzzo, lived for many years at Rome. Todini was the inventor and maker of a great number of musical contrivances, in which clockwork played an important part. He occupied himself with this manufacture for several years, and turned his house into a kind of musical museum. He published in 1676 a pamphlet describing its contents. His name is associated with our subject in having adopted a new mode of stringing the Violono, or Double-Bass, by using four strings, and playing himself upon the instrument at oratorio performances in Rome. I have mentioned in Section I. that the Violono was originally used with several strings—five, six, or seven—and with frets. Todini is therefore credited with having introduced the method of stringing the Double Bass which led to the conversion of the old Violonos into Double-Basses fitted for modern requirements.

TONONI, Carlo, Bologna. At the exhibition at Milan in 1881, an inlaid Kit, of beautiful workmanship, was exhibited of this maker.

Carolo Tunonus fecit Bononiae
in Platea Castælionis Anno Domini 1698.

Carolus Tononi Bonon fecit Venetiis
 sub Titulo S. Cecilæ Anno 1739.

TONONI, Carlo Antonio, Venice, born at Bologna, probably a son of the above. The model varies very much; those of the flat pattern are excellent instruments. They are large, and beautifully made. The varnish, though inferior to that of Santo Serafino, is similar. These Violins are branded above the tail-pin. His instruments date from about 1716.

TONONI, Giovanni, about 1700. Similar characteristics.

TONONI, Felice, Bologna.

TONONI, Guido, Bologna.

TOPPANI, Angelo de, Rome, about 1740. Scarce; workmanship resembles that of Tecchler.

TORTOBELLO, Francesco, Rome, 16—. Maggini characteristics.

TRAPANI, Raffaele, Naples, about 1800. Large pattern; flat model; purfling deeply laid; edges sharp; scroll heavy.

VALENZANO, Gio. Maria, Rome, 1771 to about 1830. Neapolitan character; neat work; varnish excellent in some specimens, being soft and transparent.

VETRINI, Battista, Brescia, about 1629. Yellow varnish of good quality; handsome wood; rather small.

VIMERCATI, Paolo, Venice, about 1700. Similar to Tononi. Jacob Stainer is said to have worked in the shop of Vimercati.

WENGER, Padua, Lute-maker, 1622.

ZANNETTO, Pellegrino, Brescia, 1547. M. Chouquet in his "Catalogue Raisonné" of the instruments at the Conservatoire in Paris, describes a six-string Viol da Gamba of this make.

ZANOLA, Giovanni Battista. Flat model; rough workmanship; German character.

Joannes Baptista Zanola, Verona, 17—

ZANOLI, Giacomo, 1740-80. Verona. Worked in Venice, Padua, and Verona. Venetian character.

ZANOTTI, Antonio, Mantua, about 1734.

Antonius Zanotus, fecit Mantuæ, anno 1734.

ZANTI, Alessandro, Mantua, 1765. He copied Pietro Guarneri, but had little knowledge of varnishing, if we are to judge from the few instruments of this maker extant.

ZANURE, Pietro, Brescia, 1509. A maker of Viols.

ZENATTO, Pietro, Treviso, about 1634.

> Pietro Zenatto fece in
> Treviso Anno 1634.

SECTION VII

The French School

The French have long occupied a foremost place in the production of articles needing delicate workmanship, and it is therefore not surprising that they should at an early period have turned their attention to the art of Violin-making, which requires in a high degree both skilful workmanship and artistic treatment. The French manufacture of Violins appears to have commenced about the same period as the English, viz., in the early part of the 17th century, François Médard and Tywersus being among the French makers, and Rayman and Wise their fellows in England. The primitive French makers, like their English brethren, copied the instruments made at Brescia and Cremona, to which course they adhered down to the days of Barak Norman, when the two nations parted company, as regards having a common type, the French continuing the path they had hitherto taken, and copying the Italians, with scarcely any deviation, to the present time. The English left the Italian form for the German one of Jacob Stainer, which they adopted, with but few exceptions, for nearly a century, recovering the Italian about the middle of the 18th century. It is remarkable that French makers should have restrained themselves from following the pattern of the famous German maker when his name was at its height and his instruments were in such demand. That in not adopting the then popular form they were rightly guided, experience has clearly demonstrated. When we scan the older works the French have left us, and consider the advantage they had in keeping to the Italian form, we cannot but feel disappointed in finding so few meritorious instruments among them. There appear to have been many makers who were quite unconcerned whether their instruments possessed merit becoming the productions of a true artist; their chief aim would seem to have been to make in dozens—in other words, quantity in place of quality. If the early French makers are carefully studied, it will be seen that Boquay, Pierray, and one or two of their pupils are the only makers deserving of praise. It must be admitted that the shortcomings of the makers of the first period were adequately supplied by those of the second period, which includes the king of French artists, Nicolas Lupot. The old French school, originating with Tywersus and Médard, includes the following makers: Nicolas Renault, of Nancy, Médard, also of Nancy, Dumesnil, Bertrand, Pierray, Boquay, Gaviniés, Chappuy, Ouvrard, Paul Grosset, Despont, Saint-Paul, Salomon, Véron, with others of less importance. Many of these makers had a fair amount of ideas, which, had they been well directed, might have led to fame. Others contented themselves with copying, without giving any place to their fancy. It will be found that many of the instruments by Boquay,

Pierray, and a few others, have varnish upon them closely resembling that of the Venetian school; it is full-bodied, very transparent, and rich in colour. Many of their works are covered with a very inferior quality of varnish, which has caused some confusion respecting the merit due to them as varnishers, they being frequently judged by their inferior instruments, without reference to their good ones. It is evident that they made two qualities of varnish, in accordance with the price they were to obtain, as was commonly done in England by the Forsters, Banks, and Wamsley, where similar confusion exists. The Italians happily avoided this objectionable practice. Their works are of one uniform quality in point of varnish. This divergence may possibly be accounted for by the difference of climate. In Italy, oil varnish, judiciously used, would dry rapidly, whereas in France or England the reverse would be the case; hence its more sparing use.

We will now glance at the second French School of makers, commencing with De Comble. Learning his art in Italy, and, it is said, under Stradivari, he brought to bear a knowledge superior to that possessed by the makers mentioned above. The form he introduced was seen to be in advance of that hitherto met with among the French and Belgian makers, and led to its being chiefly followed. The next maker was Pique, who made Violins and Violas that were excellent in point of workmanship, and had he been equally successful in varnishing he would probably have been held in the same estimation as Nicolas Lupot. From these makers sprang quite a little school of its own, comprising François Gand, in Paris, who succeeded to the business of Lupot, and Bernardel, with several others less known. Mention must not be omitted of another excellent copyist—Silvestre, of Lyons. He has left some charming specimens of his art. They are lighter in character than the works of Nicolas Lupot, and resemble the work of Stradivari from 1680 to 1710. Every portion of the work evidences the skill and judgment of the maker. The wood, with scarcely an exception, has not been manipulated in order to darken it, consequently the instruments become of increasing merit as age acts upon them.

The practice of preparing the wood for Violin-making, either by baking it or by the application of acids, may be traced, in the first instance, to a desire to obtain artificially those results which are brought about by the hand of time. In obtaining lightness and dryness in new wood, it was imagined that the object in view would be reached without the aid of Dame Nature. Experience, however, has shown that Fiddles, like all things intended to pass into green old age, mature gradually, and are not to be benefited by any kind of forcing process. The earliest account I have met with of Fiddle-baking occurred in England about 150 years since. One Jeacocke, a baker by trade, and a lover of music by nature, used to bake his Fiddles in sawdust for a week whenever their tones showed symptoms of not being up to his standard of quality. In France the practice may be said to have been introduced about eighty years ago, with a view of facilitating the creation of such mysteries as Duiffoprugcar and Morella Violins, baked and browned until they had something of a fifteenth-century hue. The same means were adopted in the production of instruments intended as copies of the works of Stradivari and Guarneri. The brown hue of the originals, and the worn and broken condition of the varnish which comes of age alone, were imitated with more or less ingenuity. Happily the error is recognised, as far as the best workmanship is concerned, in France. The legitimate imitator's art no longer includes that of depicting wear and brownness, rendering abortive so much excellent work.

It only remains now to mention Salle, Vuillaume, Chanot, Gand, Germain, Mennégand, Gaillard, and Miremont, all copyists of more or less note, who may be said to complete the modern French school. These makers are or were the chief manufacturers of Violins in France of a better class. Those made by thousands yearly at Mirecourt are not Violins in the eyes of the connoisseur. They are made, as common cabinet work is produced in England, by several workmen, each taking a portion, one making the backs, another the sides, another the bellies, and so on with the other parts of the instrument, the whole being finally arranged by a finisher. Such work must necessarily be void of any artistic nature; they are like instruments made *in* a mould, not *on* a mould, so painfully are they alike. This Manchester of Fiddle-making has doubtless been called into being by the great demand for cheap instruments, and has answered thus far its purpose, but it has certainly helped to destroy the gallant little bands of makers who were once common in France, Germany, and England, among whom were men who were guided by reverential feelings for the art, irrespective of the gains they reaped by their labours. The number of instruments yearly made in Mirecourt and Saxony[1] amounts to many thousands, and is yearly increasing. They send forth repeated copies of Amati, Maggini, Guarneri, and Stradivari, all duly labelled and dated, to all parts of the world, frequently disappointing their simple-minded purchasers, who fondly fancy they have thus become possessed of the real article at the trifling cost of a few pounds. They produce various kinds of modern antiques in Violins, some of which display an amount of ingenuity worthy of being exercised in a better cause; but usually the whole thing is overdone, and the results, in point of tone, are far more disastrous than in the common French copies. The following list of French, Belgian, and Dutch makers contains many names not included in the first edition of this book. The works wherein several of these names occur are M. J. Gallay's, "Les Luthiers Italiens aux 17ième et 18ième Siècles," 1869; M. Fétis, "Biographie Universelle des Musiciens;" M. Vidal, "Les Instruments à Archet," 1876; the "Catalogue Raisonné," of the instruments at the Conservatoire, by Gustave Chouquet, Paris, 1875; "Recherches sur les facteurs de Clavecins," by M. le Chevalier de Burbure, Antwerp, 1863; Pougin's "Supplement to the Dictionary of Fétis;" and Mendel's "Musikalisches Conversations-Lexikon," 1880.

1 Germany's yearly output of such instruments is enormous, the principal seats of manufacture being Mark-Neukirchen (Saxony) and Mittenwald (Bavaria).

SECTION VIII

French Makers

ALDRIC, Paris, 1790-1844. Copied Stradivari with great skill. He was also well known as a dealer in Cremonese instruments. He was one of the earliest French makers who dealt with Luigi Tarisio, the famous Italian connoisseur. He generally used a red varnish of good quality.

ALLAR, ——, Paris, 1788.

AMELOT, ——, Lorient; worked early in the present century. He used a highly ornamented label.

AUBRY, ——, Paris, 1840. Succeeded his uncle Aldric, mentioned above.

AUGIÈRE, ——, Paris, about 1830, was established in the Rue Saint Eustache, in partnership with Calot, and made some good instruments. Augière formerly worked in the shop of Clement of Paris.

BACHELIER, ——, Paris, 1788.

BASSOT, ——, Paris, 1788.

BERNARDEL, Auguste Sébastien Philippe, born at Mirecourt in 1802, was in the workshop of Lupot, in Paris. The instruments of this maker are excellently made, and the wood judiciously selected. He took his sons into partnership in 1859 and retired from business in 1866. He died in 1870. His sons, Ernst Auguste and Gustave Adolphe, were in partnership with Eugène Gand, and the firm was known as "Gand et Bernardel frères."

BERTRAND, Nicolas, Paris, about 1700 to 1735, used varnish of a superior kind. He made many of the Viols of the type common in Paris, for some time after the Violin had been introduced; they were named Dessus-de-Viole, Pardessus, Quinton, and Viole-haut-contre. His name is often seen branded on the backs of his instruments, inside.

BOIVIN, Claude, about 1749, Paris. M. Chouquet, in his "Catalogue Raisonné" of the instruments at the Paris Conservatoire, described a Guitar by this maker, made for a daughter of Louis XV.

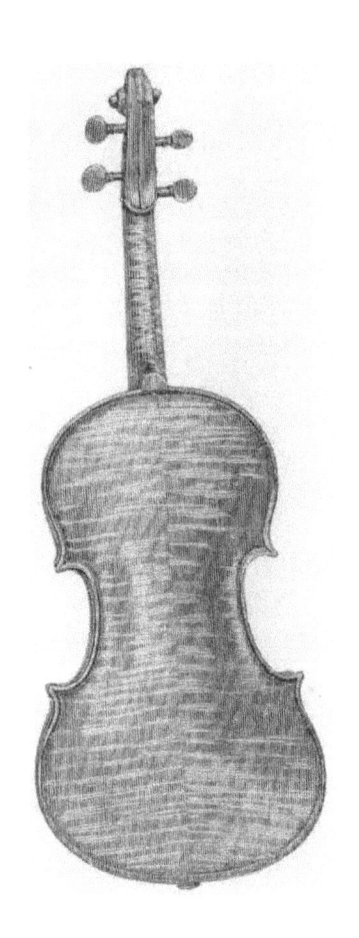

ANTONIO STRADIVARI.
1702.

ANTONIO STRADIVARI.
1722.

ANTONIO STRADIVARI.
1703.

Plate XIII.

Jacques Boquay,
rue d'Argenteuil, à Paris, 1723.

BOQUAY, Jacques, Paris, 1700-1730. One of the first of the old French school. He, with a few of his contemporaries, inherited a good amount of the Italian character of workmanship, introduced probably into France by Nicolas Renault. Boquay, with others whose names are mentioned in this list of French makers, used varnish closely allied to that of Cremona; its colour is a warm brown, very transparent, and of a soft nature. He made many instruments of small size. The model is often that of Girolamo Amati, but slightly more arched; the sound-hole is more rounded and less striking. The scroll can scarcely be considered a copy of Girolamo Amati's; it is well cut, but lacks the peculiar grace of the Italian. The tone is sweet, without much power.

BORLON, Artus or Arnould, about 1579, Antwerp, maker of stringed instruments (mentioned in the pamphlet by M. le Chevalier de Burbure).

BORLON, or PORLON, Pierre, Antwerp, about 1647, of whom M. de Burbure says: "Pierre Borlon, or Porlon, made in the year 1647 a Double-Bass for the orchestra of the Cathedral (Antwerp). The instrument is in existence, and inside is the name 'Peeter Porlon tot, Antwerpen f. 1647.'" The same author mentions another early Double-Bass made in 1636 by Maître Daniel for a chapel in Antwerp, and remarks, in passing, that in other countries the Double-Bass was not used until about half a century later. The question of priority in this matter is important and interesting; but in order to arrive at a satisfactory conclusion, it is necessary to be certain that these Belgian Basses are not, together with the Brescian and others, converted Viols.

BORLON, Joannes, Antwerp, also a maker of Viols.

BORLON, François, Antwerp, Viol-maker.

BOULLANGIER, C., 1823-1888. Worked in Paris, and for the late Mr. Withers. Was in business for many years in Frith Street, Soho, and has made many excellent instruments.

BOUMEESTER, Amsterdam, about 1650.

BOURDET, Sébastien, Mirecourt, one of the earliest Violin-makers in Mirecourt.

BOURDET, Jacques, Paris, 1751.

BOUSSU, Eterbeck, le Bruxelles, about 1750.

BRETON, 1777. This name is met with branded on the backs, "Breton à Paris." A little heavy in character, but fairly made; dark brown colour.

BRETON, Le, Mirecourt, 1812-30. Commonplace instruments. Large pattern, usually stamped with name inside.

BRUGÈRE, the name of several contemporary French makers, dating from Mirecourt and elsewhere. Some show good workmanship and varnish.

CALOT, ——, about 1830. He was in the workshop of Clément prior to date given. *See* AUGIÈRE.

CASTAGNERY, Andrea. *See* Italian list.

CASTAGNERY, Jean Paul. M. Fétis mentions this maker as having worked in Paris, 1638-62.

CHAMPION, René, Paris, about 1735. His instruments are well made, and the varnish is of good quality.

CHANOT, François, born at Mirecourt in 1788. An engineer by profession. Becoming interested in the construction of Violins, he designed one having sides like those of the guitar. M. Chouquet describes a Violin of this maker, made for Viotti, and remarks that the experiment of François Chanot opened the way to those of Savart. The date of Chanot's patent is 1818. The paper of Savart on the construction of bow instruments was read at the French Academy in the following year.

CHANOT, Georges, Paris. Brother of the above-named; born at Mirecourt, 1801. Throughout life was a most indefatigable worker. He has made a very large number of copies of Stradivari and Guarneri, chiefly of the former, which are also the best. They are well constructed instruments, and the wood is of an excellent description. He was long known as a dealer in Cremonese instruments, and many notable rarities passed into his possession. The instruments of this maker will, at no distant date, be valued higher than they are at the present time. He died in 1883.

CHANOT, Georges, London. Son of Georges Chanot, Paris. Assisted Charles Maucotel, and a short time afterwards started in business on his own behalf. He died in 1893.

CHANOT, F. Son of Georges Chanot.

CHANOT, G. A. Brother of the above-named.

CHAPPUY, Nicolas-Augustin, about 1765. His instruments are chiefly of large pattern; nearly all are branded on the button, in a similar manner to those of the Testore family. Chappuy differed greatly in his work. When he used plenty of wood we have instruments of a good kind and worthy of attention. There are many, however, having his brand that are scarcely fit to be called Violins, so inferior is the work and wood.

The Violin M. Habeneck used during thirty-seven years, when instructing his class at the Conservatoire, Paris, was made by Chappuy, and is preserved at that institution.

CHARDON, Joseph, Paris, son-in-law and pupil of Georges Chanot, Paris, to whose business he succeeded in the year 1872.

CHAROTTE, ———, born at Mirecourt, settled at Rouen. Died in 1836.

CHATERAIN, Paris, about 1759. Good workmanship.

CHEVRIER, André-Augustin, about 1838. Born at Mirecourt, worked in Paris and Brussels.

CLAUDOT, Charles, Paris, possibly came from Mirecourt. The workmanship is heavy; varnish mostly yellow. His instruments are good for orchestral purposes. His name is generally found stamped on the back, inside.

CLAUDOT, Augustin, Paris, "Strad" pattern, yellow varnish, good wood.

CLEMENT, ——, Paris, 1815-40.

CLIQUOT, Henri, Paris, about 1765.

CLIQUOT, Louis Alexandre, about 1765.

COUSINEAU, Paris, about the end of the 18th century. Well made, name often branded on button.

CUNAULT, Georges, Paris, contemporary; worked with Miremont, and afterwards alone; a careful maker.

CUNY, ——, Paris. 18th century.

CUYPERS, Johannes, 1755-18——. Worked at the Hague; varnish often yellow in colour. Well finished instruments, which are rising in value.

DANIEL, ——, 1656, is described as having made a Double-Bass for the orchestra of one of the chapels at Antwerp Cathedral.

DARCHE, Nicholas, Aix la Chapelle, died 1873. Made many useful instruments on the lines of the Cremonese Masters. Other makers of this name worked in Brussels and Mirecourt in the 19th century.

DAVID, ——. Maker to the court of Louis XVI.

    Fait à Tournay par
Ambroise de Comble, 1750.

DE COMBLE, Ambroise, Tournay, about 1760. It is said that he worked in the shop of Antonio Stradivari, and judging from the character of the work, together with that of the varnish, it is not unlikely that he did receive instructions from the great Cremonese maker. The varnish is very like Italian; the colour often a rich red, with much body. His instruments are inclined to roughness as regards workmanship, and therefore are not pleasing to the eye. There is a resemblance to the instruments of Stradivari after 1732 in form, though not in workmanship, and he would therefore seem to have copied those late instruments. They may be described as of large pattern, flat model, and having an abundance of wood. They are deserving of attention both from the professor and the amateur, the workmanship being skilful and the material excellent. The tone is large, and frequently possesses the richness so much admired in the works of the Italians. This quality is traceable to the soft and flexible nature of the superior varnish with which these instruments are covered. Several Violas and Violoncellos are extant which were made by De Comble.

DEHOMMAIS, Paris, 1870. *See* GERMAIN (Emile).

DELANOIX, ——, Bruxelles, about 1760.

DELAUNAY, ——, Paris, 1775, Viol-maker. M. Chouquet describes an instrument of this maker which is in the collection at the Conservatoire.

DELEPLANQUE, Gérard, Lille, 1768.

DERAZEY, Honoré, Mirecourt. Many of the instruments of this maker are carefully finished. They are heavy in wood. The varnish is inclined to hardness. Died 1875.

DERAZEY, J. A., Mirecourt, 1815-85. Son of Honoré; purchased the business of Nicolas. Made many useful instruments.

DESPONS, Antoine, Paris, 17th century, is said to have made excellent instruments of various patterns.

DIEULAFAIT, ——, 1720, Viol-maker. A Viol da Gamba of this maker is at the Conservatoire, Paris.

DROULOT, ——, Paris, 1788.

DUCHERON, Mathurin, Paris, 1714.

DU MESNIL, Jacques, Paris, about 1655.

EESBROECK, Jean Van, 1585, Antwerp, Lute-maker. M. C. Chevalier de Brabure states he was the son of Josse van Eesbroeck, of Maria Kerch. He gives some interesting particulars relative to the connection of music with the guild of St. Luke at Antwerp, and speaks of the makers of Clavichords seeking for admission into the Guild in 1557, adding that it was natural these makers should desire to belong to a corporation so great and honourable as that of St. Luke, which since 1480 had its Chambers of Rhetoric "dite *de Violiren, de Violier.*"

FALAISE, ——. Copied the Amatis and Stradivari. The workmanship may be likened to that of Pique. Varnish yellow and thin. There is no indication of a resort to any maturing process. Wood frequently handsome.

FENT, or FENDT, ——, Paris, 1780. A maker known among French connoisseurs; related to the Fendts who worked in London.

FLEURY, Benoist, Paris, from about 1755 to 1788. A Viol da Gamba of this maker, from the Clapisson collection, is at the Conservatoire, Paris.

FOURRIER, Nicolas, Mirecourt. *See* NICOLAS.

GAILLARD, Charles, Paris, about 1850-81. Born at Mirecourt. Worked in Paris with C. A. Gand, and later on his own account. He was one of the best modern French makers, and his instruments already take high rank and command good prices.

GAILLARD-LAJOUE, J. B., Mirecourt, brother of the above. Apprenticed to Gand, for whom he worked until about 1852. Much of his work is of a high order, and his best instruments are yearly increasing in value. He died about 1870.

GAND, Charles François, Paris. He became a pupil of Nicolas Lupot in the year 1802. During his apprenticeship he proved himself an excellent maker, and was much valued by his famous instructor. He married the daughter of Lupot, and succeeded him in the Rue Croix des Petits Champs in the year 1824. The career of François Gand was one of much activity. As a repairer of the works of the great masters he early obtained a high reputation, and perhaps restored more valuable instruments than any repairer of his time. The care that he took and the judgment which he exercised in endeavouring to bring together the various broken parts of an imperfect instrument, that the original appearance might be maintained as closely as possible, cannot be too highly praised. He often accomplished seeming impossibilities. Splintered cracks were by his ingenuity closed as though no fibre had been severed, while at other times pieces were inserted so deftly that the most experienced eyes might fail to detect their presence. It was with him a labour of love, and he did not scruple to spend days over work on which others would only spend hours. He made many Violins, several of which were given as prizes at the Paris Conservatoire. They are well-made instruments, though heavy in appearance. They are good serviceable instruments, and, the wood not having been browned by baking or other injurious process, age mellows them greatly. He died in the year 1845.

GAND, Charles Adolphe, son of Charles François Gand, was instructed by his father, and succeeded, together with his brother, to the old-established house founded by his grandfather. He died in 1866.

GAND, Charles Nicholas Eugène, Paris, brother of C. Adolphe Gand, was a connoisseur of much experience and reputation. Upon the death of his brother C. Adolphe he entered into partnership with Bernardel Brothers. The firm employed many workmen, and turned out large numbers of useful, well-made instruments, with red varnish. They were the recipients of numerous medals and decorations. C. N. E. Gand died in 1892.

>Gaviniés, rue
>S. Thomas du Louvre,
>à Paris, 17—

GAVINIÉS, François, Paris, about 1734. Father of Pierre Gaviniés, the Violinist. Old French school. The wood is often of excellent quality, and the varnish also. Many of these old French makers, like our good English ones, made instruments of two qualities, and Gaviniés was one of them.

GERMAIN, Joseph Louis, born at Mirecourt in 1822. In Paris he was employed by François Gand, and afterwards worked for Vuillaume, for whom he made several choice instruments. It is to be regretted that his exceptional abilities were not allowed to add lustre to his name, he having made for the trade. He died in 1870.

GERMAIN, Emile, Paris. Son of the above; established in Paris as a maker and restorer of Violins. He was, until 1882, in partnership with a maker named Dehommais.

GOSSELIN, ——, Paris, 1814-40.

GRAND-GERARD, Paris, about 1800. Commonplace work branded occasionally with his name.

GRANDSON, Fils, Mirecourt, about 1850.

GROSSET, Paul François, Paris, about 1750. Pupil of Claude Pierray.

GUERSAN, Louis, succeeded Paul Pierray.

>Ludovicus Guersan prope Comædiam Gallicam, Lutetiæ,
>Anno 1766.

HEL, Pierre Joseph, Lille, contemporary. Well-made instruments.

HENRY, Jean Baptiste. Born 1757, near Mirecourt. Worked in Paris.

HENRY, Jean Baptiste Felix, son of the above. Established in Paris 1817.

HENRY, Charles, brother of the above, born 1803. Made several excellent instruments.

HENRY, Octave, nephew of Charles.

HENRY, Eugène, son of Charles, born in 1843.

HOFMANS, Mathias, Antwerp, 1700-25. A Kit of this maker was exhibited at Milan in 1870.

JACOBS, Hendrik, Amsterdam, 1690-17—. A close imitator of Niccolò Amati. Few makers have been more mistaken than Jacobs; so exact was he in following the model of Amati, that numbers of his Violins are passed by the inexperienced as original. He mostly selected the grand pattern of Amati for his model, which gave him full scope for the exercise of his powers. He selected wood as nearly as possible resembling that found in the works of Niccolò Amati. The backs are mostly of even grain, and compact; the modelling can only be found fault with near the purfling, where its sharpness at once catches the attention of the critic in these matters, and divulges the true author. The varnish, though good, is not equal to that of Amati. The scroll is inferior to the body in merit. The purfling is of whalebone, like that of most of the Dutch makers.

JACOBS, ——, Amsterdam, probably a son of the above. Excellent varnish, of a deep red, very transparent; full of character, but wanting in finish. Purfling embedded.

JACQUOT, Charles, born at Mirecourt in 1804. Worked in Paris. He obtained prizes for his instruments at the Paris and other exhibitions.

JACQUOT, Pierre Charles, Nancy, son of the above.

JEANDEL, P. N., born in 1812. Worked for some years in Paris, and received prizes at the Paris and other exhibitions. He died in 1879.

KOLIKER, ——, Paris, 1789-1820.

LAMBERT, Jean Nicolas, Paris, about 1745.

LAPAIX, ——, Lille, about 1855.

LAPREVOTTE, Etienne, Paris, 1825-56.

LECLERC, ——, Paris, about 1775.

LECOMTE, ——, Paris, 1788.

LEDUC, Pierre, Paris, 1646.

LEFEBVRE, ——, Amsterdam, about 1730.

LEFEBVRE, ——, Paris, 1788.

LE JEUNE, François, Paris, 175-.

LE PILEUR, Pierre, about 1754.

LESCLOP, François Henry, Paris, 1746.

LOUIS, ——, Geneva.

LOUVET, Jean, Paris, 1750.

LUPOT, Jean, Mirecourt.

LUPOT, Laurent, Mirecourt, born 1696. Son of Jean Lupot, removed to Plombières, afterwards to Luneville, and again to Orleans.

LUPOT, François, born 1736. Son of Laurent. Born at Plombières. In the year 1758 he removed to Stuttgart, and was appointed maker to the Duke of Wurtemberg. François removed with his son Nicolas to Orleans in 1770. He died in Paris in 1804. The workmanship and style are similar to those seen in the instruments of Chappuy and other makers of that period. Scroll rather rough, varnish dark brown, broad pattern.

> N. Lupot fils, Luthier,
> rue d'Illiers, à Orléans, l'an 1791.

> Nicolas Lupot, Luthier, rue de
> Grammont; à Paris, l'an 1803.

> Nicolas Lupot, Luthier, rue Croix
> des-petits-champs, à Paris, l'an 1817.

LUPOT, Nicolas, son of François, born at Stuttgart in 1758, removed with his father to Orleans in 1770. He established himself in Paris in 1794, his fame having reached that city some time before. The attention which he soon received from the musical world of Paris proved to him that his removal was advantageous. He had not long been in Paris before he was honoured with the patronage of the Conservatoire of Music, an honour which is attended with many benefits, the chief of which is the making of a Violin annually, to be awarded as a prize to the most successful student among the Violinists. By this arrangement the maker has an opportunity of exercising to the best advantage all the skill of which he is capable, as he is at once aware that the attention of the public is directed to the constructor of the prize, as well as to the receiver, and that an immediate road to popularity is thus opened. Lupot's appointment as maker to the Conservatoire was enjoyed by his successor, François Gand, and was retained by the latter's son, in conjunction with Bernardel. Nicolas Lupot may be justly termed the French Stradivari. He was an artist in every sense of the word. He regarded the works of Stradivari with the utmost veneration. While, however, he laboured unceasingly to imitate him, he scorned all those mischievous maturing processes common to so many French copyists; he never desired that his copy should pass with the unwary as the original; it left his hands wholly unsophisticated. There is not an instance in which he did not varnish the copy all over, leaving time to do its work of wear, although by so doing he doubtless sacrificed much in his own time, inasmuch as all new Violins, so varnished, have a crude appearance, notwithstanding any amount of high finish expended upon them. What, however, Lupot lost in his own day has been awarded to his name a hundredfold since. He seldom occupied himself in copying Guarneri or Amati, although there are a few beautiful examples met with now and again in which he adopted these forms. Stradivari was his idol, and from the fact already mentioned, that he is very rarely found to have followed any other model than that of Stradivari, he would seem to have been aware of his own peculiar fitness for the great master's design. Every feature of Lupot's instruments was clearly a matter of study with him. It cannot be said of him, as of most other makers, that certain points are good, while others are weak. Every portion of his work contributes to the harmonious whole. The outline is perfect; the sound-hole is executed in a masterly manner; the model, purfling, and scroll of equal merit. He was untouched in his own day, and his productions have never been approached since. The varnish of Lupot is peculiar to him. Its qualities are good, being free from hardness. Though it is not of the Italian type, neither is it of the kind usually met with on the Violins of his contemporaries: it may be described as a quality of varnish coming between the Italian and the French. Its colour varies between light and dark red. Age has assisted in heightening its lustre, and although it will never rank with the varnish of Cremona, yet it will hold its own among the varnishes of modern times. It is said that many instruments having the name of Pique in them are the work of Lupot, and this misnomer is accounted for by the story that Pique purchased them in an unvarnished state, and varnished them with his preparation. Be this as it may, it is certain that the varnish of Pique could not serve to benefit such instruments; on the contrary, it would reduce their value. The tone of Lupot's instruments improves yearly. The quality is round and telling, and free from roughness. He died in Paris in 1824, aged 66, and was succeeded in his business by his son-in-law, François Gand.

MARQUIS DE LAIR, Mirecourt, about 1800. The name is generally branded on the back. The wood is chiefly of a plain description, and varnish wanting in transparency.

MAST, Jean Laurent, Paris, about 1750.

MAST, Joseph Laurent, Mirecourt and Toulouse. Son of Jean Laurent. A Violin dated 1816 is in the Museum of the Paris Conservatoire.

MAUCOTEL, Charles, born at Mirecourt, in 1807. In 1834 he entered the workshop of Gand in Paris. In 1844 he was employed by Davis, of Coventry Street, London, and ultimately commenced business in Rupert Street, from which he retired in 1860, and returned to France. He made several instruments, all of which have good qualities in workmanship and tone. They are strong in wood and carefully modelled.

MAUCOTEL, Charles Adolphe, Mirecourt, worked in Paris from 1839 until 1858, in which year he died. He made many excellent instruments.

Franciscus Médard fecit Parisiis 1710.

MÉDARD, François, was established in Paris about 1700. The work is excellent, and the varnish soft and transparent.

MÉDARD, Nicolas, Nancy, brother of François.

MÉDARD, Jean, Nancy, brother of Nicolas.

MENNÉGAND, Charles, born at Nancy in 1822. He is distinguished both as a maker and repairer of instruments. He entered the service of Rambaux in Paris in 1840. He has been rightly regarded as having displayed singular ability in the delicate and difficult task of "cutting" the large Italian Violoncellos and Tenors. The practice of reducing the dimensions of Cremonese instruments has happily come to be looked upon as emulative of the acts of the Goths and Vandals. It is in any case certain that numerous instruments have been operated upon with no greater skill than might have been expected at the hands of those barbarians. "These ruthless men," remarks Charles Reade, "just sawed a crescent off the top, and another off the bottom, and the result is a thing with the inner bout of a giant and the upper and lower bout of a dwarf." He rightly names this, "cutting in the statutory sense, viz., cutting and maiming," and implores the owner of an instrument in its original state to spare it, and if too large, to play on one of the value of £5, with the Cremona set before him to look at while he plays. To "cut" a Cremona, and to cut a diamond into a brilliant or a rose, are tasks equally difficult. The indifferent operator, in both cases, suffers more or less from the injury and annoyance his unskilfulness has occasioned. Borgis, a Venetian diamond-cutter, was employed by Shah Jehan to cut the Koh-i-nor, and in place of a reward was fined ten thousand ducats for his imperfect performance. Had it happened that some possessors of Cremonese gems had inflicted monetary or other punishment on incapable instrument cutters, the world would have been richer in Cremonas. Mennégand was at Amsterdam for a few years, and returned to Paris in 1857. He died in 1885.

MIREMONT, Claude Augustin, Paris. Born at Mirecourt in 1827, removed to Paris in 1844. Miremont has made several excellent Violins, copies of Stradivari and Guarneri. He was for some years in New York, but returned to Paris and died at Pontorson in 1887.

MODESSIER, ——, Paris, 1810. Made several instruments of large pattern, excellent for orchestral purposes. Wood of good quality.

MOUGENOT, Georges, Brussels, contemporary.

NAMY, ——, Paris, 1780 to 1806.

NEZOT, ——, about 1750, maker of Viols.

NICOLAS, François (Nicolas Fourrier), went from Mirecourt to Paris, where he is said to have worked from about 1784 to 1816.

NICOLAS, Didier, Mirecourt, 1757-1833. The instruments of this maker are chiefly of large size, the outline being after that of Stradivari. They are mostly stamped on the back, inside, "A la ville de Cremonne, D. Nicolas Ainé." Colour, yellow; tone very powerful, and admirably adapted for the orchestra.

NICOLAS, Joseph, son of Didier, born 1796, died 1864.

OUVRARD, Jean, pupil of Claude Pierray.

ANTONIO STRADIVARI.

Plate XIV.

PACHERELE, Michel, Paris, about 1779.

PACHEREL, Pierre, Nice, died 1871, probably related to Michel Pacherele. Good workmanship; made several copies of Stradivari.

PAUL, Saint, Paris, 17th century. Chiefly copied Amati. In the style of Boquay.

> Claude Pierray, proche la Comédie
> à Paris, 1725.

PIERRAY, Claude, Paris, from about 1700 to 1725. Was an excellent workman, and many of his productions partake of the Italian character to a considerable extent. They are of two patterns, the majority being large. Amati would seem to have been his model, but his instruments can scarcely be considered copies of that maker, the outline only being retained, while the other features are dissimilar. The wood is rarely handsome, but its quality is good; the thicknesses are variable. The work is of average merit. Varnish is of a pale red colour, of good quality. It is interesting to learn that these instruments were appreciated in England at the beginning of the eighteenth century. Tom Britton had in his collection of books and instruments at Clerkenwell a "Claude Pierray," which is described in the sale catalogue as "a very beautiful Violin, and as good as a Cremona."

PIÈTE, N., Paris, about 1780.

PILLEMENT, F., Paris, 1790-1820. Work branded inside.

> Pique, rue de Grenelle St. Honoré,
> au coin de celle des 2 Ecus, à
> Paris, 1790.

PIQUE, F. L., Paris, about 1788-1822. As a copyist of Stradivari, this maker approached, perhaps, nearest to Nicolas Lupot. It has been supposed that some Violins bearing the name of Pique were made by Lupot, and varnished by Pique. There are several specimens of Pique's instruments upon which have been lavished care and skill of a very high order. Each feature is brought out, while, at the same time, exaggeration, that common error of the copyist, is avoided. The scrolls are well executed, both in point of finish and style; the sound-hole also is cut with precision. Many of his instruments have whole backs, of well-chosen material; the bellies are of a fine quality of wood. The instruments of Pique have long been esteemed, and will grow in reputation.

PIROT, Claude, Paris, about 1800. Pressenda style and appearance.

PONS, César, Grenoble, about 1775.

PONS, ——, Paris, chiefly known as a maker of Guitars.

RAMBAUX, Claude Victor, born 1809. Worked in early life at Mirecourt, and afterwards in Paris. He was a clever repairer, and gifted with excellent judgment in his treatment of the works of the old masters. He was at one time in the workshop of Gand. He died in 1871.

RANCE, Thomas, Brussels, about 1683. Good workmanship, well purfled, flat model.

RAUT, Jean, worked at Rennes about 1760.

REMY, ——, Paris, about 1760.

REMY, Jean Mathurin, Paris, 1770-1854.

REMY, Jules, Paris, 1813-76.

REMY, ——, London, 1840. Originally from Paris. Copied the old masters with average ability, but unfortunately adopted the pernicious practice of preparing the wood, making his instruments prematurely old without the qualities of healthy age.

RENAUDIN, Léopold, Paris, about 1788.

RENAULT, Nicolas, an early maker, contemporary with Tywersus.

ROMBOUTS, Peeter, Amsterdam, about the middle of the 18th century. High model, varnish of much brilliancy, but flaky.

ROZE, ——, Orleans, about 1760. Average workmanship, yellow varnish, heavy scroll.

SACQUIN, ——, Paris, 1830-60, made several excellent instruments; oil varnish of good quality, neat work, "Strad" pattern, name branded on back, inside.

SALLE, ——, Paris, about 1825-50. Made several copies of Guarneri, many of which are excellent. He was also a clever restorer of old instruments, and had a critical eye for the works of the old Italian masters, in which he dealt to some extent.

SALOMON, Jean Baptiste Deshayes, Paris, about 1750.

SAUNIER, ——, about 1740-70.

SCHNOECK, Egidius, Brussels, 1700-30.

SILVESTRE, Pierre, Lyons. A maker of rare abilities. The finish of his instruments is of the highest order; indeed, it would be difficult to find any maker within the range of the modern French school who has surpassed him in delicate workmanship. It may be said of him, as of many others, that extreme fineness of work is obtained often at the expense of character; to develop both qualities needs the mind of a Stradivari. Silvestre was fortunate in procuring wood of beautiful quality; there is scarcely an instrument of his which is not handsome. He chiefly copied Stradivari. It is to be regretted that so few of his works are to be met with. Pierre Silvestre was born at Sommerwiller in 1801, and died at Lyons in 1859. In Paris he worked in the workshop of Lupot, and in that of his successor, François Gand.

SILVESTRE, Hippolyte, born 1808, brother of Pierre, with whom he worked in partnership at Lyons from 1831-48. Hippolyte worked in the shop of Vuillaume. He retired from business in 1865.

SILVESTRE, Hippolyte Chrétien, Lyons, succeeded to the business of his uncles, Pierre and Hippolyte, which he transferred in 1884 to Paris.

SIMON, Claude, Paris, about 1788.

SIMONIN, Charles, Paris and Toulouse, pupil of J. B. Vuillaume.

SOCQUET, Louis, Paris, about 1760-1800.

THERESS, Charles, London.

THIBOUT, Jacques Pierre, Paris, born 1777, died 1856. A well-known dealer in rare Italian instruments. To him belongs the merit of having encouraged Luigi Tarisio to bring to Paris his Cremonese gems. When Tarisio paid his first visit to Paris, the reception that he met with was not of such a nature as to warrant his returning; but having ultimately decided upon once more visiting the French capital, he met with Thibout, who, by earnest solicitation, prevailed on him to remove his rich wares to Paris. Jacques Pierre Thibout was an excellent workman, and his instruments are highly esteemed.

THOMASSIN, ——, Paris, about 1845.

TYWERSUS, ——, Nancy, 16th century.

VAILLANT, François, Paris, about 1750.

VÉRON, Pierre André, 1720-50.

VIBRECHT, Gysbert, Amsterdam, about 1700.

VUILLAUME, Jean, Mirecourt, 1700-40.

VUILLAUME, Claude, Paris, 1772-1834. The earliest maker of this family; made commonplace instruments branded with his name.

VUILLAUME, J. B., Paris, born 1798, died in 1875. There are upwards of 2,500 Violins which bear his name. Many of these he made throughout. The early ones are much appreciated, and having been wisely varnished over at first, now begin to show the good results of such handling. The career of Vuillaume was singularly eventful. Commencing life from the first stage of the ladder, he gradually mounted to the highest, by the help of the usual nurses of fortune, skill and perseverance. He was a great lover of Cremonese instruments, and was intimately associated with Tarisio. At the death of the celebrated Italian connoisseur, he purchased the whole of his collection. He employed a number of skilful workmen, some of whom have achieved independent and individual reputations, and will be found noticed in their proper places in this work.

VUILLAUME, N. F., Brussels. Brother of the above. Was well known both as a maker and connoisseur. Born in 1802; died 1876.

VUILLAUME, Claude François, born 1807.

VUILLAUME, Sébastien, Paris, nephew of J. B. Vuillaume, made a few excellent instruments. He died in the same year, 1875.

SECTION IX

The German School

There is no trace of any German Violins of the time of Gasparo da Salò, or Maggini. This is certainly remarkable, and the more so when we consider how near were the German makers of Lutes, &c., to the old Italian town where Violins were being made. It is evident from this non-production of Violins that the Tyrolese were content with their Viols and Lutes, and did not recognise the wonderful effects of the little Violin until it had become pretty nearly perfected by the Italians. The manufacture of Lutes, Viols, and Guitars in Germany had in 1650, or a little later, reached its zenith, and the exquisite pieces of workmanship, in the shape of Lutes, Viols da Gamba, and Viols d'Amore, richly inlaid with mother-of-pearl, ivory, and tortoiseshell, made at this period, evidence the high state of the art.

To Jacob Stainer is due the credit, to a great extent, of changing the system of modelling so long in vogue in Germany. Although so great a maker, he was seemingly unable to free himself entirely from the proclivities common to his countrymen as Violin makers. There remained, after all Stainer's changes, the German sound-hole and extra arching, &c. Yet it must be readily admitted that the example which Stainer put before his countrymen was of great value, and served to engender an improved style throughout the Violin manufacture of Germany. The exceptional merits of this famous German artist were soon recognised, and his followers were legion. Among them were Sebastian Kloz, George Kloz, Egidius Kloz, and other members of that, perhaps the largest, family of Fiddle-makers the world has seen (had they been as good as they were numerous, what stores of prized Violins would have been bequeathed to us!); Reiss, of Bamberg; Rauch, of Breslau; and Leopold Widhalm, of Nüremberg, who was one of Stainer's best imitators; and others less known.

There were several German makers—led, possibly, by the example of Stainer and Albani the younger—who turned their attention to Italy, as furnishing models superior to their own, and thus combined the styles of both countries; while they endeavoured to copy closely the Italian masters, without attempting to be original. Niccolò Amati was the maker whom these men chiefly copied, and most successfully did they perform their task. These copies, however, did not meet the success to which they were entitled, and the popularity of Stainer's mode was then so great that the instruments made upon systems other than his found no favour in the Fatherland. The makers who were copyists of the Italian masters were Ruppert, Bachmann, Jauch, and Eberle of Prague.

When we consider the long list of makers forming the German School, we cannot fail to feel surprised that the number of really good artists was not much larger; and our surprise increases when the close proximity of the Tyrolese workers to the chief Italian centres of the manufacture of Violins is also considered. If the names of Jacob Stainer and Mathias Albani be excepted, the list is singularly destitute of makers famous for originality. The Germans were certainly great in the manufacture of the older stringed instruments, but seem to have made a poor beginning in the making of Violins. The form selected was bad, and they failed to improve upon it to any great extent. It would be quite impossible to furnish anything approaching a complete list of German makers, their number being so extended, and so many of their instruments being anonymous, and withal so weak in character that it is hard to discern them. Every care, however, has been taken to render the following list as complete as possible.

SECTION X

German Makers

ALBANI, Mathias, Botzen. M. Fétis, quoting the Biographical Dictionary of Moritz Berman, with regard to Albani, states that he was born in 1621, and died in 1673. The form is somewhat like Stainer's, but higher and heavier in construction. The varnish is very rich. Wood of good quality.

>Mathias Albani Fecit
>Bulsani Tyrol 1651.

>Matthias Albanus Fecit
>Bulsani in Tyroli 1680.

ALBANI, Mathias, Botzen, about 1650-1712. Son of the above. This maker should, perhaps, have been classed with those of Italy, his style being Italian; but as he was the son of the well-known German maker, it was thought best that his name should follow that of his father under the head of German makers. The son has shown but faint marks of having been tutored by his parent in the art of Violin-making. He is said to have visited Cremona, in order to receive instruction there under Amati, and this circumstance may have given to his work that Italian air which is so pleasing to the connoisseur.[1] This maker is often credited with the work of the elder Albani, it having been supposed that there was but one of that name. The model is good, and the workmanship throughout demands high praise. Gerber states that the famous Violinist, Tomaso Albinoni, possessed two Violins of this maker, dated 1702 and 1709.

>1 He appears to have worked for a time in Rome, from which city some instruments are dated.

ALBANI, Paolo, Palermo, about 1633. Probably related to the Albanis of Botzen. *See* Italian makers.

ALETZIE, Paolo, Munich. *See* Italian makers.

>Paulus Aletzee hof
>Lauten und Geigenmacher
>in München 1710.

ARTMANN, ———, Weimar, near Gotha, 18th century. Was originally a joiner. Copied Amati very cleverly. The varnish is frequently of amber colour.

BACHMANN, Carl Ludwig, born at Berlin, 1716. Court musician and Violin-maker. The work is clean, and not without style. Bachmann was a performer on the Viol. In 1765 he was appointed instrument maker to the court of Frederick the Great. Bachmann, in conjunction with Ernest Benda, founded in 1770 the concerts for amateurs at Berlin. He died in 1800.

BACHMANN, O., Halberstadt, Violin-maker, and author of a handbook on the construction of bow instruments, published in 1835 at Leipsic.

BAUSCH, Ludwig C. A., Leipsic, born at Nuremberg in 1815. Pupil of B. Fritsche in Dresden.

BAUSCH, Ludwig B. Son of the above.

BAUSCH, Otto B., Leipsic, born 1841, brother of the above.

BECKMANN, Sweno, Stockholm, about 1700. The work is rough.

BEDLER, ——, about 1750.

BÈLA, Szepessy, born at Budapest in 1856. Now living in London.

BINDERNAGEL, ——, Gotha, 18th century. Copied Amati chiefly. There are a few of his instruments which are on the model of Stradivari, and are highly valued in Germany.

BUCHSTADTER, Gabriel David, Ratisbon, 18th century. His Violins are not equal in merit. Some have excellent wood, others very indifferent. When one of his best instruments can be procured, it is a good substitute for a second-class Italian.

CHRISTA, Joseph Paul, Munich, 1730.

> Josephus Paulus Christa, Lauten
> und Geigenmacher in München. 17—

DIEL, Martin (spelt Diehl by later members of the family), Mayence, worked with Nicolaus Döpfer, and later with Carl Helmer of Prague. He was a son-in-law of Döpfer.

DIEL, Nicolaus, born 1779, son of Martin, worked with his uncle Jacob Steininger of Frankfort. He succeeded to the business of his father. Died 1851.

DIEL, Johann, brother of Nicolaus.

DIEL, Jacob, son of Nicolaus, settled in Bremen 1834, later in Hamburg. Died 1873.

DIEHL, Nicolaus Louis, Hamburg, son of Jacob Diehl, died 1876.

DIEHL, Friedrich, Darmstadt, born 1814, son of Nicolaus, received a bronze medal, Paris Exhibition, 1867.

DIEHL, Johann, Mayence.

DIEHL, Heinrich, son of Johann.

DÖPFER, Nicolaus, 1768. The instruments of this maker are well made; the model is less raised than that of many German makers. He made a few large Tenors. Döpfer was the master of Martin Diehl.

DURFEL, J. G., Altenburg, 18th century. A well-known maker of Double-Basses.

EBERLE, J. Ulric, Prague, about 1730-50. Was a good copyist of the Italian masters. Eberle also made Viols d'Amour.

Joannes Udalricus Eberle,
Lautenmacher in Prag, 1730.

EDLINGER, T., Prague, about 1712.

EDLINGER, Joseph Joachim, Prague. Son of the above. Worked for some time in Italy. Died 1748.

ELSLER, Johann Joseph, Mayence, 1720-50. Made many good Viols da Gamba.

ERNST, Franz Anton, born in 1745 in Bohemia, died in 1805. He was an eminent Violinist, and received lessons from Antonio Lolli. In 1778 he was engaged as Court musician at Gotha. He took great interest in Violin-making, and made several excellent instruments.

FELDEN, M., Vienna, about 1550. Maker of Viols.

FICHTOLD, Hans, about 1612. Lute-maker.

FICHTL, Martin, Vienna, 1757. Large pattern, good varnish, wood of excellent quality.

FICKER, Johann Christian, Cremona, 1720. Said to have lived in the midst of the greatest makers the world has had; if so, he certainly did not make himself acquainted with the art of Violin-making as understood in Cremona. His instruments may have been made at Mittenwald, and dated from Cremona.

FICKER, Johann Gotlieb, Cremona, 1789.

FISCHER, Zacharie, Würtzburg, 1730. This maker adopted the practice of baking the wood for the manufacture of Violins.

FISCHER, Anton, Vienna, died 1879.

FREY, Hans, Nuremberg and Bologna, born about 1440. A celebrated maker of Lutes. He was the father-in-law of Albert Dürer. John Evelyn, in his Diary, 1645, after speaking in praise of the cheese and sausages of Bologna, refers to the great celebrity of the Lutes by the old makers of that city, and mentions Hans Frey. He says they "were of extraordinary price, and the workmen were chiefly Germans."

FRITZCHE, ——, Leipsic, about 1780-1810.

GEDLER, Johann A., Fussen, about 1750.

GEDLER, Johann B., Fussen, about 1780.

GEISSENHOF, Franz, Vienna, died 1821. The initials F. G. sometimes branded on the button. Stradivari model. Good work.

GERLE, Johann, Nuremberg, 1533 to about 1550. Maker of Lutes and Viols. He also published a book on the Lute, 1533.

GRIESSER, Matthias, Innspruck, 1727.

GRIMM, Carl, Berlin, born about 1794. He died at Berlin, 1855, and was succeeded by a son, Ludwig Grimm.

GROBITZ, A., Warsaw, about 1750.

GUGEMMOS, Fussen, Bavaria, 17——. Indifferent work.

HAENSEL, Johann A., Berlin. Contributed an article to the "Leipsic Musical Gazette" in 1811, entitled "Ueber den Bau der Violin."

HAMBERGER, Joseph, Presburg, 1845.

HAMM, Johann Gottfried, Rome, 18th century. Made instruments of a wide pattern, often with ivory edges, and branded inside with his initials.

HAMMIG, W. H., Leipsic. Now living.

HASSERT, ——, Eisenach, 18th century.

HASSERT, ——, Rudolstadt, 18th century.

HELMER, Carl, Prague, born 1740. Pupil of Eberle of Prague.

HILDEBRANDT, Michael C., Hamburg, 1770.

HILTZ, Paul, Nuremberg, 1656. Maker of Viols.

HOFFMANN, Martin, Leipsic, about 1680 to 1725. Maker of Lutes and Viols.

HOFFMANN, Johann Christian, Leipsic, about 1720. Son of Martin Hoffmann. Lute and Viol maker.

HORNSTAINER, Joseph, Mittenwald, about 1730. Made a few Double-Basses of good quality.

HORNSTAINER, Matthias, Mittenwald, about 1800.

HORIL, Jacob, Rome, about 1742.

HULLER, August, Shoeneck, about 1775.

HUMEL, Christian, Nuremberg, about 1709.

HUNGER, Christoph Friedrich, Leipsic, born at Dresden, 1718, died 1787. One of the best German makers.

JAIS, Johann, Botzen, about 1776. There were other makers of this name.

JAUCH, Johann, Gratz, Styria, Austria. Worked in Dresden about 1774.

KARB, ———, Königsberg, Maker of Viols.

KAMBL, Johann A., Munich, 1640.

> Johan Andreas Kambl Churfürstl.
> Hof Lauten und Geigenmacher
> in München.

KEMBTER, ———, Dibingen, about 1730. Stainer model. Good wood, and work well purfled.

KIAPOSSE, Sawes, St. Petersburg, 1750.

KIRCHSCHLAG, ———, Tyrol, 1780.

KLOZ, Matthias, Mittenwald, 1656-1743. Is reported to have been a pupil of Stainer. The work is good and the varnish in some cases of a mellow quality, in others somewhat thin. Some of the wood that he used was cut at the wrong season, and is consequently worm-eaten.

> Sebastian Kloz, in
> Mittenwald, An 17—

KLOZ, Sebastian, Mittenwald, 1696-1750, son of Matthias Kloz. The instruments of this maker are much esteemed. The model is flat as compared with most Violins of the German school. The varnish varies.

KLOZ, George, Tyrol, 1687-1737, brother of Sebastian Kloz. Instruments well made, chiefly yellow in colour; wood often worm-eaten.

KLOZ, Egidius, Mittenwald, 1675-1711.

KLOZ, Ægidius, Mittenwald, 1733-1805. Son of Sebastian. One of the best of this very large family of makers.

KLOZ, Joseph, Mittenwald, son of Egidius.

KLOZ, J. Karl, about 1741. Good work, dark varnish, ornamental border round label.

KNITTLE, Joseph, Mittenwald.

KNITTING, Philip, Mittenwald, 1760.

KOHL, Johann, Munich, 1580. Lute-maker to the Bavarian Court.

KOLDITZ, J., Rumburg, died 1796.

CHAPEL OF THE ROSARY.
CHURCH OF ST. DOMENICO, CREMONA.

Plate XV.

KOLDITZ, Mathias Johann, Munich, 1720.

Mathias Joannes Koldjz,
Lauten und Geigenmacher in
München 17—

KRAMER, H., 1717, Viol-maker.

KRINER, Joseph, Mittenwald, 1786.

LASKA, Joseph, Prague, born at Rumburg, 1738, died 1805. Worked with J. Kolditz.

LEMBÖCK, Gabriel, Budapest, 19th century. Maker; also known as a repairer of old instruments.

MANN, Hans, Naples.

MAUSSIELL, Leonard, Nuremberg, 1745. Stainer pattern, excellent workmanship. Thin yellow varnish, raised edges. The style and work is not unlike that of Tecchler.

MAHER (MAIER), Andreas Ferdinand. Good varnish, sometimes with lion scrolls.

Andreas Ferdinandus Mahr,
Hof Laut und Geigenmacher
in Salzburg. Anno 17—

MEUSIDLER, Johann, Nuremberg, about 1550. Maker of Viols.

MOHR, Philip, Hamburg, 17th century. Viol-maker.

MOLDONNER, Fussen, Bavaria, 18th century.

NIGGEL, Simpertus, Fussen, 17—. Flat model, good workmanship. Branded inside with initials S. N.

OHBERG, Johann, Stockholm, 1773. Workmanship of average merit. Varnish mostly of yellow colour.

OTT, Johann, Nuremberg, about 1463. Lute-maker.

OTTO, Jacob August, born at Gotha, 1762, died 1830. Violin-maker to the Court of Weimar. Received instructions from Franz Anton Ernest. He published a work in 1817 entitled, "Ueber den Bau und die Erhaltung der Geige und aller Bogeninstrumente," and another work with more information in 1828, the first English edition of which was published in 1848.

OTTO, Georg August, son of Jacob August, born 1807, died 1859. Succeeded to the business of his father at Jena.

OTTO, Christian, Halle, second son of Jacob August. Born 1813, died 1876.

OTTO, Heinrich, Berlin, third son of Jacob August. Born 1815, died 1858.

OTTO, Carl, Ludwigslust, fourth son of Jacob August. Born 1825. Violin-maker to the Court of Mecklenburg. Died in 1883.

OTTO, C. U. F., Stockholm, fifth son of Jacob August. Died 1884.

OTTO, Ludwig, St. Petersburg, son of Georg August. Born at Cologne; died 1887.

OTTO, Louis, Dusseldorf, son of Carl, now living.

OTTO, Hermann, St. Petersburg, son of Ludwig. Died 1884.

PARTH, Andreas Nicholas, Vienna, 18th century.

PFRETZSCHNER, Johann Gottlob, Cremona, 1750. Very commonplace.

PFRETZSCHNER, Carl Friedrich, Cremona, son of the preceding; no merit.

PLACK, F., Schoenbock, 1730-45.

POSSEN, L., Schoengau, Bavaria, about 1553. Maker of Viols and Lutes.

RAUCH, ——, Wurtzburg.

RAUCH, Jacob, Manheim, 1720-50. Brother of the above. Court Violin-maker.

RAUCH, Sebastian, Hamburg, 1725. High model, rough workmanship. A maker of this name is said to have worked at Leitmeritz, Bohemia, about 1750. Possibly the same.

RAUCH, ——, Breslau, about 1750.

REICHEL, Johann Gottfried, Absam, 18th century.

REICHEL, Johann Conrad, Neukirchen, 18th century.

REICHERS, August, Berlin, 19th century. Pupil of Bausch of Leipsic.

RIESS, ——, Bamberg, about 1750.

RÖSCHER, C. H. W., Bremen, about 1871.

ROTH, Christian, Augsburg, 17th century.

RUPPERT, Franz, Erfurt, 18th century.

RUPPERT, J. N., Erfurt, 1719-28.

SAINPRAE, Jacques, Berlin, 17th century. A Baryton Viol of this maker is among the musical instruments at the Kensington Museum. It is said to have belonged to Johann Quantz, the famous flute-player.[2] The Baryton was a favourite instrument with Haydn. He composed several pieces for the instrument, and was fond of playing it. The Baryton, or Viol di Bordone, is of the character of the Viole d'Amour, being strung with sympathetic metal strings. It is, however, a large and more complicated instrument.

> 2 The flute-playing of Johann Joachim Quantz in 1728 gave so much pleasure to the Crown Prince of Prussia, afterwards Frederick the Great, that he decided to take lessons from Quantz, who was then in the service of Augustus, Elector of Saxony and King of Poland. Quantz was stationed alternately in Dresden and Warsaw. He became a member of the orchestra of Augustus in 1718, when Jean Baptiste Volumier was its director, of whom mention has been made (page 208) relative to his having been sent to Cremona in 1715 to await the completion of twelve Violins ordered of Stradivari.

SAWICKI, C. N., Vienna, 1792-1850.

SCHEINLEIN, Mathias F., 1710-71. High built; dark varnish.

SCHEINLEIN, Johann Michael, Langenfeld, son of the above. Similar characteristics.

SCHELL, Sebastian, Nuremberg, 1727. Lute-maker.

SCHLICK, ——, Leipsic.

SCHMIDT, ——, Cassel, 1800-25. Copied Stradivari indifferently; wood of an inferior kind.

SCHONFELDER, Johann A., Neukirchen, about 1743.

SCHONGER, Franz, Erfurt, 18th century.

SCHONGER, Georg, Erfurt, son of the above.

SCHORN, Johann, Innspruck, about 1680. An excellent maker; the varnish is similar to that of Albani; high modelled. He appears to have removed to Salzburg. There are Viols of his make dated from there in 1696 and 1699.

SCHORN, Johann Paul, Salzburg, about 1700-16. Court instrument-maker.

SCHOTT, Martin, Prague. Chiefly known as a maker of Lutes.

SCHWARTZ, Strasbourg, about 1845. Several of this name worked in Strasbourg.

SCHWEITZER, J. B., Budapest, died 1875. Flat model, neat workmanship. Made a few Tenors.

STADELMANN, Daniel, Vienna, 1680-1744. Good work, model of Jacob Stainer. Thin varnish, sometimes yellow colour.

STADELMANN, Johann Joseph, Vienna, 18th century. Copied Stainer; average merit.

>   Jacobus Stainer in Absam
>   prope Oenipontum. 16—

STAINER, Jacob, Absam, born July 14, 1621, at Hall. The celebrity of this maker is second only to that of the great Cremonese artists. His admirers in Germany and England were, at one time, more numerous than those of the principal Italian makers. In a manuscript note which Sir John Hawkins added to his own copy of his History of Music (1776), he says, "The Violins of Cremona are exceeded only by those of Stainer, a German, whose instruments are remarkable for a full and piercing tone." To the connoisseur of to-day such commendation may seem inexplicable, and cause him to believe that Fiddle admirers of past times were incapable of appreciating true beauty of form, and its bearing upon sound, or else that fashion made its influence felt on the Fiddle world as elsewhere. It would be absurd to deny that the greatest German maker of Violins that ever lived was a man of rare abilities, because it is indelibly written on his chief works that he was a thorough artist. Therefore an expression of surprise that Jacob Stainer has been estimated higher than even Stradivari by the Germans and English, must not be understood as a reflection on his abilities, since it refers to the form that he chose to give to his works. To account for the apparent inconsistency in the works of Stainer, and to strike the balance between his exceptional abilities on the one side and his model on the other, is not easy. His form was not a borrowed one; it is as original as that of Stradivari—a fact which makes it more than ever unintelligible that he should have been content with it. To arrive at anything approaching to a satisfactory solution, we must endeavour to trace the history of this model. Jacob Stainer was born in the Tyrol, and passed there his early years, and probably received his first instructions from one of the old Tyrolean Lute and Viol makers, at a period when they raised their model, and introduced into the German School the scooping round the sides of the backs and bellies, the inelegant sound-hole, the harsh outline, and uncouth scroll. As experience ripened his understanding, he may have felt that these characteristics of the German School were not such as could be moulded with advantage by an artist, whatever his talent might be, and resolved to do his best to unlearn much that he had acquired. In order to do so with any chance of success, but one course was open to him—that of studying the works of the Italian masters. It has been stated that he went to Italy when very young. With this view I do not concur. In all cases where there is an absence of direct evidence, opinions can only be formed from particular analogies bearing on the case under consideration. Now in the case of Stainer we have nothing to guide us but his variations of style, and dates of time and place. What is the result of a careful investigation of every particle of evidence that we can glean? The style is ever German, although the great maker is head and shoulders above all his countrymen who followed his art. I am thus forced to believe that had so excellent an artist visited Italy in his youth, as reported, there would have remained but the faintest trace of its origin. That men of less ability should be unable to entirely sever themselves from their national style of work, even under circumstances most favourable for such a release, I can readily understand; it is an incapacity which has been exemplified over and over again; but Jacob Stainer was not one of these ordinary men; he had not his superior in the school of Cremona as a finished workman, with the single exception of Antonio Stradivari. I believe, therefore, that the German style was deeply rooted within him when he ceased to be young, and that if he went to Cremona or Venice, it was not until he recognised the inferiority of the school in which he had been bred, as compared with that of Cremona or Venice. That he did not go far enough in his "second thought" is pretty well acknowledged on all sides. His originality was conceived in the German School, amid the worst examples, and it was too late to undo what had gone before. Here, then, lies, I consider, the key to the seeming anomaly that so great a maker as Stainer should have adopted and clung to so clumsy a model. That he became acquainted with much of the best work of the Italians is evidenced by his improved style. The varnish he used furnishes even stronger evidence of his having possessed a knowledge of the subject equal to that of the Cremonese makers. Whether he acquired this knowledge in Cremona or Venice cannot be stated with certainty, but I am inclined to believe that he gained it in the first-named city. Who but an artist acquainted with the best work of Italy in Violin-making could have made those exquisite Violins known as "Elector Stainers"? The wood, selected for its rare loveliness, the finished workmanship, and charming rose-coloured varnish, render these works of art of which one glimpse is a never-fading memory. These works show the diligent zeal with which Stainer laboured in his studies of the Italian masters. He contrived to give these instruments an air of grace quite foreign to the best efforts of his brother German makers. In the sound-hole and scroll is observable his seeming desire to leave behind the German preferences; and although it must be admitted that he was but partially successful in his endeavours to stamp out early tendencies, the connoisseur cannot but be impressed with the results of the artist's manipulations. Had such skill been exercised on a form nearer akin to the Italian, the result would have been perfect.

Prior to the publication of the interesting facts obtained by Herr S. Ruf, relative to the personal history of Jacob Stainer, we had no really reliable account of this famous maker.[3] The industry and research of Herr Ruf has not only supplied all the ascertainable facts with regard to Stainer, but also served to trace the history of Stainer fiction. The last-mentioned portion of Herr Ruf's labours is singularly instructive as to the manner in which romance is spliced on to what is intended to be sober history, and which results oftentimes in the graft being rendered invisible, or even unsuspected. He tells us that the first mention of Jacob Stainer is that made by Johann Primisser, about a century after the death of the Violin-maker, and that he merely states that there lived in Absam in 1673 a celebrated maker named Stainer.

> [3] The notice of Jacob Stainer in the "Biographie Universelle des Musiciens" contains information supplied by J. B. Cartier, the well-known Violinist, which formed a portion of the history of the Violin which Cartier proposed publishing, also from notes made by Paul L. de Boisgelou, who brought together much curious information relative to music and musicians.

Early in the present century Counsellor Von Sardagna collected certain particulars concerning Stainer, which were published in 1822. He states that Stainer lived at Absam, that it is traditionally reported that he went to Venice or Cremona, and died a madman. It appears that this slight material was at once utilised for the manufacture of nearly all the romantic accounts of Stainer with which we are familiar. Herr Ruf says that in the year 1825 there appeared in a German literary publication a poetical effusion entitled "Jacob Stainer," and that in 1829 Dr. Johann Schuler published a novel of great merit on the same subject.

Herr Ruf states that August Lewald in 1835 made the novel of Dr. Schuler the basis of the romantic account of Stainer, published in his "Guide Book to Tyrol," under the title of "An Evening in Absam," but without any acknowledgment whatever. Notwithstanding the growth of Stainer literature down to 1835, not a single historical fact concerning the maker had been brought to light. In the year 1839 Herr Ruf began his labours of research. He discovered at Hall a register of the parish of Absam, wherein he found all the information we possess as regards the birth and death of Stainer and his family. About this period the poem of Dr. Johann Schuler, "Jacob Stainer," was dramatised by Theodore Rabenalt. Other poems based on the same material appeared in 1843, but still the facts of Stainer's life were all but unknown. At length Herr Ruf was prevailed upon by Dr. Schafhaült (an ardent admirer and collector of Stainer's Violins) to prosecute his inquiries concerning the great maker.

In the archives of the town and salt mines at Hall, Herr Ruf found much information, which he published in the local newspapers, the ephemeral nature of which naturally placed his valuable contributions beyond the reach of those likely to value them. In the meantime Nicolaus Diehl, of Hamburg, published a little book on Violins, into which was imported a portion of the romance traceable to the novels or poems on Stainer. Herr Ruf, feeling disappointed that his labours in discovering the facts relative to Stainer had failed to clear away the cloud of Stainer fiction, published in 1872 his book, "Der Geigenmacher Jacob Stainer von Absam in Tirol," which gives us a full account of his researches, and should have secured to him the full credit due to his industry. His facts, however, like the good fiction found in Dr. Schuler's novel, "Jacob Stainer," have been used by German writers on the subject of the Violin without any acknowledgment. Herr Ruf died at Hall in the year 1877.

It is said that Stainer was apprenticed to an organ-builder at Innsbrück, but owing to his weak constitution he was unable to continue in the business, and chose instead the trade of Violin-making. Amongst the rumours concerning this maker may be mentioned that of his having been a pupil of Niccolò Amati. It is certain there is no direct evidence in support of it, neither is it shown that his work is founded on that of Amati. I am satisfied that Stainer was assisted neither by the Brothers Amati nor Niccolò Amati, and I am strengthened in this opinion by the steadfastly German character of a model which no pupil of Amati could have persisted in using, even though based on his earliest traditions.

The marriage of Stainer took place October 7, 1645. On the 9th of October, 1658, he was appointed by the Archduke Leopold (of Austria, Governor of Tyrol) one of the "archducal servants," and on the 9th of January, 1669, he obtained from the Emperor the title of "Violin-maker to the Court." About this period he is said to have incurred the displeasure of the Jesuits, which led to his being accused of the crime of heresy. The accusation seems to have been based on the fact of books of a controversial kind—chiefly Lutheran—having been found in his possession. The penalty he suffered for daring to indulge in polemical literature was six months' imprisonment, and his future prospects were completely shattered. Prior to this misfortune he appears to have been in pecuniary difficulties, and frequently at law with one Salomon Hübmer, of Kirzchdorf, from whom he had obtained money loans. In the year 1677 he petitioned the Emperor Leopold—who was a great patron and lover of music—to render him pecuniary assistance, but failed to procure it. Over-burdened with troubles, he was bereft of his reason, and died insane and insolvent in the year 1683.

"Alas! misfortunes travel in a train,
 And oft in life form one perpetual chain."

His widow was left with a family of eight daughters, she dying in poverty in 1689, which chronological fact disposes of the fiction, so widely circulated, that in consequence of the great grief he experienced upon the death of his wife he withdrew from the world, and became an inmate of a Benedictine monastery, and that he made within its walls the famous instruments known as "Elector Stainers," which he presented to the twelve Electors. Whether he made them to order, in the usual manner, whether he presented them, or where he made them, matters little; they are works of great merit, and need no mysterious surroundings to call attention to them. The followers of Stainer have been numerous, and are mentioned in the lists of German and English makers. Probably no maker is more mistaken than Stainer: the array of German instruments called by his name is at least ten times greater than the number he actually made. Nearly every high-built tub of a Violin sails under his colours. Instruments without any resemblance whatever to those of Stainer are accepted by the multitude as original Jacob Stainers. Much of this has arisen from the variety of style and work said to have been shown in the instruments of this maker. That this marked variety exists I do not believe. The pattern varies, but the same hand is traceable throughout.

STAINER, Markus, Kufstein, Tyrol, about 1659, described as a brother of Jacob. He styled himself on his label "Citizen and Violin-maker." Citizenship carried with it special privileges, and this maker apparently recognised the honour by having "Burger" after his name.

STAINER, Andreas, Absam, about 1660. Mention is made of a maker of Baryton Viols of this name.

STAUGTINGER, Mathias W., Würzburg, about 1671. Maker of Viols and Lutes.

STEININGER, Jacob, Frankfort, about 1775. Son-in-law of the Violin-maker Döpfer, and uncle of Nicolas Diehl, to whom he gave instructions in Violin-making.

STEININGER, Franz, St. Petersburg, son of Jacob Steininger.

STOSS, ———. Makers of this name worked at Prague, Vienna, and Fussen, about the end of the 18th century.

STOSS, Martin, Vienna, about 1824. Flat model, good workmanship. Stradivari pattern, indifferent varnish.

STRAUBE, ———, Berlin, about 1775.

STRAUSS, Joseph, Neustadt, about 1750.

TIEFFENBRUCKER. There appear to have been several Lute-makers of this name working in the 16th century in Germany and elsewhere. No genuine Violins are known. *See* DUIFFOPRUGCAR.

TIELKE, Joachim, Hamburg, about 1539-92. The name of Tielke is associated with the most remarkable instruments of the Lute and Guitar kind ever produced in relation to rich and chaste ornamentation. It is said there are glowing accounts in old German books of the magnificent instruments by Tielke, with elaborate designs in silver, gold, and jewels.[4] The ornamentation and workmanship seen in the best instruments of this maker bear the impress of Italian art of a high order, and evidence the employment of Italian draughtsmen by the house of Tielke. In the collection of instruments at Kensington is a Chiterna (an instrument of the Lute kind) of this make. The body is ornamented with tortoiseshell, with mythological figures in ivory and precious stones. It is signed, and dated 1539. In the possession of Mr. George Donaldson is a Guitar of this maker, signed, and dated 1592, which is considered to be the most artistic and highly ornamented work known by Joachim Tielke. It is wonderfully preserved, and admirably shows the style and character of the art-work of the period.

> 4 Engel's "Descriptive Catalogue of the Musical Instruments in Kensington Museum," 1874.

TIELKE, Joachim, Hamburg, about 1660-86. Viol and Violin maker. The dates met with on the instruments signed "Tielke" cover a period of upwards of a century and a half, and thus evidence the existence of the house, in connection with the manufacture of musical instruments, through two or more generations. There is, of this maker, a Viola di Bordone in the collection at Kensington, dated 1686. Mention is made by Fétis of a Violin dated 1670, which was in the possession of André of Offenbach; and a Chiterna dated 1676, similar to that in the Kensington collection, is owned by Mr. George Donaldson. M. Chouquet, in his catalogue of the collection of instruments at the Conservatoire, Paris, refers to a Lute (No. 136) by Tielke.

VOEL, E., Mayence, about 1840. Excellent workmanship, scroll well cut. Stradivari model. The character of work is not unlike that of Bernard Fendt.

VOGEL, Wolfgang, Nuremberg, 1650.

ANTONIO STRADIVARI.
Date 1708.
(HECTOR HAVEMEYER, ESQ.)

ANTONIO STRADIVARI.
1736.

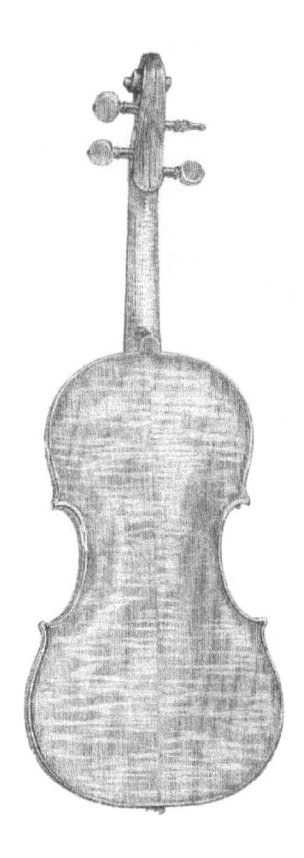

GIUSEPPE GUARNERI DEL GESÙ.
Date 1735.
(G. HART.)

Plate XVI.

VOGLER, Johann Georg, Würzburg, about 1750.

> Johann Georg Vogler, Lauten
> und Geigenmacher in Würzburg. 17—

VOIGT, Martin, Hamburg, about 1726.[5]

> 5 About thirty makers named Voigt or Voight hail from Germany, some contemporary and others dating from the 18th and 19th centuries. Their work is not of sufficient importance to require special notice.—EDITORS.

WAGNER, Joseph, 1730, Constance.

WEICKERT, Halle, 1800.

WEIGERT, ——, Lintz, about 1721. Maker of Viols.

WEISS, Jacob, Salzburg, 18th century.

> Jacob Weiss, Lauten und
> Geigenmacher in Salzburg.

WENGER, G. F., Salzburg, 18th century.

> Leopold Widhalm Lauten und
> Geigenmacher, Nürnberg Fecit, A.

WIDHALM, Leopold, Nuremburg, 18th century. One of the best imitators of Stainer. The wood is frequently handsome, the work finished with care. Varnish, although wanting the delicacy of that of Stainer, is generally of good quality; its colour is mostly pale red. Nearly all his instruments are branded with the initials inside. His name has frequently been spelt Withalm.

WITTING, J. G., Mittenwald, about 1775.

WYEMANN, Cornelius, Amsterdam, 18th century.

ZWERGER, Antoni, Mittenwald, about 1750. Neat work, good wood, varnish of the character of that seen on the instruments of Kloz.

SECTION XI

The English School

It is somewhat remarkable that the Continental writers on the Violin should have omitted to mention any English maker, either ancient or modern. Such an omission must have occurred either from want of information concerning our best makers, or, if known, they must have been deemed unworthy of the notice of our foreign friends. There is no mention of an English maker in the work of Fétis, "Antoine Stradivari," 1856, although numerous very inferior German and Italian makers are quoted. The same omission is also conspicuous in "Luthomonographie Historique et Raisonné," 1856, and Otto's "Ueber den Bau der Bogeninstrumente," &c., 1828. It may be that Continental connoisseurs have credited themselves with the works of our best makers, and expatriated them, while they have inexorably allowed bad English Fiddles to retain their nationality. However, it is my desire that my foreign brothers should be enlightened on this point, and in all candour informed of the array of makers that England has at different times produced, and is yet capable of producing, did but the new Violin command the price that would be a fair return for the time and skill required in the production of an instrument at once useful and artistic. It will be my endeavour to show forth the qualities of those of our makers whose names, as yet, seem never to have crossed the Channel, so that when these pages on the English School are read by distant connoisseurs, and the merits and shortcomings of the makers therein are fairly weighed by them, the good shall be found so to outweigh the indifferent as to entirely change the opinions formed of us as makers of the leading instrument.

Until the early nineteenth century makers of Violins in England would appear to have been comparatively numerous, if we take into consideration the undeveloped state of stringed instrument music at that period in this country. Among those makers were men of no ordinary genius—men who worked lovingly, guided by motives distinct from commercial gain, so long as they were allowed to live by their work. When, however, the duties on foreign musical instruments were removed, the effect was to partially swamp the gallant little band of Fiddle-makers, who were quite unable to compete with the French and German makers in *price* (not *excellence*, be it distinctly understood, for we were undoubtedly ahead of our foreign competitors, both in style and finish, at this period). The prices commanded by many English makers previous to the repeal of the duty were thoroughly remunerative. Five to twenty pounds were given for English Violins, while Violoncellos and Tenors commanded prices proportionately high. The English Violin-makers were thus enabled to bestow artistic care in the making of their instruments. When, however, they were suddenly called upon to compete on equal terms with a legion of foreign manufacturers, the result was not so much that their ardour was damped, as that they themselves were extinguished, and served as another instance of the truth of the adage that "the good of the many is the bane of the few."

In matters of magnitude, whether artistic or otherwise, competition is undoubtedly healthy, there being always a small body of patrons who are willing to check the tendency to deteriorate, common to all productions, by encouraging the worker with extra remuneration, in order that a high degree of excellence may be maintained; but in matters confined to a small circle, as in the case of Violin-making, the number of those willing to encourage artistic workmanship is so minute as to fail even to support *one* maker of excellence, and thus, when deprived suddenly of its legitimate protection, the art, with other similar handicrafts, must drift into decadence. If we look around the Violin world, it is everywhere much the same. In Italy there is no Stradivari in embryo, in France no coming Lupot, in Germany no Jacob Stainer, and in England no future Banks or Forster. Why so? The answer is twofold. Partly there is fault in the *demand*, arising from the marked preference of this age for cheapness at the expense of goodness; partly, too, there is a fault in the *supply*, a foolish desire on the part of the makers to give maturity to their instruments, wherein they always completely fail, yet they will not give up their conceit. Here, again, were we dealing with matters of greater magnitude, the evil influence would be lessened, the artistic impulses would still be felt, though in a less degree; whereas so contracted is the circle of the Violin world, that under any stress the support given to makers willing to bestow an artist's care on their work is totally inadequate.

The case of modern Violin-makers is unfortunate. Old Violins being immeasurably superior to modern productions, the demand must necessarily set steadily for the former, and the modern maker has only the few patrons of new work to support him. It cannot be expected that the players of to-day should patronise the modern Violin in order that the next generation should reap the benefit. Years since it was quite a different matter. The makers were well paid for their work, and new instruments were then made to supply wants similar to those which the horrid Mirecourt or Saxon copy fulfils at present. As with other things, so is it also with Violins; if they are to be produced with the stamp of artistic merit, they must be paid for accordingly; without patronage the worker necessarily becomes careless. Finding that his skill fails to attract attention, he gradually sinks down into the mere routine of the ordinary workman. When Italy shone brightest in art, the patronage and remuneration which the workers received was considerable. Had it been otherwise, the powers of its Raffaele, its Cellini, and last (though not least to the admirers of the Violin), its Stradivari, would have remained simply dormant. Art, like commerce, is regulated in a great measure by supply and demand. In Raffaele's day, sacred subjects were in demand; the Church was his great patron, and aided him in bringing forth the gift which nature had implanted within him. In modern times, landscape-painting became the favoured subject, particularly in England; the result of which preference has been to place us in the foremost rank in that branch of art. The stage furnishes another instance of the effect that patronage has in bringing forth latent talent. If the history of dramatic art be traced, it will be found that its chief works were written when the taste of an appreciative public could be securely counted upon. As it waned, so the writers of merit became rarer; or perhaps it would be more correct to say, the plays produced became less meritorious, the authors being constrained to pander to the prevailing tastes.

As further evidence of the effect of patronage on art, a case in point is found in the manufacture of Venetian glass. The Venetians, centuries ago, became famous for their works in glass, and the patronage they enjoyed was world-wide; but their country being thrown into an unsettled condition, capital drifted from it, until the blowing of glass, together with other industries, was comparatively extinguished. Within recent years the art of making glass has shown signs, even in Venice itself, of reviving with all its former vigour in the workshops of Salviati, the success of which is due in great measure to English capital.

With regard to English Violin manufacture, there would be no reason why Violins should not, at the present moment, be produced in England which should fully reach the standard of merit maintained in our forefathers' days, if only the patronage of the art occupied a larger area. The present dearth of English makers does not arise from any national want of talent for this particular handicraft; in fact, we have plenty of men quite as enthusiastic as our foreign friends for a vocation which, in England also, must be pronounced to be alike venerable in its antiquity and famed for the dexterity of its genius.

The earliest makers of Viols in England seem to have been Jay, Smith, Bolles, Ross, Addison, and Shaw, names thoroughly British. We may take this as good evidence that the making of Viols in England originated with the English, and was not commenced by settlers from the Continent. Doubtless the form of the English Viol and its brethren was taken from the Brescian makers, there being much affinity between these classes of instruments. In the few Violins extant by Christopher Wise the Italian character is very striking. In them we see a flat model, excellent outline, and varnish of good quality. The Viols of Jay have the same Italian character. Later on we have names of some reputation—Rayman, Urquhart, and Barak Norman. In the absence of any direct evidence as regards the nationality of these makers it is requisite to endeavour to trace the style belonging to their works. It will be observed that there was a great improvement in the style of work and varnish of instruments made in England, commencing with the time of Rayman, and it is probable that this step in advance was obtained from intercourse with Italy or the German Tyrol. Starting with Rayman, there is a German ring in the name which makes me think that he came from Germany, and, if so, brought with him the semi-Italian character of work common to the makers who lived so near Brescia. If the work and style of Rayman be carefully examined, it will be seen that there is much in common with the inferior Brescian makers. The outline is rugged, the sound-hole is of that Gothic form peculiar to Brescia; the head is distinct from that of the early English type. At the same period Urquhart made instruments of great merit, the varnish of which is superior to that of Rayman, but is evidently composed of similar ingredients. Its superiority may have arisen from a different mode of mixing only. The name of Urquhart has a North British sound, and it is probable that he was born in Scotland, and settled in London as an assistant to Rayman, who would impart to him the style of foreign work.

The semi-Italian character pervading the instruments made in England at this period seems to have culminated in the productions of Barak Norman, whose best works bear even a more marked Brescian character than those of Rayman. The model varies very much, sometimes being high, at other times very flat; in the latter case the results are instruments of the Maggini type. Barak Norman frequently double-purfled his instruments, and inserted a device in the purfling, evidently following Maggini in these particulars. With Barak Norman ends the list of English copyists of the Brescian makers.

We now arrive at the copyists of Jacob Stainer and the Amati, a class of makers who possessed great abilities, and knew how to use them. The first name to be mentioned is Benjamin Banks, of Salisbury, who may with propriety be termed the *English Amati*. He was the first English maker who recognised the superior form of Amati's model over that of Stainer, and devoted all his energies to successful imitation. Too much praise cannot be lavished on Banks for the example which he selected for himself and his fellow-makers.

Next follow the names of Forster, Duke, Hill, Wamsley, Betts, Gilkes, Hart, and Kennedy, together with those of Panormo, Fendt, and Lott, who, although not born in England, passed the greater part of their lives here, and therefore require to be classed with the English School. The mention of these makers will bring the reader to the present time.

Upon scanning this goodly list, there will be found ample evidence that we in England have had makers of sufficient merit to entitle us to rank as a distinct school—a school of no mean order. We may therefore assume that the Continental writers who from time to time have published lists of makers of the Violin, and have invariably ignored England, have erred through want of information regarding the capabilities of our makers, both ancient and modern.

The following list will be found to enumerate nearly the whole of the English makers, and indicate the distinctive character of their respective works.

SECTION XII

English Makers

ABSAM, Thomas, Wakefield, 1833.

Made by
Thomas Absam,
Wakefield, Feb. 14,
1833.

ADAMS, Garmouth, Scotland, 1800.

ADDISON, William, London, 1670.

AIRETON, Edmund. Was originally employed in the workshop of Peter Wamsley, at the "Harp and Hautboy," in Piccadilly. He made a great many excellent Violins and Violoncellos, and chiefly copied Amati. Varnish of fair quality; colour yellow. He died at the advanced age of 80, in the year 1807.

ALDRED, ——, about 1560. Maker of Viols.

ASKEY, Samuel, London, about 1825.

BAINES, about 1780.

BAKER, ——, Oxford. Mention is made of a Viol of this maker in the catalogue of the music and instruments of Tom Britton, the small-coal man.

BALLANTINE, Edinburgh and Glasgow, 1850.

Benjamin Banks,
Musical Instrument Maker
In Catherine Street, Salisbury.
1780.

BANKS, Benjamin, Salisbury, born 1727, died 1795. To this famous maker must be given the foremost place in the English School. He was a thorough artist, and would not have been thought lightly of had he worked in Cremona's school, and been judged by its standard. This may be considered excessive praise of our native maker; but an unprejudiced judge of work need only turn to the best specimens of Banks's instruments, and he will confess that I have merely recorded a *fact*.

Banks is, again, one of the many instances of men who have gained a lasting reputation, but whose histories have never reached the light to which their names have attained. How interesting would it be to obtain the name of his master in the knowledge of making instruments! No clue whatever remains by which we could arrive at a satisfactory conclusion on this point. That he was an enthusiast in his art is certain, and also that he was aware to some extent that he possessed talent of no mean description. This is evidenced by the fact that many of his instruments are branded with the letters B. B. in several places, as though he felt that sooner or later his works would be highly esteemed, and would survive base imitations, and that by carefully branding them he might prevent any doubt as to their author. Many of his best instruments are found to have no brand: it would seem, therefore, that he did not so mark them for some time. He appears to have early shown a preference for the model of Niccolò Amati, and laboured unceasingly in imitation of him, until he copied him with an exactness difficult to surpass. Now that time has mellowed his best works, they might pass as original Amatis with those not perfectly versed in the characteristics of the latter. Many German makers excelled as copyists of Amati; but these makers chiefly failed in their varnish, whereas Banks was most happy in this particular, both as regards colour and quality. If his varnish be closely examined, its purity and richness of colour are readily seen. It has all the characteristics of fine Italian varnish, being beautifully transparent, mellow, and rich in its varieties of tints. It must be distinctly understood that these remarks apply only to the very finest works of this maker, there being many specimens which bear the label of Banks in the framing of which he probably took but a small share, leaving the chief part to be done by his son and others. Banks cannot be considered as having been successful in the use of his varnish on the bellies of his instruments, as he has allowed it to clog the fibre, a blemish which affects the appearance very much, and has been the means of casting discredit on the varnish among those unacquainted with the real cause. The modelling is executed with skill. Fortunately, sufficient wood has been left in his instruments to enable time to exert its beneficial effects, a desideratum overlooked by many makers of good repute. The only feature of his work which can be considered as wanting in merit is the scroll, which is somewhat cramped, and fails to convey the meaning intended, viz., the following of Amati; but as this is a point having reference to appearance, and therefore solely affecting the connoisseur, it may be passed over lightly, and the more so when we consider that Banks was not the only clever workman who has failed in head-cutting. He made Violins, Tenors, and Violoncellos, all excellent; but the last-named have the preference. His large Violoncellos are the best; those of the smaller pattern are equally well made, but lack depth of tone. The red-varnished instruments are the favourites.

BANKS, Benjamin, son of the above, born in September, 1754; died January, 1820. Worked many years with his father at Salisbury, afterwards removed to London, and lived at 30, Sherrard Street, Golden Square.

James and Henry Banks,
Musical Instrument Makers
and Music Sellers,
18   Salisbury.   02

BANKS, James. Brother of the above. For some years carried on the business of his father at Salisbury, in conjunction with his brother Henry. They ultimately sold the business and removed to Liverpool. The instruments of James and Henry Banks are of average merit.

BARNES, Robert, 1710. Worked with Thomas Smith at the "Harp and Hautboy" in Piccadilly. Afterwards partner with John Norris.

John Barrett, at the Harp and
Crown in Pickadilly, 17—

Made by John Barrett at ye Harp &
Crown in Pickadilly, London, 17—

BARRETT, John, 1714. An average workman, who followed the model of Stainer. His shop bore the sign of the "Harp and Crown." Barrett was one of the earliest copyists of Stainer, and in the chain of English makers is linked with Barak Norman and Nathaniel Cross. The wood is generally of a very good quality, the varnish yellow.

BARTON, George, Old Bailey, London, about 1780-1810.

Jo. Betts, No. 2,
near Northgate the
Royal Exchange,
London, 17—

BETTS, John, born 1755, at Stamford, Lincolnshire, died in 1823. Became a pupil of Richard Duke. He commenced business in one of the shops of the Royal Exchange, where he soon enjoyed considerable patronage. John Betts does not appear to have made a great number of instruments, but employed many workmen, into whose instruments he inserted his trade label. He was, perhaps, the earliest London dealer in Italian instruments. His quaintly-worded business card runs:—

"John Betts, Real Musical Instrument Maker, at the Violin and German Flute, No. 2, under the North Piazza of the Royal Exchange, makes in the neatest manner, Violins the patterns of Antonius Stradivarius, Hièronymus Amati, Jacobus Stainer, and Tyrols. Equal for the fine, full, mellow tone to those made in Cremona. Tenors, Violoncellos, Pentachords, &c., &c., &c."

The sound-holes of Betts' instruments are rather wide; broad purfling; scroll well cut.

BETTS, Edward, nephew of John Betts; was a pupil of Richard Duke, whose work he copied with considerable skill. Of course, in trying to imitate Duke he was copying Amati, Richard Duke having spent his life in working after the Amati pattern, without attempting to model for himself. The care bestowed by Edward Betts on his instruments was of no ordinary kind. The workmanship throughout is of the most delicate description; indeed, it may be said that neatness is gained at the expense of individuality in many of his works. Each part is faultless in finish, but when viewed as a whole the result is too mechanical, giving as it does the notion of its having been turned out of a mould. Nevertheless, this maker takes rank with the foremost of the English copyists, and in his instruments we have as good specimens of undisguised work as can be readily found. They will be yearly more valued.

THE "BETTS" STRADIVARI.
1704.
(R. D. WADDELL, ESQ.)

Plate XVII.

BOLLES, ——, An early maker of Lutes and Viols.

BOOTH, William, 1779 to about 1858, Leeds.

BOOTH, ——, son of the above, Leeds, died 1856.

BOUCHER, ——, London, 1764.

BROWN, James, London, born 1770, died 1834. Worked with Thomas Kennedy.

BROWN, James, London, son of the above, born 1786, died 1860.

BROWNE, John, London, about 1743. Worked at the sign of the "Black Lion," Cornhill. Good work. Amati pattern. Scroll well cut; hard varnish.

CAHUSAC, ——, London, 1788. Associated with the sons of Banks.

CARTER, John, London, 1789, worked with John Betts, and afterwards at Drury Lane on his own account.

CHALLONER, Thomas, London. Similar to Wamsley.

COLE, Thomas, London, 1690.

<blockquote>Thomas Cole, near Fetter Lane
In Holborn, 16—</blockquote>

COLE, James, Manchester, 19th century.

COLLIER, Samuel, 1750.

COLLIER, Thomas, 1775.

COLLINGWOOD, Joseph, London, 1760.

CONWAY, William, 1750.

CORSBY, ——, Northampton, 1780. Chiefly made Double-Basses.

CORSBY, George. Lived upwards of half a century in Princes Street, Leicester Square, where he worked and dealt in old instruments.

CRAMOND, Charles, Aberdeen, 19th century.

CRASK, George, Manchester. He made a large number of instruments, chiefly imitations.

CROSS, Nathaniel, London, about 1700-50. Worked with Barak Norman. He made several good Violins. Purfling narrow; excellent scroll.

CROWTHER, John, 1760-1810.

CUTHBERT, London, 17th century. Maker of Viols and Violins. Many of the latter have merit. Model flat, and wood of good quality. Very dark varnish.

DAVIDSON, Hay, Huntley, 1870.

DAVIS, Richard. Worked with Norris and Barnes.

DAVIS, William, London. Succeeded Richard Davis in the business now carried on by Edward Withers.

DEARLOVE, Mark, Leeds.

Dearlove and Fryer,
Musical Instrument Manufacturers,
Boar Lane, Leeds, 1828.

DELANY, John, Dublin. Used two kinds of labels, one of them very small—

Made by John Delany,
No. 17, Britain Street, Dublin. 1808.

In the other, which is larger, he states that he made Violins that his name might be of immortal memory.

Made by John Delany,
In order to perpetuate his memory in future ages.
Dublin. 1808.
Liberty to all the world
black and white.

DENNIS, Jesse, London, 1805.

DEVEREUX, John, Melbourne. When in England he worked with B. Simon Fendt.

DICKINSON, Edward, London, 1750. Made instruments of average merit. The model is high.

Edward Dickinson,
Maker, at the Harp and Crown in the Strand,
near Exeter Change,
London. 17—

DICKESON, John, 1750-80, a native of Stirling. He would seem to have lived in various places, some instruments dating from London and some from Cambridge. He was an excellent workman, and chiefly copied Amati. His work much resembles that of Cappa.

DITTON, London, about 1700. Mention is made of an instrument by this maker in Tom Britton's Catalogue.

T. Dodd,
Violin, Violoncello
and Bow Maker,
New Street,
Covent Garden.

DODD, Thomas, son of Edward Dodd, of Sheffield. He was not a maker of Violins. Numerous instruments bear his name, but they are the work of John Lott and Bernard Fendt. The merit of these instruments is of the highest order, and they are justly appreciated by both player and connoisseur. Thomas Dodd deserves to be mentioned in terms of high praise, notwithstanding that the work was not executed by him, for his judgment was brought to bear upon the manufacture during its various stages, and more particularly in the varnishing, in which he took the liveliest interest. He had a method of mixing colours, the superior qualities of which he seems to have fully known, if we may judge from the note on his labels, which runs thus: "The only possessor of the recipe for preparing the original Cremona varnish. Instruments improved and repaired." This undoubtedly savours of presumption, and is certainly wide of the truth. Nevertheless there is ample evidence that the varnish used by Thomas Dodd was very excellent, and had a rich appearance rarely to be met with in instruments of the English school. Dodd was encouraged in the art of varnish-making by persons of taste, who readily admitted the superior qualities of his composition, and paid him a handsome price for his instruments. He was thus enabled to gratify his taste in his productions by sparing no means to improve them. He ultimately attained such a reputation for his instruments as to command no less a sum than £40 or £50 for a Violoncello. Commanding such prices, it is evident that he spared no expense, or, what was to him a matter of still greater importance, no time. He was most particular in receiving the instruments in that incomplete stage known in the trade as "in the white," *i.e.*, without varnish. He would then carefully varnish them with his own hands, guarding most warily the treasured secret of the composition of his varnish. That he never departed from this practice may be inferred from the fact that the varnish made by the workmen in his employ, apart from the establishment, for their own instruments, is of an entirely different stamp, and evidently shows that they were not in their master's secrets.

The instruments bearing the Dodd label are not valued to the extent of their deserts, and there can be but little doubt that in the course of time they will be valued according to their true merits. They were made by men of exceptional talent, who were neither restricted in price nor material. Under such favourable conditions the results could not fail to be good.

DODD, Thomas, London. Son of Thomas Dodd, musical instrument dealer, of St. Martin's Lane. The father, although not a maker of Violins, possessed excellent judgment, both as regards work and makers, which enabled his son to profit considerably during his early years whilst working with Fendt and Lott.

DORANT, William, London, 1814.

    Richd. Duke,
    Londoni fecit 17—

Richard Duke, Maker,
Holborn, London. Ann. 17—

DUKE, Richard, worked from 1750-80. The name of this maker has long been a household word with English Violinists both amateur and professional. Who has not got a friend who is the fortunate owner of a veritable "Duke"? The fame of His Majesty Antonio Stradivari himself is not greater than that of Richard Duke in the eyes of many a Fiddle fancier. From his earliest fiddling days the name of Duke became familiar to him; he has heard more of him than of Stradivari, whom he somehow confuses with Cremona. He fondly imagines that Cremona was a celebrated *maker*, and Stradivari something else; inquires, and becomes more confused, and returns again to "Duke," with whom he is thoroughly at home.

Many excellent judges have wondered how it came to pass that Richard Duke should have been so highly valued, there being, in their estimation, so little amongst his remains worthy of the reputation he gained. The truth is that no maker, with the exception of the great Cremonese artists, has been so persistently counterfeited. The name of Duke has been stamped upon every wretched nondescript, until judges who had not the opportunity of seeing the genuine article mistook the copies for the original, and hence the confusion. When, however, a really fine specimen of Duke is once seen, it is not likely to be forgotten. As copies of Amati such instruments are scarcely surpassed, varnish, work, and material being of the best description. The copies of Stainer were not so successful.

DUKE, Richard, London. Son of the above.

DUNCAN, ——, Aberdeen, 1762.

DUNCAN, George, Glasgow, contemporary.

EGLINGTON, ——, London, 1800.

EVANS, Richard, London, 1750. His label is a curiosity—

Maid in the Paris of
Lanirhengel, by Richard
Evans, Instrument maker,
in the year 17—

FENDT, Bernard, born at Innsbruck, in the Tyrol, 1756, died 1832. He was evidently a born Fiddle-maker, genius being stamped, in a greater or less degree, upon all his works. To Thomas Dodd belongs the credit of bringing his talent into play. Dodd obtained the services of Fendt upon his arrival in

England, which the latter reached at an early age. He remained with Dodd many years, frequently making instruments with John Frederick Lott. The instruments so made bear the label of Thomas Dodd. Lott being also a German, reciprocity of feeling sprung up between him and Fendt, which induced Lott to exchange the business to which he was brought up for that which his fellow countryman Fendt had adopted, and henceforth to make Violins instead of cabinets. By securing the services of these admirable workmen, Dodd reaped a rich harvest. He found in them men capable of carrying out his instructions with an exactness that could not be surpassed. Dodd was unable to use the tools himself; but in Fendt and Lott he had men who were consummate masters of them. When the instruments were finished, as far as construction was concerned, they were clothed in coats of the master's livery—"Dodd's varnish," the secret of making which he kept carefully to himself. With these coats of varnish upon them the work was doubly effective, and every point of excellence was made to shine with the happiest effect. Upon leaving the workshop of Thomas Dodd, Bernard Fendt worked for John Betts, making many of those copies of Amati which are associated with the name of Betts, and which have so high a value.

Although Fendt was German by birth, his style of work cannot be considered as German in character. Having early quitted his post of trade in Paris for England, and having in this country placed himself under the guidance of Dodd, who steadfastly kept before his workmen the originals of the great Italian masters for models, his work acquired a distinctive stamp of its own, and in its turn gave rise to a new and independent class of makers.

FENDT, Bernard Simon, London, born in 1800, died in 1852. Son of the above. He was an excellent workman. It is to be regretted that he did not follow the excellent example set by his father, and let time do its work, without interruption, upon his instruments. Had he done so they would, in many instances, have been equal to those of his parent; but, unfortunately, he worked when the mania for obtaining supposed maturity by artificial means was at its height, and shared the general infatuation, and, in consequence, very frequently destroyed all the stamina of his instruments. Subsequently he became a partner of George Purdy, and carried on a joint business at Finch Lane, in the City of London, from whence most of his best instruments date. Purdy and Fendt had also a shop in the West End about 1843. He was a most assiduous worker. The number of Violins, Tenors, Violoncellos, and Double-Basses that he made was very great; indeed, his reputation would have been greater had he been content to have made fewer instruments and to have exercised more general care. His copies of Guarneri are most numerous, numbering some hundreds. They are mostly varnished with a glaring red colour, of a hard nature. He made many good Double-Basses of the Gasparo da Salò form, the varnish on which is superior to that on his Violins. He made also an excellent quartette of instruments—Violin, Viola, Violoncello, and Double-Bass—for the Exhibition of 1851. They were certainly the best contemporary instruments exhibited, but he failed to obtain the prize medal.

FENDT, Martin, London, born 1812, died 1845. Brother of the above. Worked for Betts.

FENDT, Jacob, London, born 1815, died 1849. Third son of Bernard Fendt. The best maker among the sons of Bernard. His instruments are beautifully finished, and free from the stereotyped character belonging to those of his brother Bernard. As specimens of the imitator's art they are unsurpassed. One cannot but regret that such a consummate workman should have been obliged to waste his energies in making new work resemble that of a hundred years before. The patronage that he obtained was not of much value, but had he brought his work into the market in its natural condition he could not have lived by his trade. He was, therefore, compelled to foster that which he no doubt felt to be degrading. The copies of Stradivari by Jacob Fendt are among his best efforts. The work is well done; the discoloration of the wood cleverly managed, the effects of wear counterfeited with greater skill than had ever been done before, and finally, an amount of style is thrown into the work which transcends the ingenuity of any other copyist. Had he been allowed to copy the form of the old masters, as Lupot did, without imitating the actual wear of the instrument, we should have had a valuable addition to our present stock of instruments of the Panormo class.

FENDT, Francis, London. Fourth son of Bernard; also worked in Liverpool about 1856.

FENDT, William, London, born 1833, died 1852. Son of Bernard Simon Fendt. Was an excellent workman, and assisted his father in the manufacture of several of his Double-Basses.

FERGUSON, Donald, Huntley, Aberdeenshire.

FIRTH, G., Leeds, 1836.

> William Forster,
> Violin Maker,
> in Brampton.

FORSTER, William, born in 1713, died 1801. The family of the Forsters have played no unimportant part in the history of Violins. The attention they commanded as makers, both from artists and amateurs, has probably never been equalled in England. Their instruments claimed attention from the moment they left their makers' hands, their construction being excellent in every way. William Forster was a native of Brampton, in Cumberland, where he followed the trade of a spinning-wheel maker, occupying his spare time in the making and repairing of Violins and musical instruments generally. His labours, as far as they relate to Violin-making, appear to have been of a very unpretending nature, but they served to impart a taste for the art to his son William, who was the best maker of the family.

> William Forster,
> Violin Maker,
> in St. Martin's Lane, London,
> 17—

FORSTER, William, London, born 1739, died 1807. Son of William Forster mentioned above. Worked with his father at Brampton in Cumberland, making spinning-wheels and Violins—two singularly diverse occupations. It was, however, to the latter industry he gave the most attention, and he soon became the great maker of the neighbourhood. He afterwards added another string to his bow, viz., that of playing country-dances at the village festivities. Thus armed with three occupations, he must have been well employed. He seems to have early discovered that his abilities required a larger field in which to show themselves to advantage, and accordingly took the usual course in such circumstances—came to the Metropolis, in which he settled about the year 1759. He soon obtained employment at a musical instrument seller's on Tower Hill, and gave up, then and for ever, the making of spinning-wheels, while by throwing all his soul into the manufacture of Violins he soon gave his master's patrons the highest satisfaction. He ultimately commenced business on his own behalf in the neighbourhood of Duke's Court, St. Martin's Lane, where his abilities attracted considerable attention, and secured him the patronage of the *dilettanti* in the musical world. For several years he followed the path trodden by the makers of the period, and copied Stainer. His instruments of this date are very excellent both in workmanship and material, but are not equal to those of the Amati pattern, which he commenced to make about the year 1770. These are beautiful works, and have a great charm from their being so varied. Some are copies of Antonio and Girolamo Amati, variously modelled; others are copies of Niccolò Amati. The wood and varnish also vary very much, but the high standard of goodness is well maintained throughout. His varnish was, during the last twenty years of his life, very fine in quality, and in the manufacture of it he is said to have been assisted by a friend who was an excellent chemist. He made only four Double-Basses, three of which were executed for the private band of George III. Forster's instruments were the favourite equipment of Robert Lindley, and their value in his day was relatively far higher than at the present moment. When Lindley died attention was turned to Italian Violoncellos, and a vast number having been brought to England, the value of Forster's productions was very considerably depreciated; now, however, that the cultivation of stringed instrument music has been so much extended, they are rapidly rising again to their former level, Italian instruments being a luxury not obtainable by every one, and age having so benefited the tone of Forster's Violoncellos as to render them excellent substitutes.

FORSTER, William, London, born in 1764, died 1824. Son of William Forster, the second of the family. Although this maker did not attain to the celebrity of his father, his instruments are often fully as good. The workmanship is very neat, and the modelling excellent, the varnish being equal to that on his father's instruments.

> William Forster, Junr., Violin,
> Violoncello, Tenor & Bow Maker,
> 18— Also Music Seller No 43
> to their Royal Highnesses the
> Prince of Wales and the Duke of
> Cumberland.

FORSTER, William, London, born in 1788, died 1824. Son of William Forster, mentioned above. He was a very good workman: he made but few instruments.

FORSTER, Simon Andrew, London, born in 1801, died about 1870. Brother of William, mentioned above. He learned his business from his father and Samuel Gilkes, who worked for William Forster. He made several instruments between the years 1828 and 1840, which are of average merit. Best known as joint author with W. Sandys of a "History of the Violin" (London, 1864).

FRANKLAND, ——, London, about 1785.

> John Furber, Maker,
> 13, John's Row, top of Brick Lane,
> Old St., Saint Luke. 1813.

FURBER, ——, London. There were several makers of this family, some of whom worked for Betts, of the Royal Exchange. Many of their instruments are excellent, and should unquestionably be more valued than they are. John Furber made several Violins of the grand Amati pattern, and also copied with much ability the "Betts" Stradivari, when the instrument belonged to Messrs. Betts in the Royal Exchange, for whom he worked.

FURBER, Henry John, son of John Furber, London. He has made several excellent instruments, and maintained the character for good workmanship which has been associated with the name of Furber for upwards of a century.

GIBBS, James, 1800-45. Worked for Samuel Gilkes and others.

> Gilkes.
> From Forster's,
> Violin and Violoncello Maker,
> 34, James Street, Buckingham Gate,
> Westminster.

GILKES, Samuel, London, born in 1787, died in 1827. Was born at Morton Pinkney, in Northamptonshire. He became an apprentice of Charles Harris, whose style he followed to some extent. Upon leaving Harris he engaged himself to William Forster, making many instruments for him, retaining, however, all the features of the style of Harris. In the year 1810 he left the workshop of Forster, and commenced business on his own account in James Street, Buckingham Gate, where the few instruments bearing his name were made. Too much cannot be said in praise of much of the work of this excellent maker. The exquisite finish of many of his instruments evidences that the making of them was to him a labour of love. Amati was his favourite model.

GILKES, William, London, born 1811, died 1875. Son of Samuel Gilkes. Has made a great number of instruments of various patterns, chiefly Double-Basses.

GOUGH, Walter. An indifferent workman.

HARBOUR, ———, London, about 1785.

HARDIE, Matthew, Edinburgh, date from about 1800. He was the best maker Scotland has had. The model is that of Amati; the work throughout excellent. The linings are mostly of cedar. He died about 1825-26.

HARDIE, Thomas, Edinburgh. Worked with his father, Matthew Hardie. He was born in 1804, died 1856.

HARE, John, London. About 1700. His label shows that he was in partnership, his name being joined to that of Freeman, and the address is given as "Near the Royal Exchange, Cornhill, London." Much resembles the work and style of Urquhart. Varnish of fine quality.

HARE, Joseph, London, probably a son of John Hare, above-mentioned. Varnish of excellent quality.

Joseph Hare, at yᵉ Viol and Flute,
near the Royal Exchange, in Cornhill, London.
172—

HARRIS, Charles, London, 1800. This maker is known only to a few dealers, as he made chiefly for the wholesale merchants of his day. His name was rarely affixed to his instruments, but those thoroughly acquainted with his work agree in giving him a foremost place among the makers of this country. He was, like many other makers of that period, engaged in two occupations differing very much from each other, being at the same time a Custom-house officer and a maker of Violins. The former circumstance brought him into contact with mercantile men, and enabled him to obtain commissions to make Violins for the export trade. His business in this direction so increased that he obtained the services of his relative, Samuel Gilkes, as his assistant. He never aimed at producing a counterpart of the instrument that he copied by resorting to the use of deleterious means to indicate upon the surface of an instrument the ravages of time. He faithfully copied the form, and thus did what Lupot was doing at the same period. The finish of these instruments is excellent, and as they are covered with a good quality of varnish, they have every recommendation of appearance.

HARRIS, Charles. Son of the above. Neat workmanship. Well-cut scroll. Sound-holes not well formed. Yellow varnish. Worked for a short time for John Hart.

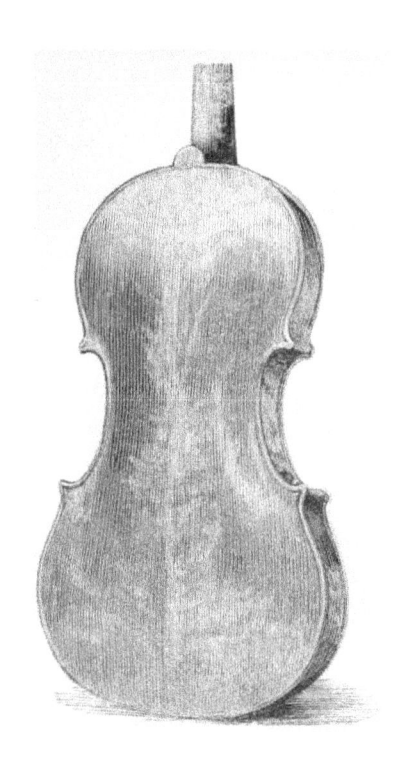

GIUSEPPE GUARNERI DEL GESÙ.
(THE "VIEUXTEMPS.")

ANTONIO STRADIVARI (INLAID).
Date 1687.
(FROM THE PLOWDEN COLLECTION.)

Plate XVIII.

John Hart,
Maker,
14, Princes Street, Leicester Square,
London. Anno 18—

HART, John Thomas, born December 17, 1805, died January 1, 1874. He was articled to Samuel Gilkes in May, 1820, of whom he learned the mechanical branch of his profession. He afterwards centred his attention upon the peculiar characteristics of the Cremonese and Italian Violin-makers generally, and in a comparatively brief space of time obtained an extensive acquaintance in that direction. His unerring eye and powerful memory of instruments once brought under his notice secured for him the highest position among the connoisseurs of his time. Commencing business at a period when the desire to possess instruments by the famous Italian makers was becoming general among amateurs, and being peculiarly fortunate in securing an early reputation as a judge of them, he became the channel through which the greater part of the rare Italian works passed into England, and it has frequently been said that there are very few distinguished instruments in Europe with which he was unacquainted. Among the remarkable collections that he brought together may be mentioned that of the late Mr. James Goding, the remnant of which was dispersed by Messrs. Christie and Manson in 1857; the small but exquisite collection of Mr. Charles Plowden, consisting of four Violins of Stradivari and four of Guarneri, with other instruments of less merit, the whole of which again passed into Mr. Hart's possession upon the death of their owner; and, lastly, a large portion of the well-known collection of the late Mr. Joseph Gillot, sold by Christie and Manson shortly after the famous sale of pictures belonging to the same collector.

HAYNES, Jacob, London, 1746. Copied Stainer. The style resembles that of Barrett.

HEESOM, Edward, London, 1748. Copied Stainer.

HILL, Joseph, London, 1715-84. Pupil of Peter Wamsley. His Violoncellos and Tenors are well-made instruments.

>Joseph Hill, Maker,
>at the Harp and Flute,
>in the Hay Market.
>London.

HILL, William, London, 1741. Son of the above. Very good work.

>William Hill, Maker, in Poland Street,
>near Broad Street, 17—

HILL, Joseph, London, 1800-40. Son of the above.

HILL, Lockey, London, 1800-35. Brother of the above. Made many excellent instruments.

HILL, William Ebsworth, London, 1817-95. Son of Lockey Hill. Made several instruments in his younger days, but, like the rest of our English makers, he long since discovered that new work was unremunerative, and turned his attention to repairing and dealing in old instruments, and became the founder of the well-known firm of W. E. Hill and Sons, of Bond Street. He exhibited at the Exhibition of 1862 a Violin and Tenor, thus showing that Violin-making was not quite extinguished in England.

HOLLOWAY, J., London, 1794.

HUME, Richard, Edinburgh, 16th century. A maker of Lutes, &c.

JAY, Henry, London, 17th century. Maker of Viols, which are capital specimens of the work of the period. The varnish is excellent.

JAY, Thomas, London. Related to the above. Excellent work.

>   Made by Henry Jay,
> in Long Acre, London. 1746.

JAY, Henry, London, about 1744-77. A maker of Kits chiefly. At this period these juvenile Violins were in much demand by dancing-masters. A few years ago a very choice collection of these instruments was made by an Irish gentleman residing at Paris, who obtained specimens from all parts of Europe. Henry Jay also made Violoncellos, some of which have the names of Longman and Broderip on the back.

>   Made and sold by John Johnson,
> at the Harp and Crown, in Cheapside,
>   17   London.   53

JOHNSON, John, London, 1750. The Violins bearing his label are dated from Cheapside. Johnson was a music and musical instrument seller. In "The Professional Life of Dibdin," written by himself, we have the following reference to this City music-seller: "My brother introduced me to old Johnson, who at that time kept a capital music-shop in Cheapside.[1] I soon, however, grew tired of an attendance on him. He set me down to tune Harpsichords, a mere mechanical employment, not at all to my taste." "I saw plainly that I might have screwed up Harpsichords in old Johnson's shop to all eternity, without advancing my fortune; and as to the songs and sonatas that I brought him for sale, they had not been performed at the theatres nor Vauxhall, nor any other place, and Johnson would not print them." "The Thompsons, however, of St. Paul's Churchyard, published six ballads for me, which sold at three-halfpence a-piece, and for the copyright of which they generously gave me three guineas." Though we may not feel disposed to apply the term "generous" to a payment of half-a-guinea for a Dibdin ballad, yet in all probability we are indebted to the Thompsons for this particular recognition of merit. Happily true genius, when in straits, generally finds relief. Were it otherwise, and had the Thompsons been as deaf to Dibdin as John Johnson appears to have been, "Tom Bowling," "Poor Jack," and many other compositions of sterling merit, might never have been written.[2]

> 1 Dibdin's brother was captain of a merchant vessel, and
> was intimate with Johnson the music-seller. On the death
> of Captain Dibdin his brother composed "Tom Bowling,"

the music and words of which bespeak the fraternal love of the composer.

2 Dibdin was evidently discouraged in consequence of Johnson's refusal to publish his songs: he says, "After I had broken off with Johnson, I had some idea of turning my thoughts to merchants' accounts—the very last thing upon earth for which I was calculated."

KENNEDY, Alexander, London, 1700-86. Was a native of Scotland. He was the first maker of Violins in his family, which was connected with the manufacture for nearly two centuries.

> Alexander Kennedy, Musical Instrument
> Maker, living in Market Street, in Oxford
> Road, London, 17—

KENNEDY, John, London, born 1730; died 1816. Nephew of Alexander Kennedy. Made Violins and Tenors.

KENNEDY, Thomas, London, born 1784; died about 1870. Son of the above. Probably made more instruments than any English maker, with the exception of Crask.

LENTZ, Johann Nicolaus, London, 1803. He used mostly one kind of wood, viz., close-grained maple. Varnish nearly opaque.

> Johann Nicolaus Lentz, fecit
> near the Church, Chelsea. 1803.

LEWIS, Edward, London, 1700. The work is well executed throughout, and the varnish superior.

LISTER, George, 18th century.

LONGMAN AND BRODERIP, Cheapside, London, about 1760. They were music-publishers and instrument-sellers, and were not Violin-makers. Benjamin Banks, Jay, and others, made many of the instruments upon which the name of Longman is stamped. Muzio Clementi was at one time a partner in the firm. The business ultimately passed to Collard and Collard.

LOTT, John Frederick, 1775-1853. Was a German by birth. He was engaged in the cabinet business early in life. He was induced by Fendt to turn his attention to making Violins, and ultimately obtained employment under Thomas Dodd, making many of the Violoncellos and Double-Basses that carry the label of Dodd within them. His work was of a most finished description. His Double-Basses are splendid instruments, and will bear comparison with Italian work. His varnish was far from equal to his finish. The time he spent in making these instruments was double that which any other English maker expended over similar work. There is not a single portion of any of his Double-Basses that has been carelessly made; the interior is as beautifully finished as the exterior. The machines on many of his Basses were made by himself—a very unusual circumstance. The scrolls are finely cut. He was certainly the king of the English Double-Bass makers.

LOTT, George Frederick, London, born 1800; died 1868. Son of the above. Many years with Davis, of Coventry Street. Was an excellent judge of Italian instruments, and a clever imitator.

LOTT, John Frederick, London, younger brother of the above, died about 1871. Was articled to Davis. Has made many clever imitations. He was also an ardent lover of Cremonese instruments, and thoroughly understood their characteristics. His career was both chequered and curious, sufficiently so, indeed, to cause our eminent novelist, Charles Reade, to make it the subject of "Jack of all Trades: a Matter-of-Fact Romance." Jack Lott (as he was familiarly styled) therefore shares with Jacob Stainer the honour of having supplied subject-matter for writers of fiction. It must, however, be said that whilst Dr. Schuler's "Jacob Stainer" is mainly pure fiction, "Jack of all Trades" is rightly entitled "a matter-of-fact romance." I have many times heard John Lott relate the chief incidents so graphically described by Charles Reade.

MACINTOSH, Dublin. Succeeded Perry and Wilkinson. Died about 1840.

MARSHALL, John, London, 1750.

MARTIN, ——, London, about 1790.

MAYSON, Walter H., Manchester, 1835-1904. A prolific maker. His later work is highly spoken of.

MEARES, Richard, about 1677. Maker of Viols.

>Richard Meares, without Bishopsgate,
>near to Sir Paul Pinder's, London. Fecit 1677.

MIER, ——, London, about 1786.

MORRISON, John, London, about 1780-1803.

NAYLOR, Isaac, Headingly, near Leeds, about 1778-92.

NICHOLS, Edward, 18th century.

>Edwardus Nichols,
>Fecit ad exemplar Antoni Straduarii Cremonensis, 1763.

NORBORN, John, London, about 1723.

✠
Barak Norman
and
Nathaniel Cross,
at the Bass Viol in St.
Paul's Church Yard,
London. Fecit 172—

NORMAN, Barak, London, 1688-1740. The instruments of this maker are among the best of the Old English school. His instructor in the art of Viol and Violin-making is unknown, but judging from the character of his work it is very probable he learned from Thomas Urquhart. This opinion is strengthened upon examining his earliest instruments. We there find the same peculiarities which mark the individuality of Urquhart. Later in life he leaned much to the model of Maggini.

During his early years he was much esteemed as a maker of Viols, many of which have all the marks of careful work upon them. On all of these instruments will be found his name, surrounded with a design in purfling, under the finger-board, or his monogram executed in purfling. The same trade token will be found in his Violoncellos. All endeavours to discover any existing English Violoncello, or record of one, anterior to Barak Norman, have failed, and, consequently, it may be assumed that he was the first maker of that instrument in England. Here, again, is evidence of his partiality for the form of Maggini, as he copied this maker in nearly all his Violoncellos. All the Violoncellos of Barak Norman have bellies of good quality; the modelling is executed skilfully, due care having been observed in leaving sufficient wood. His Tenors are fine instruments. Many of these were made years before he began the Violoncellos—a fact which satisfactorily accounts for the marked difference in form peculiar to them. The build is higher, and the sound-hole German in character; the varnish is very dark. About the year 1715 Barak Norman entered into partnership with Nathaniel Cross, carrying on the joint business at the sign of the Bass Viol, St. Paul's Churchyard. In a Viol da Gamba which belonged to Walter Brooksbank, Esq., of Windermere, is a label in the handwriting of Nathaniel Cross, in which he adds the power of speech to the qualities of the quaint Gamba; the words are, "Nathaniel Cross wrought my back and belly," the sides and scroll being the work of his partner.

NORRIS, John, London, born 1739; died 1818. Articled to Thomas Smith, the successor of Peter Wamsley. Similar work to that of Thomas Smith. He became a partner of Robert Barnes.

Made by Norris and Barnes,
Violin, Violoncello, and Bow
Makers, To their Majesties,
Coventry Street, London.

Edward Pamphilon,
April the 3rd, 1685.

PAMPHILON, Edward, London, 17th century. The Violins of this maker were formerly much prized. The model is very high, and the appearance somewhat grotesque. It is to be regretted that the splendid varnish often found on these instruments was not put upon better work.

PANORMO, Vincent. (*See* Italian School.)

PANORMO, Joseph, London. Son of Vincent Panormo. His work was excellent. His Violoncellos are decidedly superior to his Violins.

PANORMO, George Lewis, London. Brother of the above. Made Violins of the Stradivari pattern.

PANORMO, Louis, London. Made Guitars chiefly.

PARKER, Daniel, London, 18th century. This is another maker of the English school, who was possessed of exceptional talent, and whose instruments are well worthy of attention from those in search of good Violins at a moderate cost. To Parker belongs, in conjunction with Benjamin Banks, the merit of breaking through the prejudice so long in favour of preference for the Stainer model.

The dates of his instruments extend from the year 1740 to 1785. He left his Violins thick in wood, which has certainly enhanced their value now that time has ripened them. He used excellent material, which is often very handsome. The varnish is of a mellow quality, and fairly transparent. A large number of these Violins have been passing under other makers' names, and have been but little noticed.

PEARCE, James, London, 18th century.

PEARCE, W., London, contemporary.

PEMBERTON, Edward, London, 1660. This maker has been often mentioned as the author of a Violin said to have been presented to the Earl of Leicester by Queen Elizabeth, and to suit this legend Pemberton's era has been put back a century. The date given above will be found in the Violins of this maker.

PERRY AND WILKINSON, Dublin, 17— to 1830. The instruments bearing the labels of these makers are frequently excellent in tone, material, and finish.

POWELL, Thomas, London, 18th century.

> Made by Thomas
> Powell, No. 18, Clemens
> Lane, Clare Market.
> 1793.

PRESTON, London, about 1724. Appears to have used his trade label in the instruments he sold, made by makers he employed.

PRESTON, John, York, 18th century.

> John Preston, York,
> 1791. Fecit.

RAWLINS, Henry, London, about 1781. He appears to have been patronised by Giardini, the Violinist, according to the label here given. Giardini held the post of leader at the Italian Opera at this period.

> Restauratus Henricus Rawlins
> Auspicio Giardini
> Londini 1781.

> Jacob Rayman dwelling in
> Blackman Street, Long—Southwark.
> 1641.

> Jacob Rayman, at ye Bell
> Yard in Southwark,
> London, 1648.

RAYMAN, Jacob, London, 17th century. The subject of this notice was probably a German, from the Tyrol, who settled in England about 1620, and may be considered as the founder of Violin-making in this country, there being no trace of any British Violin-maker previous to that time. His work is quite different from that of the old English Viol-makers. The instruments of Rayman are of a somewhat rough exterior, but full of character. The form is flat, considering the general style of the work. The sound-holes are striking, although not graceful in any way. The scroll is diminutive, but well cut. The varnish is very fine. In the catalogue of the effects of Tom Britton, mention is made of "an extraordinary Rayman."

RICHARDS, Edwin, London, contemporary. Maker and repairer.

ROOK, Joseph, Carlisle, about 1800.

ROSSE (or Ross), John, Bridewell, London, about 1562. Made Viols and Bandoras.

ROSS, John, London, about 1596. Son of the above. Maker of Viols. The varnish is excellent in quality.

SHAW, London, 1655. Viol maker.

SIMPSON, London, 1785.

> John Simpson,
> Musical Instrument Maker,
> At the Bass Viol and Flute,
> In Sweeting's Alley,
> Opposite the East door of the Royal Exchange,
> London.

SMITH, Henry, London, 1629. Maker of Viols.

SMITH, Thomas, London. Pupil of Peter Wamsley, and his successor at the Harp and Hautboy.

> Made by Thos. Smith, at the Harp and
> Hautboy, in Pickadilly, London. 1756.

SMITH, William, London, about 1770.

TARR, William, Manchester. Made many Double-Basses from about 1829.

TAYLOR, London, about 1800. A maker of much merit. Instruments of the character of Panormo.

THOMPSON, London, 1749.

THOROWGOOD, Henry, London. Little known.

TILLEY, Thomas, London, about 1774.

TOBIN, Richard, London, 1800. Pupil of Perry, of Dublin. His instruments are much appreciated by the best judges. In cutting a scroll he was unequalled amongst English makers.

TOBIN, London. Son of the above.

URQUHART, London, 17th century. Nothing is known concerning the history of this excellent maker. The style may be considered as resembling that of Jacob Rayman, and it is possible he worked with him. His varnish is equal to that on many Italian instruments.

VALENTINE, William, London, died about 1877. Made many Double-Basses for Mr. Hart, which are highly valued.

WAMSLEY, Peter, London, 18th century. One of the best English makers. His copies of Stainer are very superior.

> Made by Peter Wamsley,
> At ye Golden Harp, in Piccadilly,
> London. 17—

WISE, Christopher, London, about 1650. Yellow varnish, neat workmanship, flat model, small pattern.

WITHERS, Edward, Coventry Street. Succeeded William Davis.

WITHERS, Edward. Son of the above. Wardour Street, Soho. Was instructed by John Lott.

YOUNG, London, about 1728. Lived in St. Paul's Churchyard. Purcell has immortalised father and son in the first volume of his Catches.

"You scrapers who want a good Fiddle well strung,
You must go to the man that is old while he's Young;
But if this same Fiddle you fain would play bold,
You must go to his son, who'll be Young when he's old.
There's old Young and young Young, both men of renown,
Old sells, and young plays, the best Fiddles in town;
Young and old live together, and may they live long,
Young, to play an old Fiddle; old, to sell a new song."

SECTION XIII

The Violin and its Votaries

Sterne (himself a votary of the Fiddle) has well said, "Have not the wisest of men in all ages, not excepting Solomon himself, had their hobby-horses—their running-horses, their coins and their cockle-shells, their drums and their trumpets, their Fiddles, their pallets, their maggots and their butterflies? And so long as a man rides his hobby-horse peaceably and quietly along the king's highway, and neither compels you nor me to get up behind him,—pray, sir, what have either you or I to do with it?" He further tell us, "There is no disputing against hobby-horses;" and adds, "I seldom do: nor could I, with any sort of grace, had I been an enemy to them at the bottom; happening at certain intervals and changes of the moon, to be both Fiddler and painter."

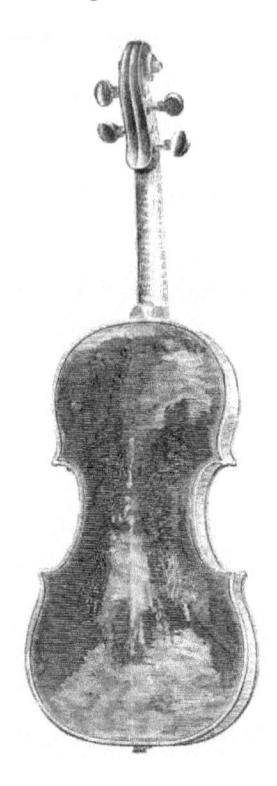

GIUSEPPE GUARNERI DEL GESÙ.
1733.

GIUSEPPE GUARNERI DEL GESÙ.
1741.
(LATE R. D. HAWLEY, ESQ.)

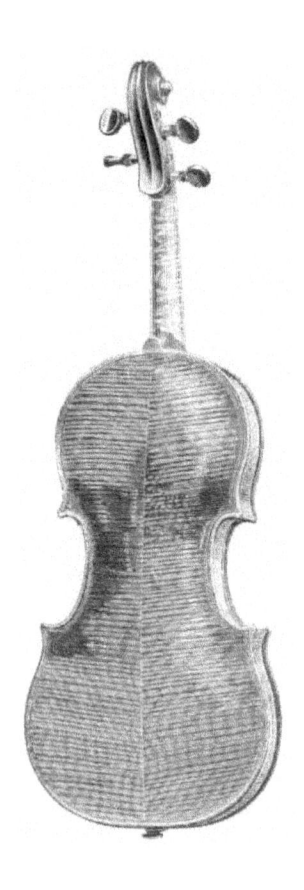

ANTONIO STRADIVARI.
1726.

Plate XIX.

The leading instrument is singularly favoured. It may be said to have a double existence. In addition to its manifold capabilities, it has its life of activity on the one hand, and inactivity on the other. At one time it is cherished for its powers of giving pleasure to the ear, at another for the gratification it affords to the eye. Sometimes it is happily called upon to perform its double part—giving delight to both senses. When this is so, its existence is indeed a happy one. The Violin thus occupies a different position from all other musical instruments. Far more than any other musical instrument it enters into the life of the player. It may almost be said to live and move about with him; the treasure-house of his tenderest and deepest emotions, the symbol of his own better self. Moreover, the Violin is a curiosity as well as a mechanical contrivance. Thus it is cherished, perhaps for its old associations—it may have been the companion of a valued friend, or it may be prized as a piece of artistic work, or it may be valued, independently of other associations, for the simple purpose for which it was made, viz., to answer the will of the player when touched with the bow. The singular powers centred in the Violin have been beautifully expressed by Oliver Wendell Holmes, who says: "Violins, too. The sweet old Amati! the divine Stradivari! played on by ancient maestros until the bow hand lost its power, and the flying fingers stiffened. Bequeathed to the passionate young enthusiast, who made it whisper his hidden love, and cry his inarticulate longings, and scream his untold agonies, and wail his monotonous despair. Passed from his dying hand to the cold *virtuoso*, who let it slumber in its case for a generation, till, when his hoard was broken up, it came forth once more, and rode the stormy symphonies of royal orchestras, beneath the rushing bow of their lord and leader. Into lonely prisons with improvident artistes; into convents from which arose, day and night, the holy hymns with which its tones were blended; and back again to orgies, in which it learned to howl and laugh as if a legion of devils were shut up in it; then, again, to the gentle *dilettante*, who calmed it down with easy melodies until it answered him softly as in the days of the old maestros; and so given into our hands, its pores all full of music, stained, like the meerschaum, through and through with the concentrated hue and sweetness of all the harmonies which have kindled and faded on its strings." The gifted author of "The Autocrat of the Breakfast-Table" has evidently made himself acquainted with the various life-phases of a Violin.

The fancy for the Violin as a curiosity has been a matter of slow growth, and has reached its present proportions solely from the intrinsic merits of its object. The Violin has not come suddenly to occupy the attention of the curious, like many things that might be named, which have served to satisfy a taste for the collection of what is rare or whimsical, and to which an artificial value has been imparted. In those days when the old Brescian and Cremonese makers flourished, the only consideration was the tone-producing quality of their instruments; the Violin had not then taken its place among curiosities. The instruments possessing the desired qualities were sought out until their scarcity made them legitimate food for the curious. Beauties, hitherto passed over, began to be appreciated, the various artistic points throughout the work of each valued maker were noted, and in due time Violins had their connoisseurs as well as their players.

Besides Italy, England, France, and Germany have had their great men in the Fiddle world, whose instruments have ever been classed as objects of *virtu*. Mace, in his "Musick's Monument," published in 1676, gives, perhaps, the earliest instance of curiosity prices in England. "Your best provision (and most compleat) will be a good chest of Viols; six in number, viz., two Basses, two Tenors, and two Trebles, all truly and proportionally suited; of such there are no better in the world than those of Aldred, Jay, Smith; (yet the highest in esteem are) Bolles and Ross (one Bass of Bolles I have known valued at £100). These were old." From the above curious extract we glean that the Fiddle family was receiving some attention. The makers in England whose instruments seem to have reached curiosity prices are Bolles, Jay, Barak Norman, Duke, Wamsley, Banks, and Forster: the value attached at different periods to the works of these men has nearly approached the prices of Cremonese work. Of course, the high value set upon the instruments of the makers above named was confined to England.

Turning to France, we find that many of the old French makers' instruments brought prices greatly in excess of their original cost. The favourite French makers were Médard, Boquay, Pierray, of the old school, and Lupot and Pique of the modern.

In Germany there have been makers whose works have brought very high prices. Stainer, Albani, Widhalm, Scheinlein, are names that will serve to associate high values with German work. In the case of Jacob Stainer, the celebrity of his instruments was not confined to Germany; they were highly prized by the English and French, and at one period were more valued than the best Amatis. It was not until the vast superiority of Italian Violins over all others was thoroughly recognised, that the love of the instrument as a curiosity reached its present climax. In Italy, the value set upon the chief Cremonese works, though great, was comparatively insignificant, as far as the Italians themselves are concerned, and when France and England came into competition with them for the possession of their Violins by Amati, Stradivari, Guarneri, and the gems of other makers, they at once yielded the contest.

The introduction of Italian instruments into Great Britain was a matter of slow growth, and did not assume any proportions worthy of notice until the commencement of the present century, when London and Paris became the chief marts from whence the rare works of the old Italians were distributed over Europe. By this time the taste of the Fiddle world had undergone a considerable change. The instruments in use among the *dilettanti* in France and England had hitherto been those built on the German model of the school of Jacob Stainer. The great German maker was copied with but little intermission for upwards of a century, dating from about 1700 to 1800, a period of such considerable extent as to evidence the popularity of the model. Among the Germans who were following in the footsteps of Stainer were the family of Kloz, Widhalm, Statelmann, and others of less repute. In England there was quite an army of Stainer-worshippers. There were Peter Wamsley, Barrett, Benjamin Banks, the Forsters, Richard Duke, and a whole host of little men. Among the makers mentioned there are three, viz., Banks, Forster, and Richard Duke, who did not copy Stainer steadfastly. Their early instruments are of the German form, but later they made many copies of the

Cremonese. To Benjamin Banks we are indebted for having led the English makers to adopt the pattern of Amati. He had long laboured to popularise the school which he so much loved, but met with little encouragement in the beginning, so strong was the prejudice in favour of the high model. However, he triumphed in the end, and completely revolutionised the taste in England, till our Fiddle-fanciers became total ab-*Stainers*! Then commenced the taste for instruments of flat form. Where were they to be found? If the few by the early English makers be excepted, there were none but those of the Italians to be had, and perhaps a few old French specimens. Attention was thus directed to the works of the Cremonese, and the year 1800 or thereabouts may be put down as the time when the tide of Italian Violins had fairly set in towards France and England. The instruments by the Amati were those chiefly sought after; the amount of attention they commanded at this period was probably about equal to that bestowed upon the works of Stradivari and Guarneri at the present time. Violins of Amati and other makers were, up to this time, obtainable at nominal prices. The number in Italy was far in excess of her requirements, the demand made upon them for choir purposes in former days had ceased, and the number of Violins was thus quite out of proportion to the players. The value of an Amati in England in 1799 and 1804 may be gathered from the following extracts from the day-book of the second William Forster, who was a dealer as well as maker—"20th April, 1799. A Violoncello by Nicholas Amati, with case and bow, £17 17s. 0d.;" and further on—"5th July, 1804, an Amati Violin £31 10s. 0d." These prices were probably less than those which William Forster received for many instruments of his own make. It is certain that these low prices did not long continue; the price increased in due proportion to the vanishing properties of the supply. The call for Violins by the Amati was so clamorous as speedily to effect this result; the prices for them were doubled, trebled, and often quadrupled, until they no longer found a home in their native land. The value set on them by the French and English so far exceeded that which the Italians themselves could afford, even though inclined to indulge in such things, that the sellers were as eager to sell as the buyers to buy. During the time of this scramble for instruments of Cremona, the theory of the flat model was fast gaining ground. The circulation of the works of Cremona among the players of France and England led to a comparison of the various forms, and it was found that the elevated model was inferior in every way when tested by the works of the great Italian makers. Hitherto no distinction had been drawn as regards value among the productions of the several members of the Amati family. Andrea had been looked upon as equivalent to Girolamo, Antonio, or Niccolò; but attention now began to be directed towards the works of the brothers, and to those of Niccolò in particular, as the flat model gained in the appreciation of the Fiddling world. Grand Amatis became the coveted Fiddles; they were put up frequently at twice the value of the smaller patterns—a position they still maintain. The taste for the flat form having thus been developed, the works of Antonio Stradivari came to the front, slowly but surely; their beauties now became known outside the circle in which they had hitherto been moving: a circle made up chiefly of royal orchestras (where they were used at wide intervals), convent choirs, and private holders, who possessed them without being in the least aware of their merits. They were now eagerly sought by soloists in all parts of Europe, who spread their fame far and wide. Their exquisite form and finish captivating the *dilettanti*, the demand increased to an extent far beyond that commanded by the works of the Amati at the height of their popularity.

There were a few Stradivari instruments in England when Amati was the favourite maker, and their value at that period may be estimated, if it be true that Cervetto, the father of the famous Violoncellist, was unable to dispose of a Stradivari Violoncello for five pounds—a circumstance which shows how blind our forefathers were to the merits of the greatest maker the world has had. Among the artists of the early part of the present century who used the instruments of Stradivari were Boccherini, Viotti, Rode, Kreutzer, Habeneck, Mazas, Lafont, and Baillot.

About the year 1820 the fame of Giuseppe Guarneri as a great maker was published beyond Italy, chiefly through the instrumentality of Paganini. That wonderful player came to possess a splendid specimen of Guarneri del Gesù, dated 1743, now sleeping in the Museum at Genoa, which Paganini used in his tour through France and England. He became the owner of this world-famed Violin in the following curious manner. A French merchant (M. Livron) lent him the instrument to play upon at a concert at Leghorn. When the concert had concluded, Paganini brought it back to its owner, when M. Livron exclaimed, "Never will I profane strings which your fingers have touched; that instrument is yours." A more fitting present or higher compliment could not have been offered. The names of Amati and Stradivari became familiar to the musical world gradually, but Guarneri, in the hands of a Paganini, came forth at a bound. This illustrious Violin was often credited with the charm which belonged to the performer; the magical effects and sublime strains that he drew forth from it must, it was thought, rest in the Violin. Every would-be Violinist, whose means permitted him to indulge in the luxury, endeavoured to secure an instrument by the great Guarneri. The demand thus raised brought forth those gems of the Violin-maker's art, now in the possession of wealthy amateurs and a few professors. When the various works of the gifted Guarneri were brought to light, much surprise was felt that such treasures should have been known to such a handful of obscure players, chiefly in the churches of Italy. The Violin used by Paganini belongs to the last period of the great maker, and consequently, is one of those bold and massive instruments of his grandest conception, but lacks the beautiful finish of the middle period. The connoisseurs of those days had associated Giuseppe Guarneri with Violins of the type of Paganini's only; their surprise was great when it was discovered that there were three distinct styles in the works of Guarneri, one evidencing an artistic grandeur, together with a high finish, but little inferior to those of Antonio Stradivari. The marked difference between these epochs of Guarneri's manufacture has led to a great amount of misconception. Fifty years since, the world possessed little information on the subject, and the connoisseur of those times could not believe it possible that these varied styles emanated from one mind. The opportunities given to the connoisseur of later days of comparing the various instruments of the several epochs of Guarneri have set at rest all doubts concerning them. They no longer require dates or labels; they are as easily distinguished and classed as the works of Amati or Stradivari.

Attention was claimed for the works of Maggini by the charming Belgian Violinist, Charles de Bériot, who, early admiring the large proportions and powerful tone of Maggini's instruments, decided to use one for public playing. That an artist so refined as De Bériot, and one who attached so much importance to that sympathy between the Violin and player which should make it the vehicle for presenting its master's inward feelings, should have selected a Violin of large size, and adapted for giving forth a great volume of tone, was a matter of surprise to a great many of his contemporaries. Those who judged only from his school of playing anticipated that he would have selected Amati as embodying the qualities he so passionately admired. It is certain, however, that he succeeded in bringing the penetrating power of his Maggini thoroughly under his control. In the instruments of Maggini, De Bériot doubtless recognised the presence of vast power, together with no inconsiderable amount of purity of tone, and to bring forth these qualities to the best advantage was with him a labour of love. The popularity of Maggini's Violins rapidly raised their value. Instruments that, before De Bériot made them widely known, might have been purchased for ten pounds, realised one hundred. The Violin known as "De Bériot's Maggini" remained in his possession till within a short time of his death, when it was disposed of to his friend and patron, the Prince de Chimay, it is said, for the enormous sum of six hundred pounds—a price far in excess of the average value of Maggini's instruments. In this instance, the association of De Bériot with the instrument is sufficient, perhaps, to account for the rare price set upon it.

We now reach the time when Carlo Bergonzi began to be regarded as a maker of the first class. As a Cremonese maker, he was one of the latest to receive the attention to which his exceptional merits fairly entitled him. To English connoisseurs belongs the credit of appreciating this great maker.

The recognised merits of the makers already named naturally caused a demand for Italian instruments generally. If the masters could not be had, the pupils must be found; hence a whole host of Italian makers, quite unknown in England fifty years since, became familiar to the connoisseur. The works of Guadagnini, Gagliano, Grancino, Santo Serafino, Montagnana, and others whose names it is unnecessary to give, passed from Italy into France and England, until the various schools of Italian Violin manufacture were completely exhausted. When we look back, it is surprising that so much has been achieved in such a brief space of time. The knowledge of Italian works in 1800 was of the slenderest kind, both in France and England; in less than three-quarters of a century those countries contrived to possess themselves of the finest specimens of Cremonese instruments, together with those of other Italian schools. We here have an example of the energy and skill that is brought to bear upon particular branches of industry when once a demand sets in. Men of enterprise rise with it unnoticed, and lead the way to the desired end. In the case of Italian Violins it was Luigi Tarisio who acted as pioneer—a being of singular habits, whose position in the history of the Violin, considered as a curiosity, is an important one. This remarkable man was born of humble parents, wholly unconnected with the musical art. In due time he chose the trade of a carpenter, which vocation he followed with assiduity, if not with love. He amused himself during his leisure hours in acquiring a knowledge of playing on the Violin—an accomplishment that was destined to exercise an influence on his future life, far greater than was ever contemplated by the young carpenter. That his playing was not of a high order may be readily imagined: it was confined chiefly to dance-music, with which he amused his friends, Fiddling to their dancing. His first Violin was a very common instrument, but it served to engender within him that which afterwards became the ruling passion of his life. His study of this little instrument was the seed from which grew his vast knowledge of Italian works. So much was his attention absorbed by the form of the instrument that any skill in playing upon it became quite a secondary consideration. He endeavoured to see all the Violins within his reach, and to observe their several points of difference. The passion for old Violins, thus awakened, caused him to relinquish his former employment entirely, and to devote the whole of his attention to the art which he so loved. He soon became aware of the growing demand for Italian works, and felt that, possessed with a varied and proficient knowledge of the different styles of workmanship belonging to the Italian schools of Violin-making, he could turn his present acquirements to a profitable as well as pleasurable use. He resolved to journey in search of hidden Cremonas. His means were, indeed, very limited. His stock-in-trade consisted only of a few old Violins of no particular value. With these he commenced his labours, journeying in the garb of a pedlar, on foot, through Italian cities and villages, and often playing his Violin in order to procure the bare means of existence. Upon entering a village he endeavoured to ingratiate himself with the villagers, and thus obtain information of the whereabouts of any inhabitants who were possessed of any member of the Fiddle family, his object being to examine and secure, if possible, such instruments as were possessed of any merit. It can readily be conceived that at the commencement of the present century, numbers of valuable Cremonese and other instruments were in the hands of very humble people. Luigi Tarisio knew that such must be the case, and made the most of his good fortune in being the first connoisseur to visit them. His usual method of trading was to exchange with the simple-minded villagers, giving them a Violin in perfect playing order for their shabby old instrument that lacked all the accessories. It was indeed the case of Aladdin's Lamp, and as potent were these Fiddles as the wonderful lamp or ring itself. In the possession of Luigi Tarisio they drew forth from the purses of the wealthy gold that would have enabled the humble villagers to have ceased labour. It is an axiom, however, that everything on this earth is only of value providing it is in its proper place, and these rare old instruments, in the keeping of the poor peasants, could scarcely be considered to be in their proper element; their ignorant possessors were alike unable to appreciate their sterling worth, as works of art, or their powers of sound. Luigi Tarisio, after gathering together a number of old rarities, made for his home, and busied himself in examining the qualities of his stock, selecting the best works, which he laid aside. With the residuum of those instruments he would again set out, using them as his capital wherewith to form the basis of future transactions among the peasantry and others. He visited the numerous monasteries throughout Italy that he might see the valuable specimens belonging to the chapel orchestras. He found them often in a condition ill becoming their value, and tendered his services to regulate and put them into decent order—services gladly accepted and faithfully performed by the ardent connoisseur. By the handling of these buried treasures, his knowledge and experience were greatly extended. Makers hitherto unknown to him became familiar. When he met with instruments apparently beyond the repairer's skill, he would make tempting offers of purchase, which were often accepted. Having accumulated many instruments of a high order during these journeys, he began to consider the best means of disposing of them. He decided upon visiting Paris. He took with him the Violins he valued least, resolving to make himself acquainted with the Parisian Fiddle market before bringing forth his treasures. It is said that he undertook his journey on foot, depriving himself often of the common necessaries of life, that he might have more money to buy up his country's Fiddles. His first visit to Paris was in 1827, an eventful year in the history of Italian Violins, as far as relates to Paris. Upon arriving in the French capital, he directed his steps to the nearest luthier, one Aldric, to whom he had been recommended as a purchaser of old instruments of high value. Upon arriving at the shop of M. Aldric, Tarisio hesitated before entering, feeling suddenly that his appearance was scarcely in keeping with his wares, his clothes being of the shabbiest description, his boots nearly soleless, and his complexion, naturally inclined to blackness, further darkened by the need of ordinary ablutions. However, he set aside these thoughts, and introduced himself to the luthier as having some Cremona Violins for sale. Aldric regarded him half-contemptuously, and with a silent intent to convey to Tarisio that he heard what he said, but did not believe it. The Italian, to the astonishment of the luthier, was not long in verifying his statement; he opened his bag and brought forth a beautiful Niccolò Amati, of the small pattern, in fine preservation, but having neither finger-board, strings, nor fittings of any kind. The countenance of the luthier brightened when he beheld this unexpected specimen of the Italian's wares. He carefully examined it, and did his best to disguise the pleasurable feelings he experienced. He demanded the price. The value set on it was far in excess of that he had anticipated; he erroneously arrived at the probable cost from an estimate of the shabby appearance of the man. He had been comforting himself that the Italian was unaware of the value put upon such instruments. He decided to see further the contents of the bag before expressing an opinion as to the price demanded for the Amati. Violins by Maggini, Ruggeri, and others, were produced—six in number. Tarisio was asked to name his price for the six. After much giving and taking they became the property of the luthier. This business was not regarded as satisfactory by Tarisio; he had overestimated the value of his goods in the Paris market; he had not learned that it was he himself who was to create the demand for high-class Italian instruments by spreading them far and wide, so that their incomparable qualities might be observed. He returned to Italy with his ardour somewhat cooled; the ready sale at the prices he had put upon his stock was not likely to be realised, he began to think. However, with the proceeds of his Paris transaction he again started in search of more Cremonas, with about the same satisfactory results. He resolved to visit Paris again, taking with him some of his choicest specimens. He reached the French capital with a splendid collection—one that in these days would create a complete *furore* throughout the world of Fiddles. He extended his acquaintance with the Parisian luthiers, among whom were MM. Vuillaume, Thibout, and Chanot senior. They were all delighted with the gems that Tarisio had brought, and encouraged him to bring to France as many more as he could procure, and at regular intervals. He did so, and obtained at each visit better prices.

GASPARO DA SALÒ.　　　　GIUSEPPE GUARNERI DEL
(LATE LORD AMHERST OF　　　　　GESÙ.
HACKNEY.)　　　　　　　　1735.
　　　　　　　　　　　　　(PRINCE FREDERICK
Plate XX.　　　　　　　WILLIAM OF PRUSSIA.)

This remarkable man may be said to have lived for nought else but his Fiddles. Mr. Charles Reade, who knew him well, says:[1] "The man's whole soul was in Fiddles. He was a great dealer, but a greater amateur; he had gems by him no money would buy from him." It is related of him that he was in Paris upon one occasion, walking along the Boulevards with a friend, when a handsome equipage belonging to a French magnate passed, the beauty of which was the talk of the city. Tarisio's attention being directed to it by his friend, he calmly answered him that "*he would sooner possess one 'Stradivari' than twenty such equipages.*" There is a very characteristic anecdote of Tarisio, which is also related by Mr. Reade in his article on Cremona Violins, entitled the "Romance of Fiddle-dealing":

"Well, one day Georges Chanot, senior, made an excursion to Spain, to see if he could find anything there. He found mighty little, but coming to the shop of a Fiddle-maker, one Ortega, he saw the belly of an old Bass hung up with other things. Chanot rubbed his eyes, and asked himself was he dreaming? the belly of a Stradivari Bass roasting in a shop window! He went in, and very soon bought it for about forty francs. He then ascertained that the Bass belonged to a lady of rank. The belly was full of cracks; so, not to make two bites of a cherry, Ortega had made a nice new one. Chanot carried this precious fragment home and hung it up in his shop, but not in the window, for he was too good a judge not to know that the sun will take all the colour out of that maker's varnish. Tarisio came in from Italy, and his eye lighted instantly on the Stradivari belly. He pestered Chanot till the latter sold it him for a thousand francs, and told him where the rest was. Tarisio no sooner knew this than he flew to Madrid. He learned from Ortega where the lady lived, and called on her to see it. 'Sir,' says the lady, 'it is at your disposition.' That does not mean much in Spain. When he offered to buy it, she coquetted with him, said it had been long in her family; money could not replace a thing of that kind, and, in short, she put on the screw, *as she thought*, and sold it him for about four thousand francs. What he did with the Ortega belly is not known; perhaps sold it to some person in the toothpick trade. He sailed exultant for Paris with the Spanish Bass in a case. He never let it go out of his sight. The pair were caught by a storm in the Bay of Biscay; the ship rolled; Tarisio clasped his Bass tightly and trembled. It was a terrible gale, and for one whole day they were in real danger. Tarisio spoke of it to me with a shudder. I will give you his real words, for they struck me at the time, and I have often thought of them since. '*Ah, my poor Mr. Reade, the Bass of Spain was all but lost!*'

"Was not this a true connoisseur—a genuine enthusiast? Observe, there was also an ephemeral insect called Luigi Tarisio, who would have gone down with the Bass; but that made no impression on his mind. *De minimis non curat Ludovicus!*

"He got it safe to Paris. A certain high-priest in these mysteries, called Vuillaume, with the help of a sacred vessel, called the glue-pot, soon re-wedded the back and sides to the belly, and the Bass now is just what it was when the ruffian Ortega put his finger in the pie. It was sold for 20,000 fr. (£800). I saw the Spanish Bass in Paris twenty-five years ago, and you can see it any day this month you like, for it is the identical Violoncello now on show at Kensington numbered 188. Who would divine its separate adventures, to see it all reposing so calm and uniform in that case?—*Post tot naufragia tutus.*"

1 "Cremona Violins," *Pall Mall Gazette*, August, 1872.

The love of Tarisio for the masterpieces of the great makers was so intense, that often when he had parted with the works he so admired, he never lost sight of them, and waited a favourable opportunity for again making himself their owner.

It is related of him that upon one occasion he disposed of a beautiful Stradivari, in perfect preservation, to a Paris dealer. After having done so he hungered for it again. For years he never visited Paris without inquiring after his old favourite, and the possibility of its again being offered for sale, that he might regain possession of it. At last his perseverance was rewarded, inasmuch as he heard that it was to be bought. He instructed his informant to obtain for him a sight of it. The instrument was fetched, and Tarisio had scarcely patience enough to wait the opening of the case, so anxious was he to see his old companion. He eagerly took up the Violin, and turned it over and over, apparently lost to all about him, when suddenly his keen eye rested upon a damage it had received, which was hidden by new varnish. His heart sank within him; he was overcome by this piece of vandalism. In mingled words of passion and remorse he gave vent to his feelings. He placed it in its case, remarking sadly that it had no longer any charm for him.

In the year 1851 Tarisio visited England, when Mr. John Hart, being anxious that he should see the chief collections of Cremonese instruments in this country, accompanied him to the collection, amongst others, of the late Mr. James Goding, which was then the finest in Europe. The instruments were arranged on shelves at the end of a long room, and far removed from them sat the genuine enthusiast, patiently awaiting the promised exhibition. Upon Mr. Goding taking out his treasures he was inexpressibly astonished to hear his visitor calling out the maker of each instrument before he had had time to advance two paces towards him, at the same time giving his host to understand that he thoroughly knew the instruments, the greater number having been in his possession. Mr. Goding whispered to a friend standing by, "Why, the man must certainly smell them, he has not had time to look." Many instruments in this collection Tarisio seemed never tired of admiring. He took them up again and again, completely lost to all around—in a word, spell-bound. There was the "King" Guarneri—the Guarneri known as Lafont's—the beautiful Bergonzi Violin—the Viola known as Lord Macdonald's—General Kidd's Stradivari Violoncello—the Marquis de la Rosa's Amati—Ole Bull's Guarneri—the Santo Serafino 'Cello—and other remarkable instruments too numerous to mention. Who can say what old associations these Cremona gems brought to his memory? For the moment, these Fiddles resolved themselves into a diorama, in which he saw the chief events of his life played over again. With far greater truthfulness than that which his unaided memory could have supplied, each Fiddle had its tale to relate. His thoughts were carried back to the successful energies of his past.

Tarisio may be said to have lived the life of a hermit to the time of his death. He had no pleasures apart from his Fiddles; they were his all in this world. Into his lodgings, in the Via Legnano, near the Porta Tenaglia, in Milan, no living being but himself was ever permitted to enter.[2] His nearest neighbours had not the least knowledge of his occupation. He mounted to his attic without exchanging a word with any one, and left it securely fastened to start on his journeys in the same taciturn manner. He was consequently regarded as a mysterious individual, whose doings were unfathomable. The time, however, has arrived when the veil hiding the inner life of this remarkable man should be lifted, and here I am indebted for particulars to Signor Sacchi, of Cremona, who received them from a reliable source. Tarisio had been seen by his ever-watchful neighbours to enter his abode, but none had noticed him quit it for several days. The door was tried and found locked; no answer was returned to the sundry knockings. That Tarisio was there the neighbours were convinced. The facts were at once brought under the notice of the municipal authorities, who gave instructions that an entry should be made by force into the mysterious man's apartment. The scene witnessed was indeed a painful one. On a miserable couch rested the lifeless body of Luigi Tarisio; around, everything was in the utmost disorder. The furniture of the apartment consisted mainly of a chair, table, and the couch upon which lay the corpse. A pile of old Fiddle-boxes here and there, Fiddles hung around the walls, others dangling from the ceiling, Fiddle-backs, Fiddle-heads, and bellies in pigeon-holes; three Double-Basses tied to the wall, covered with sacking. This was the sight that met the gaze of the authorities. Little did they imagine they were surrounded with gems no money would have bought from their late eccentric owner. Here were some half-dozen Stradivari Violins, Tenors, and Violoncellos, the chamber Gasparo da Salò Double-Bass now in the possession of Mr. Bennett, and the Ruggeri now belonging to Mr. J. R. Bridson, besides upwards of one hundred Italian instruments of various makers, and others of different nationalities. All these were passed over by the visitors as so much rubbish in their search for something more marketable. At last they alighted on a packet of valuable securities together with a considerable amount of gold. A seal was placed upon the apartment, pending inquiries as to the whereabouts of the dead man's relatives. In due time, some nephews came forth and laid claim to the goods and chattels of the Italian Fiddle connoisseur.

> 2 The house is now turned, with those adjoining, into a manufactory. When Luigi Tarisio lived there it was a small restaurant, similar to those seen in the side streets of Soho.

Luigi Tarisio died in October, 1854. Three months later, upon the news being communicated to M. Vuillaume, of Paris, he soon set out for Milan, and had the good fortune to secure the whole of the collection, at a price which left him a handsome profit upon the transaction, besides the pleasurable feeling of becoming the possessor of such a varied and remarkable number of instruments.

Having given the reader all the information I have been able to collect concerning Tarisio, I will only add that he had advantages over all other connoisseurs, inasmuch as he found the instruments mostly in their primitive condition, and free from any tampering as regards the labels within them. He was thus enabled to learn the characteristics of each without fear of confusion. The days of taking out the labels of unmarketable names and substituting marketable counterfeits had not arrived.

The principal buyers of Italian instruments on the Continent, when dealing in this class of property was in its infancy, were Aldric, MM. Chanot senior, Thibout, Gand, Vuillaume of Paris, and Vuillaume of Brussels. In London, among others, were Davis, Betts, Corsby, and John Hart. There is yet another, the omission of whose name would be a blemish in any notice of the Violin and its connoisseurs. I refer to Mr. Charles Reade, the novelist, who in early life took the highest interest in old Italian Violins. We are indebted to him in a great measure for bringing into this country many of the most beautiful specimens we possess. Impressed with the charms of the subject, he visited the Continent for the pleasure it afforded him of bringing together choice specimens, and thus opened up the intercourse between England and the Continent for the interchange of old Violins which continues to this day. It would be difficult to find an instance where the intricacies of the subject were so quickly mastered as in his case. Without assistance, but solely from his own observation, he gained a knowledge which enabled him to place himself beside the Chief Continental connoisseurs, and compete for the ownership of Cremonese masterpieces. These were the men who laid bare the treasures of Cremona's workshops, and spread far and wide love and admiration for the fine old works. Connoisseurship such as theirs is rare. To a keen eye was united intense love of the art, patience, energy, and memory of no ordinary kind, all of them attributes requisite to make a successful judge of Violins.

Charles Lamb, on being asked how he distinguished his "ragged veterans" in their tattered and unlettered bindings, answered, "How does a shepherd know his sheep?" It has been observed that, "Touch becomes infinitely more exquisite in men whose employment requires them to examine the polish of bodies than it is in others. In music only the simplest and plainest compositions are relished at first; use and practice extend our pleasure— teach us to relish finer melody, and by degrees enable us to enter into the intricate and compounded pleasure of harmony." Thus it is with connoisseurship in Violins. Custom and observation, springing from a natural disposition, make prominent features and minute points of difference before unseen, resulting in a knowledge of style of which it has been well said "Every man has his own, like his own nose."

As an ardent votary of the Violin, regarded from a point of view at once artistic and curious, Count Cozio di Salabue takes precedence of all others. He was born about the time when the art of Italian Violin-making began to show signs of decadence, and having cultivated a taste for Cremonese instruments, he resolved to gratify his passion by bringing together a collection of Violins which should be representative of the work and character of each maker, and serve as models to those seeking to tread the path of the makers who made Cremona eminent as a seat of Violin manufacture. Virtuosity emanating from a spirit of beneficence is somewhat rare. When, however, utility occupies a prominent place in the thoughts of the virtuoso, he becomes a benefactor. The virtuosity of Count Cozio was of this character. His love for Cremonese instruments was neither whimsical nor transient. From the time when he secured the contents of the shop of Stradivari to the end of his life—a period of about fifty years—he appears to have exerted himself to obtain as much information as possible relative to the art, and to collect masterpieces that they might in some measure be the means of recovering a lost art. When in the year 1775 he secured ten instruments out of ninety-one which Stradivari left in his shop at the time of his death, he must surely have considered himself singularly fortunate, and the happiest of collectors.[3] That such good fortune prompted him to make fresh overtures of purchase cannot be wondered at. We learn from the correspondence of Paolo Stradivari that the Count had caused two letters to be sent by the firm of Anselmi di Briata to Paolo inquiring if he was willing to part with the tools and patterns used by his father Antonio, and that Paolo replied on May 4, 1776: "I have already told you that I have no objection to sell all those patterns, measures, and tools which I happen to have in my possession, provided that they do not remain in Cremona, and you will recollect that I have shown you all the tools I have, and also the box containing the patterns.... I place all at your disposal, and as it is simply a friendly matter" (Paolo Stradivari appears to have had large dealings in cloth and other goods with the firm of Anselmi di Briata, of Casale, a small city on the Po), "I will give you everything for twenty-eight giliati."[4] It does not appear that Paolo's correspondents were moved in their answer by any feelings of sentimentality or of friendship: on the contrary, the tone of the letter was clearly commercial, they having made an offer of twenty-three giliati less than demanded. Paolo Stradivari in his reply, dated June 4, 1776, says: "Putting ceremony aside, I write in a mercantile style. I see from your favour of the 13th ultimo (which I only received by the last courier), that you offer me five giliati for all the patterns and moulds which I happen to possess, as well as for those lent to Bergonzi, and also for the tools of the trade of my late father; but this is too little; however, to show you the desire I have to please you, and in order that not a single thing belonging to my father be left in Cremona, I will part with them for six giliati, providing that you pay them at once into the hands of Domenico Dupuy & Sons, silk stocking manufacturers. I will send you the things above-mentioned, conditionally that I keep the five giliati and use the other one to defray expenses for the case, the packing, and the custom-house duty, which will be necessary to send them, and I shall let you have back through Messrs. Dupuy, residing under the Market Arcades in Turin, any balance that should remain, or (if you like) you may pay the said Messrs. Dupuy seven giliati, and I shall then defray all the expenses, and send also the two snake-wood bows which I possess.—(Signed) PAOLO STRADIVARI."

> 3 These instruments and the tools appear to have been in the possession of Paolo from the year 1743, when Francesco died, and Paolo opened the shop in the Piazza S. Domenico as a cloth warehouse. He therefore seems to have only decided to dispose of his father's tools when he was in a feeble state of health, he having died, as already noticed, before the purchase was settled, aged 68.

> 4 A giliati was a Tuscan gold coin bearing the arms of Florence, the value of which was 9s. 6½d. Its present purchasing power would probably be three times as much, and therefore the sum asked by Paolo Stradivari would be equal to £38 12s. 10½d.

In reply to this interesting letter, Messrs. Anselmi di Briata appear to have written accepting the terms offered by Paolo Stradivari, and to have explained to him that they had been in treaty with a certain Signor Boroni, relative to the purchase of a Violin, and having come to terms they wished the instrument to be packed with the tools and moulds. Paolo, in acknowledging this communication, June 25, 1776, says: "In reply to your favour of the 10th instant, Signor Boroni will hand me over the Violin upon hearing that the money has been paid to Messrs. Dupuy. I shall then have no objection to place it in the same case together with the patterns and implements left by my father." From this and subsequent correspondence we learn that Messrs. Anselmi di Briata, being wholesale traders, were in a suitable position to act as intermediaries in the purchase of Violins on behalf of Count Cozio. Their business necessitated their visiting Cremona, and thus they appear to have seen the Violin of Signor Boroni, and also another belonging to a monk or friar named Father Ravizza, both of which were subsequently bought, as seen by the following extracts from a letter of Paolo Stradivari:—

"Cremona, July 10, 1776. We learn from Messrs. Dupuy of the receipt of the seven giliati, which you have paid on our account.... As we have already prepared everything, we shall therefore inform Father Ravizza and Signor Boroni; I have, however, to mention that I did not think I possessed so many things as I have found. It being according to what has been promised, it cannot be discussed over again.... It will be a very heavy case, on account of the quantity of patterns and tools, and consequently it will be dangerous to put the Violins in the same package." The writer refers to the two instruments before mentioned: "I fear without care they will let it fall in unloading it, and the Violins will be damaged; I inform you therefore of the fact.... You must let me know how I have to send the case. If by land, through the firm of Tabarini, of Piacenza, or to take the opportunity of sending by the Pò." In passing, it may be remarked that the distance between Cremona and Casale by the river Pò is about sixty miles. The later correspondence makes known the fact of the precious freight having been consigned to the firm of Anselmi di Briata by way of the Pò, and that it was entrusted to the care and charge of a barge-master named Gobbi.

It is by no means uncommon to discover the memories of men kept green in our minds from causes strangely curious and unexpected. Many seek to render their names immortal by some act the nature of which would seem to be imperishable, and chiefly fail of their object; whilst others, obscure and unthought of, live on by accident. Imagine the paints and brushes, the pencils and palettes, the easel and the sketches of Raffaele having been given over to a Pò barge-master, and that chance had divulged his name. Would he not in these days of microscopic biography have furnished work for the genealogist, and been made the subject of numberless pictures? Hence it is that the admirers of Stradivari cannot fail to remember the name of honest Gobbi, who carried the chest wherein were the tools with which the Raffaele of Violin-making wrought the instruments which have served to render his memory immortal.

Soon after the date of Paolo's last letter, he became seriously ill, dying on the 9th of October, 1776. The correspondence was then taken up by his son Antonio. He says in his letter dated November 21, 1776: "I shall send you the case with the patterns and tools of my late grandfather Antonio, which was packed and closed before my father was bedridden. You will find it well-arranged, with mark on it, and with red tape and seal as on the Violins already sent to you." He next refers to other patterns which he found locked up in a chest and which he believes were unknown or forgotten by his father, and offers to dispose of them, with a Viola, and concludes by promising to send the receipts, the copies of which show that the remnants of the tools and patterns were bought for three giliati.

It is unnecessary in this place to make further reference to Count Cozio as a collector, the chief information concerning him being spread over the section of Italian makers. The facsimile of one of the Count's letters here given will serve both as an interesting remembrance of him and as evidence of his keen interest in all relating to the art of which he was so distinguished a votary.

Probably the earliest collector of Italian Violins in England was William Corbett. He was a member of the King's orchestra, and having obtained permission to go abroad, went to Italy in 1710, and resided at Rome many years, where he is said to have made a rare collection of music and musical instruments. How he managed to gratify his desire in this direction seems not to have been understood by his friends, his means, in their estimation, not being equal to such an expenditure. Hence arose a report that he was employed by the Government to watch the Pretender. Corbett died at an advanced age in 1748, and bequeathed his "Gallery of Cremonys and Stainers" to the authorities of Gresham College, with a view that they should remain for inspection under certain conditions, leaving ten pounds per annum to an attendant to show the instruments. Whether the wishes of the testator were carried out in any way there is no information, but the instruments are said to have been disposed of by auction a short time after his decease.

The principal early collectors in this country were the Duke of Hamilton, the Duke of Cambridge, the Earl of Falmouth, the Duke of Marlborough, Lord Macdonald, and a few others. Later, Mr. Andrew Fountaine, of Narford Hall, Norfolk, became the owner of several fine Italian instruments, and made himself better acquainted with the subject, perhaps, than any amateur of his time. Among the Stradivari Violins which Mr. Fountaine possessed was that which he purchased from M. Habeneck, the famous professor at the Paris Conservatoire in the early part of the nineteenth century. Another very fine specimen of the late period, 1734, was also owned by him, a Violin of grand proportions in a high state of preservation, and of the richest varnish. The Guarneri Violins that he possessed were of a very high class. Among these may be mentioned a very small Violin by Giuseppe Guarneri, probably unique, which instrument was exhibited among the Cremonese Violins at the South Kensington Museum in 1872, together with another of the same size by Stradivari, and a third by the brothers Amati.

The number of rarities brought together by the late Mr. James Goding was in every respect remarkable. At one period he owned twelve Stradivari Violins, and nearly the same number by Giuseppe Guarneri, all high-class instruments. It would take up too much time and space to name the particular instruments which were comprised in this collection. The remnant of this group of Cremonese Fiddles was dispersed by Messrs. Christie and Manson in 1857. Mr. Plowden's collection was another remarkable one, consisting of eight instruments of the highest class.

The late Joseph Gillott was a collector, who, in point of number, exceeded all others. He did not confine himself solely to the works of the greatest makers, but added specimens of every age and clime; and at one time he must have had upwards of 500 instruments, the chief part of which belonged to the Italian School. When it is remembered that the vast multitude of stringed instruments disposed of by Messrs. Christie and Manson in 1872 did not amount to one-half the number originally owned by Mr. Gillott, some idea of the extent of his collection may be gained. Among the many curious instances of the love of collecting Violins, which sometimes possesses those unable to use them, perhaps that of Mr. Gillott is the most singular.

Notable collections, be they of Fiddles, medals, pottery, or pictures, have sometimes had their rise in accidents of a curious kind. Lord Northwick dated his passion for coins to a bag of brass ones, which he purchased in sport for eight pounds. His lordship ended by purchasing, in conjunction with Payne Knight, the collection of Sir Robert Ainslie, for eight thousand pounds, besides sharing with the same collector the famous Sicilian coins belonging to the Prince Torremuzza. The Gillott collection of Fiddles had its origin in a picture deal. Mr. Gillott happened to be making terms in his gallery at Edgbaston relative to an exchange of pictures with Edwin Atherstone,[5] poet and novelist, who collected both Violins and pictures. A difficulty arose in adjusting the balance, when Mr. Atherstone suggested throwing a Fiddle in as a counterpoise. "That would be to no purpose," remarked Mr. Gillott, "for I have neither knowledge of music nor of the Fiddle." "I am aware of that," rejoined his friend; "but Violins are often of extraordinary value as works of art." Mr. Gillott, becoming interested in the subject, agreed to accept the Fiddle as a make-weight, and the business was settled. A few months later the floor of his picture gallery on all sides was lined with cases, single and double, containing Violins in seemingly endless profusion. It was about the year 1848 he conceived the notion of bringing together this mammoth collection; and in about four years he had made himself master of the largest number of Italian instruments ever owned by a single individual. He suddenly relinquished the pursuit he had followed with such persistency; he disposed of a great number, and laid the remainder aside in his steel-pen works at Birmingham, where they slumbered for upwards of twenty years. The time at last arrived when this pile of Fiddles was to be dispersed. It fell to my lot to classify them, and never shall I forget the scene I witnessed. Here, amid the din of countless machines busy shaping magnum-bonums, swan-bills, and divers other writing implements, I was about to feast my eyes on some of the choicest works of the old Italian Fiddle-makers. Passing through offices, warehouses, and workshops, I found myself at a door which my conductor set himself to unlock—an act not often performed, I felt assured, from the sound which accompanied his deed. To adequately describe what met my eyes when the door swung back on its hinges, is beyond my powers of description. Fiddles here!—Fiddles there!—Fiddles everywhere, in wild disorder! I interrogated my friend as to the cause of their being in such an unseemly condition, and received answer that he had instructions to remove most of the instruments from their cases and arrange them, that I might better judge of their merits. I was at a loss to understand what he meant by arranging, for a more complete disarrangement could not have been effected. Not wishing to appear unmindful of the kindly intentions of my would-be assistant, I thanked him, inwardly wishing that this disentombment had been left entirely to me. The scene was altogether so peculiar and unexpected as to be quite bewildering. In the centre of the room was a large warehouse table, upon which were placed in pyramids upwards of seventy Violins and Tenors, stringless, bridgeless, unglued, and enveloped in the fine dust which had crept through the crevices of the cardboard sarcophagi in which they had rested for the previous quarter of a century. On the floor lay the bows. The scene might not inappropriately be compared to a post-mortem examination on an extended scale. When left alone I began to collect my thoughts as to the best mode of conducting my inquiry. After due consideration I attacked pyramid No. 1, from which I saw a head protruding which augured well for the body, and led me to think it belonged to the higher walks of Fiddle-life. With considerate care I withdrew it from the heap, and gently rubbed the dust off here and there, that I might judge of its breeding. It needed but little rubbing to make known its character; it was a Viola by Giuseppe Guarneri, filius Andreæ, a charming specimen (now in the ownership of the Earl of Harrington). Laying it aside, I pulled out from the pile several others belonging to the same class. Being too eager to learn of what the real merits of this huge pile of Fiddles consisted, I rapidly passed from one to the other without close scrutiny, leaving that for an after pleasure. So entirely fresh were these instruments to me, that the delight I experienced in thus digging them out may well be understood by the connoisseur. After thus wading through those resting on the table, I discovered some shelves, upon which were a number of cases, which I opened. Here were fine Cremonese instruments in company with raw copies—as curious a mixture of good and indifferent as could be well conceived. Not observing any Violoncellos, when my attendant presented himself I inquired if there were not some in the collection. I was unable to make him understand to what I referred for some little time, but when I called them big Fiddles, he readily understood. He had some faint idea of having seen something of the kind on the premises, and started off to make inquiry. Upon his return, I was conducted to an under warehouse, the contents of which were of a varied character. Here were stored unused lathes, statuary, antique pianos, parts of machinery, pictures, and picture-frames. At the end of this long room stood, in stately form, the "big Fiddles," about fifty in number—five rows, consequently ten deep. They looked in their cases like a detachment of infantry awaiting the word of command. Years had passed by since they had been called upon to take active service of a pacific and humanising nature in the ranks of the orchestra. Had they the power of speech, what tales of heroism might they have furnished of the part they played at the "Fall of Babylon" and the "Siege of Corinth," aye! and "Wellington's Victory" (Beethoven, Op. 91). A more curious mixture of art and mechanism could not easily be found than that which the contents of this room exhibited. With what delight did I proceed to open these long-closed cases! The character of the Violins naturally led me to anticipate much artistic worth in the Violoncellos, and I had not judged erroneously. Bergonzi, Amati, Andrea Guarneri, Cappa, Grancino, Testore, Landolfi, and men of less note, were all well represented in this army of big Fiddles. Having glanced at the merits and demerits of these instruments, I observed to my conductor that I imagined I had seen all. "No," he answered; "I was about to mention that there are a few Violins at Mr. Gillott's residence, and perhaps we had better go there at once." I readily assented, and in due time reached Edgbaston. There seemed no doubt as to the whereabouts of these instruments, and I was at once ushered into the late Mr. Gillott's *bedroom*. Pointing to a long mahogany glazed case occupying one side of the chamber, the attendant gave me to understand I should there find the Violins. At once I commenced operations. Pushing aside the first sliding door, I saw a row of those cardboard cases made to hold the Violin only, which many of my readers will doubtless remember seeing at the time of the sale at Messrs. Christie's. By this time it may readily be imagined that an idea had taken possession of my mind, that I had not, after all, seen the best portion of the collection. The circumstance of Violins being deposited in the sleeping apartment of their owner was sufficient to give birth to this conjecture. Upon removing the lid of the first cardboard case, my eyes rested on a charming Stradivari of the Amati period, a gem of its kind. Gently laying it on the table, that I might examine it later, I opened the next case. Here rested a magnificent Giuseppe Guarneri, the instrument afterwards bought by Lord Dunmore, date 1732. Pursuing my delightful occupation, I opened another case, the contents of which put the rest completely in the shade—here rested the Stradivari, date 1715, the gem of the collection. Unable to restrain my curiosity, I rapidly opened sixteen cases in all, from which I took out six Stradivari, two Guarneri, one Bergonzi, two Amati, and five other Violins of a high class.

> 5 Edwin Atherstone, born 1788, died 1872; was the author of "The Fall of Nineveh" and "The Last Days of Herculaneum," two poems in blank verse, and of a novel, "The Sea Kings of England," of which Sir Walter Scott wrote approvingly.

It was observed at the time of the sale of this remarkable collection, which took place shortly after the dispersion of Mr. Gillott's gallery of pictures, that "Every well-ordered display of fireworks should have its climax of luminous and detonating splendour, throwing into shade all the preliminary squibs, crackers, and rockets, the Catherine wheels, the Roman candles, and the golden rain. The French, with modest propriety, term this consummation a *bouquet*." I cannot find anything more applicable than this word to the scene I have attempted to describe. It only remains for me to say, in reference to this array of Fiddles, that I passed a week in their company, and a more enjoyable one I have never had during my professional career.

Dr. Johnson, who understood neither Fiddling nor painting, who collected neither coins nor cockle-shells, maggots nor butterflies, was clearly of the same opinion as the author of "Tristram Shandy," that there is no disputing against hobby-horses. He says: "The pride or the pleasure of making collections, if it be restrained by prudence and morality, produces a pleasing remission after more laborious studies; furnishes an amusement, not wholly unprofitable, for that part of life, the greater part of many lives, which would otherwise be lost in idleness or vice; it produces a useful traffic between the industry of indigence and the curiosity of wealth, and brings many things to notice that would be neglected."

SECTION XIV

Sketch of the Progress of the Violin

It may be said that the Violin made its appearance about the middle of the sixteenth century. There are instances where reference is made to Violins and Violin-playing in connection with times prior to that above-named, but no reliance can be placed on the statements. Leonardo da Vinci, who died in 1523, is spoken of as having been a celebrated performer on the Violin. The instrument he used is described as having had a neck of silver, with the singular addition of a carved horse's head.[1] This description, however, is sufficiently anomalous to make one rather sceptical, as to whether the instrument denoted possessed any particular affinity to the present Violin. Reference is made to the picture of the "Marriage at Cana," by Paolo Veronese, as furnishing evidence of the form of instruments used in Italy in the 16th century, and a description is given of the musical part of the subject as follows: "In the foreground, in the vacant space of the semicircle formed by the table, at which the guests of the marriage at Cana are seated, Titian is playing on the Double-Bass, Paolo Veronese and Tintoretto on the Violoncello; a man with a cross on his breast is playing on the Violin, Bassano is blowing the Flute, and a Turkish slave the Sackbut."

    1 "Lives of Haydn and Mozart," translated from the French by L. A. C. Bombet. 1818.

The naming of the performers is presumably correct, and greatly heightens our interest in the group musically. It is clear, however, that the nomenclature of the instruments is erroneous. In the engraved section of the famous picture here given, Paolo Veronese is represented taking part in the performance of a Madrigal, wearing an expression of countenance indicative of rapt pleasure, engendered by the mingling of the tones of his Tenor Viol in the harmonies. Behind Paolo Veronese is seated Tintoretto, playing an instrument identical with that in the hands of the painter of the picture. On the opposite side of the table is Titian, with the point of his bow almost touching the dog, playing the fundamental tones on the Violono. He apparently displays an amount of real relish for his task, which bespeaks a knowledge of the responsibility belonging to the post of Basso. The ecclesiastic seated next to Titian, wearing the chain with crucifix, is performing on a Soprano Viol. The instruments, in short, are Italian Viols, the Tenors of which were strung with six strings, and the Violono, or Bass, with six or seven. It is this order of Viols to which reference is made in the work of Ganassi del Fontego, and they are, therefore, distinct from the four-stringed Viols made at Brescia and Mantua.

The earliest player on the Violin of whom we have any account worthy of attention was Baltazarini, a native of Piedmont. He removed to France in the year 1577, whither he was sent by Marshal de Brissac to superintend the music of Catherine de Medici. He was probably the introducer of Italian dances into Paris, and he delighted the Court as much by his skill on the Violin as by his writing of ballet music.

During the last half of the sixteenth century a new species of music made way in Italy which exercised a marked effect on the progress of the Violin, namely, that of the concert orchestra. It was chiefly cultivated at Venice and Ferrara. At the latter place the Duke of Ferrara maintained a great number of musicians in his service. At this period there were no concerts of a public character; they were given in the palaces of the wealthy, and the performers were chiefly those belonging to their private bands.

The opera, in which instruments were used to accompany the voice, began to be put upon the stage of the public theatres in Italy about the year 1600. The opera "Orfeo," by Claudio Monteverde, a Cremonese, famous both as a composer and Violist, was represented in 1608. The opera in those times differed essentially from that of modern days. Particular instruments were selected to accompany each character; for instance, ten Treble Viols to accompany Eurydice, two Bass Viols to Orpheus, and so on. No mention is made of Violins further than that two small Violins (duoi Violini piccoli alla Francese) are to accompany the character of Hope, from which it is inferred that a band of Violins was in use not much later.

It is to the introduction of the Sonata that the rapid progress in the cultivation of Violin-playing is due. Dr. Burney tells us the earliest Sonatas or Trios for two Violins and a Bass he discovered were published by Francesco Turini, organist of the Duomo, at Brescia, under the following title: "Madrigali à una, due, e tre voci, con alcune Sonate à due e à tre, Venezia, 1624." He says: "I was instigated by this early date to score one of these Sonatas, which consisted of only a single movement in figure and imitation throughout, in which so little use was made of the power of the bow in varying the expression of the same notes, that each part might have been as well played on one instrument as another."

In this branch of composition Corelli shone forth with considerable lustre, and gave great impetus to the culture of the Violin. It was at Rome that his first twelve Sonatas were published, in 1683. In 1685 the second set appeared, entitled "Balletti da Camera"; four years later the third set was published. The genius of Corelli may be said to have revolutionised Violin-playing. He had followers in the chief cities of Italy. There was Vitali at Modena, Visconti at Cremona (who, it is said, tendered his advice to Stradivari upon the construction of his instruments—advice, I think, little needed); Veracini at Bologna, and a host of others. Dibdin, the Tyrtæus of the British navy, said: "I had always delighted in Corelli, whose harmonies are an assemblage of melodies. I, therefore, got his Concertos in single parts, and put them into score, by which means I saw all the workings of his mind at the time he composed them; I so managed that I not only comprehended in what manner the parts had been worked, but how, in every way, they might have been worked. From this severe but profitable exercise, I drew all the best properties of harmony, and among the rest I learnt the valuable secret, that men of strong minds may violate to advantage many of those rules of composition which are dogmatically imposed."

ANTONIO STRADIVARI.
1690.
(Made for Cosimo III. de Medici, Grand Duke of Florence.)

Plate XXI.

We must now retrace our steps somewhat, in order to allude to another Violinist, who influenced the progress of the leading instrument out of Italy, viz., Jean Baptiste Lulli. The son of a Tuscan peasant, born in the year 1633, Lulli's name is so much associated with the romantic in the history of Violin-playing that he has been deprived in a great measure of the merits justly his due for the part he took in the advancement of the instrument. The story of Lulli and the stew-pans[2] bristles with interest for juvenile musicians, but the hero is often overlooked by graver people, on account of his culinary associations. When Lulli was admitted to the Violin band of Louis XIV., he found the members very incompetent; they could not play at sight, and their style was of the worst description. The king derived much pleasure from listening to Lulli's music, and established a new band on purpose for the composer, namely, "Les petits Violons," to distinguish it from the band of twenty-four. He composed much music for the Court ballets in which the king danced.

> 2: Lulli having shown a disposition for music, received some instructions on the rudiments of the art from a priest. The Chevalier de Guise, when on his travels in Italy, had been requested by Mademoiselle de Montpensier, niece of Louis XIV., to procure for her an Italian boy as page, and happening to see Lulli in Florence, he chose him for that purpose, on account of his wit and vivacity, and his skill in playing on the guitar. The lady, however, not liking his appearance, sent him into her kitchen, where he was made an under scullion, and amused himself by arranging the stew-pans in tones and semitones, upon which he would play various airs, to the utter dismay of the cook.

Lulli contributed greatly to the improvement of French music. He wrote several operas, and many compositions for the Church, all of which served to raise the standard of musical taste in France. To him also belongs the credit of having founded the French national opera.

We will now endeavour to trace the progress of the Violin in England. It is gratifying to learn that, even in the primitive age of Violin-playing, we were not without our national composers for the instrument. Dr. Benjamin Rogers wrote airs in four parts for Violins so early as 1653 (the year Corelli was born). John Jenkins wrote twelve sonatas for two Violins and a Bass, printed in London in 1660, which were the first sonatas written by an Englishman. About this date Charles II. established his band of twenty-four Violins. During his residence on the Continent he had frequent opportunities of hearing the leading instrument, and seems to have been so much impressed with its beauties that he set up for himself a similar band to that belonging to the French Court. The leader was Thomas Baltzar, who was regarded as the best player of his time. Anthony Wood met Baltzar at Oxford, and says he "saw him run up his fingers to the end of the finger-board of the Violin, and run them back insensibly, and all in alacrity and in very good time, which he nor any one in England saw the like before." Wood tells us that Baltzar "was buried in the cloister belonging to St. Peter's Church in Westminster." The emoluments attached to the Royal band, according to Samuel Pepys, appear to have been somewhat irregular. In the Diary, December 19, 1666, we read: "Talked of the King's family with Mr. Kingston, the organist. He says many of the musique are ready to starve, they being five years behindhand for their wages; nay, Evens, the famous man upon the Harp, having not his equal in the world, did the other day die for mere want, and was fain to be buried at the alms of the parish, and carried to his grave in the dark at night without one linke, but that Mr. Kingston met it by chance, and did give 12d. to buy two or three links."

The state of the Merry Monarch's exchequer in 1662, according to an extract from the Emoluments of the Audit Office, seems to have been singularly prosperous. An order runs as follows: "These are to require you to pay, or cause to be paid, to John Bannister, one of His Majesty's musicians in ordinary, the sum of forty pounds for two Cremona Violins, by him bought and delivered for His Majesty's service, as may appear by the bill annexed; and also ten pounds for strings for two years ending 24th June, 1662."

The King's band was led in 1663 by the above-named John Bannister, who was an excellent Violinist. His name is associated with the earliest concerts in England, namely, those held at "four of the clock in the afternoon" at the George Tavern, in Whitefriars. Roger North informs us the shopkeepers and others went to sing and "enjoy ale and tobacco," and the charge was one shilling and "call for what you please."

In the year 1683, Henry Purcell, organist of the Chapel Royal, published twelve sonatas for two Violins and a Bass. These famous instrumental compositions were written, the author tells us, in "just imitation of the most famed Italian masters, principally to bring the seriousness and gravity of that sort of musick into vogue." Purcell, in conformity with an age of dedications, thus addressed the Merry Monarch:—

"May it please your Majesty, I had not assum'd the confidence of laying ye following compositions at your sacred feet, but that, as they are the immediate results of your Majestie's Royal favour and benignity to me (which have made me what I am), so I am constrained to hope I may presume amongst others of your Majestie's over-obliged and altogether undeserving subjects that your Majesty will, with your accustomed clemency, vouchsafe to pardon the best endeavours of your Majestie's

"Most humble and obedient subject and servant,
"H. PURCELL."

Charles II. is said to have understood his notes, and to sing in (in the words of one who had sung with him) a plump bass, but that he only looked upon music as an incentive to mirth, not caring for any that he could not "stamp the time to." The endeavour of his accomplished and gifted young organist to lead the King and his people to admire what he terms "the seriousness and gravity" of Italian music, and "to loathe the levity and balladry of our neighbours," was indeed worthy of England's greatest musician.

In the year 1678, Thomas Britton, known as the "musical small-coal man," gave concerts in this country, and a long series it was, extending over a period of forty-six years. The shape the movement took was that of a musical club, which was maintained at Britton's expense.

The concert-room of Tom Britton was over his coal-shop in Aylesbury Street, leading from Clerkenwell Green to St. John Street. From the year 1678 to the time of his death, in 1714, the concerts of Britton were attended by persons of all ranks.

"Tho' mean thy rank, yet in thy humble cell,
Did gentle peace and arts unpurchased dwell.
Well pleased, Apollo thither led his train,
And Music warbled in her sweetest strain.
Cyllenius too, so fables tell, and Jove
Came willing guests to poor Philemon's grove.
Let useless pomp behold, and blush to find
So low a station, such a liberal mind."[3]

> [3] These verses were written by Mr. John Hughes, who was a frequent performer on the Violin at Britton's concerts. (Hawkins.)

Thus the first germ of the great musical societies gave a marked impulse to the culture of stringed music in England. Attention was turned to the subject; its humanising effects were recognised, and parties met in several places for the practice of chamber music. Our progress in Violin-playing at this date was clearly satisfactory. We had a Violinist named John Henry Eccles, belonging to a clever family of musicians. He became a member of the band of Louis XIV., and was regarded as an excellent player and musician. He published in Paris some solos for the Violin in 1720. His brother Thomas was also a good Violinist. Fortune, however, did not smile upon him. He is described as being one of those itinerant musicians—perhaps the last of them—who in winter evenings went to taverns, and for a slender subsistence bore the insults of those disinclined to listen to their performance. This order of itinerant musicians may be described as having descended from the Fiddling minstrels, whom the wealthy in earlier times often retained in their houses, giving them coats and badges bearing the family arms. These musicians, in place of amusing the nobility, ultimately attended wakes and fairs. They were sometimes retained at the large inns, where the guest while eating, an old English writer says, was "offered music, which he may freely take or refuse, and if he be solitary the musicians will give him the good day, with music in the morning." In Puritan times this class of musician was thought to have so much increased as to need a special act for their suppression, which gave rise to Butler's creation, the "Champion Crowdero." Returning to our subject with Thomas Eccles, we have the following interesting account of the unfortunate Violinist, by a musician: "It was about the month of November, 1753, that I, with some friends, were met to spend the evening at a tavern in the City, when this man, in a mean but decent garb, was introduced to us by the waiter; immediately upon opening the door I heard the twang of one of his strings from under his coat, which was accompanied by the question, 'Gentlemen, will you please to hear my music?' Our curiosity, and the modesty of the man's deportment, inclined us to say yes, and music he gave us, such as I had never heard before, nor shall again under the same circumstances. With as fine and delicate a hand as I ever heard, he played the whole fifth and ninth solos of Corelli, and two songs of Mr. Handel; in short, his performance was such as would command the attention of the nicest ear, and left us his auditors much at a loss to guess what it was that constrained him to seek his living in a way so disreputable. He made no secret of his name; he said he was the youngest of three brothers, and that Henry, the middle one, had been his master, and was then in the service of the King of France. He lodged in the Butcher Row, near Temple Bar, and was well known to the musicians of his time, who thought themselves disgraced by this practice of his, for which they have a term of reproach not very intelligible; they call it *going a-busking*."[4]

> 4 The term "busker" is still applied to musicians who perform outside public-houses, on steamboats, and elsewhere.

I have now to mention a Violinist whose talents raised the instrument greatly, particularly in England, viz., Francesco Geminiani. He was instructed by Corelli, and imbibed much of his master's breadth of style. He came to England in the year 1714. In 1716 he published a set of twelve sonatas, which attracted some notice at the time from their novelty. In these he plunged into difficulties deemed then very unusual, but withal his compositions were elegantly written. He afterwards wrote and published solos and concertos, besides a "Treatise on Good Taste," and the "Art of Playing on the Violin," the latter being the first instruction book for the instrument deserving of the name. The instrumental music at this period was composed for four Violins, Tenor, Violoncello, and Double-Bass, and was called the Concerto Grosso.

Having lightly sketched the progress of the Violin in England down to about the year 1750, it will, perhaps, be better to take the thread of the instrument's progress in Italy, which we brought to the days of Corelli.

The first half of the 18th century was rich in Italian Violinists and writers for the instrument, of whom the chief was Giuseppe Tartini, born 1692. Dr. Burney says of his compositions: "Though he made Corelli his model in the purity of his harmony and simplicity of his modulation, he greatly surpassed that composer in the fertility and originality of his invention; not only in the subjects of his melodies, but in the truly *cantabile* manner of treating them. Many of his *adagios* want nothing but *words* to be excellent pathetic opera songs. His *allegros* are sometimes difficult; but the passages fairly belong to the instrument for which they were composed, and were suggested by his consummate knowledge of the finger-board and the powers of the bow. As a harmonist he was, perhaps, more truly scientific than any other composer of his time, in the clearness, character, and precision of his Basses, which were never casual, or the effect of habit or auricular prejudice and expectation, but learned, judicious, and certain." It would be difficult to add to this judgment of the compositions of Tartini. The truth of Burney's remarks is better understood at this moment than when penned. During the space of nearly a century the sonatas of Tartini lay dormant, and only within recent years have their beauties been again recognised. Such works as Tartini's are all-important links in the chain of musical progress.

Pietro Locatelli, a pupil of Corelli, introduced a style of playing quite in advance of his time. His compositions abound with novel combinations; double stops, harmonics, and arpeggios are displayed with wonderful results. Burney says that "Locatelli had more hand, caprice, and fancy than any Violinist of his time."

The immediate follower of the style of Locatelli was Lolli, born 1728, who wrote pleasing airs and used novel effects, but failed to go further. It was one of his feats to play on one string—a performance very properly held in contempt in our day, having neither sense nor grace to recommend it.

Felice Giardini was another musician of the style of Locatelli.[5] He was born at Turin, in the year 1716. His performance at Naples and Berlin excited considerable notice. In 1742 he visited England, and created some sensation, his style being new to the British public.

> 5 In "Les Maîtres Classiques," edited by M. Alard, and the "Hohe Schule," edited by Ferdinand David, will be found some of the best examples of this composer, as well as of many others noticed here.

Boccherini probably did more towards furthering the cultivation of stringed instrument music than any composer of his day, with the exception of Haydn. There are in his compositions movements of varied styles, well written for their respective instruments. His quintettes are among his chief productions, and their elegance and brilliancy are remarkable. The part allotted to his own instrument, the Violoncello, often bristles with difficulties, and hence it is that these compositions are so seldom heard. Boccherini was the first composer who wrote quintettes with two Violoncello parts.

We now reach a stage in the history of the progress of the Violin the importance of which cannot be over-estimated; I refer to the influence which the compositions of Giovanni Battista Viotti exerted upon the cultivation of our instrument. With the famous Viotti sprang up a school of Violin-playing as marked in style as that introduced by Corelli. Viotti was a pupil of Pugnani, and owed his success to the rare teaching of that master. The sensation that Viotti created in Paris was great. His varied style, his rich tone and elegance in playing, were far beyond anything that the Parisian public had previously experienced. With Viotti was ushered in a new era in solo playing. His concertos exhibit the capabilities of the instrument in elegantly constructed passages, such as none but a master of the Violin could pen. He wrote upwards of twenty concertos, those in A minor, in G, in D, and in E minor being the favourites, and to this day highly esteemed by Violinists of every school. His duos and trios are pleasing and effective, and, though long since superseded by works of greater erudition, they form a landmark in the history of the progress of the instrument.

Campagnoli, born in 1751, was a composer of rare ability. Had he written nothing but the "Studies on the Seven Positions of the Violin" he would have left enough to mark the character of his genius. Happily he has bequeathed to us many other writings. The "Fantasias and Cadences," forming a book of upwards of 100 pages, is a work full of interest to the Violinist. His modulations are singularly effective. He has also written some Studies for the Tenor, and, lastly, a "Violin School." I cannot but think that Campagnoli's educational compositions do not receive the attention which they merit, and are too often laid aside as old-fashioned. There is a certain quaintness in his writings, but this much may be said of many other compositions whose beauties are not neglected on that account. It would be difficult to find material more solid than that afforded by the writings of Campagnoli, if the foundation of Violin-playing of the highest character is to be laid.

We reach the pinnacle of the Italian school of Violin-playing in the wondrous Paganini; born February 18, 1784, died May 27, 1840. It is needless to recount the extraordinary achievements of this remarkable man. M. Fétis and others have collected the most interesting particulars relative to Paganini and his compositions, and to their entertaining accounts the reader can turn for information. It is sufficient to mention that Paganini carried the marvellous in Violin-playing as far as seems possible. The number of his imitators has been enormous, and many of them, withal, so barbarous as to render anything savouring of "à la Paganini" contemptible. The compositions of Paganini are no longer Paganini's when played by others. He, above all Violinists that ever lived, possessed an individuality in his style of playing which has hitherto defied imitation.

From Paganini to his pupil Camillo Sivori is the next step in my notice. The artistic career of Sivori was a glorious one. Elegance of style and charming purity of tone were qualities peculiarly his.

Antonio Bazzini, both as a solo Violinist and composer for the instrument, has achieved lasting fame.

Having endeavoured to lightly sketch the history of Italian performers, and of Italian music bearing on the instrument to the present time, it remains to notice a remarkable follower of the Italian school of Violin-playing in the Norwegian, Ole Bornemann Bull. The executive skill of this famous Violinist was of the highest order, and perhaps no other artist, with the exception of Paganini, gained such a world-wide renown.

It is now necessary to refer to the course of events touching the Violin in France. As the influence of Viotti resulted in a remodelling of the French style of playing, our survey will make it necessary to go back the greater part of a century.

Jean Marie Leclair, the pupil of Somis, is the first Violinist deserving of mention. He was born at Lyons in 1697. In 1729 he visited Paris, where he was engaged at the opera. He wrote several sonatas for Violin and Bass, and for two Violins and Bass, besides other compositions. The difficulties occurring in many of these writings are of no ordinary character, and if they were rendered with anything approaching to exactness, the progress made on the Violin must have been very rapid between the days of Lulli and those of Leclair.

Pierre Gaviniès claims attention both as an executant and composer. There is a freshness about his compositions which has caused many of them to be recently roused from their long sleep, and re-issued in the improved garb of a modern edition. His best-known works are the twenty-four Studies, Concertos, and Sonatas.

Although there were several Violinists in France of average ability between the time of Gaviniès and that of Rode, they scarcely claim attention in this somewhat hasty sketch; and I will, therefore, pass to the players linked with Viotti to his pupil Rode. He was born at Bordeaux in 1774. Fétis remarks,

"From Corelli to Rode there is no *hiatus* in the school, for Corelli was the master of Somis, Somis of Pugnani, Pugnani of Viotti, and Viotti of Rode."

His twenty-four Caprices, and his Concertos and Airs, are much admired by all Violinists for their elegance and effectiveness. Paganini played the concertos of Rode publicly upon several occasions; Baillot and Kreutzer were associated with Rode at the Paris Conservatoire, and likewise in the compilation of the well-known Instruction Book written expressly for the use of the pupils at the Conservatoire. Baillot was famed for his admirable bowing and refined playing. Kreutzer is, of course, better known from his Forty Studies than from anything else that he has written. His concertos partake more of the study than of the name they bear, and are valued accordingly.

Lafont was instructed by both Rode and Kreutzer, and held a high position among the Violinists of his time.

François Antoine Habeneck was a pupil of Baillot at the Paris Conservatoire, where he distinguished himself, and became a professor. Among his pupils were Alard, Sainton, and Deldevez.

M. Alard was born in 1815. He succeeded Baillot at the Conservatoire in 1843, holding the position for many years, and retiring shortly after the death of his father-in-law, M. Vuillaume. M. Alard was the master of Sarasate. M. Sainton was born in 1813 at Toulouse. He took the first prize at the Conservatoire in 1834. He settled in London in 1845. Shortly afterwards he became principal professor of the Violin at the Royal Academy of Music, and leader under Signor Costa.

It now remains for me to notice the Belgian school. The first to name is Charles de Bériot, one of the most delicious players we have had. As a composer for his instrument, he opened up entirely fresh ground; he banished all that was dry, and gave us those fresh and pleasant Airs with Variations, and Morceaux de Salon, teeming with novel effects. It can never be said that De Bériot alarmed the amateurs with outrageous difficulties; on the contrary, he gave them passages comparatively easy to execute, full of effect, and yet withal *astonishing* to the listener. De Bériot probably made more amateur Violinists than any composer of his time.

Henri Vieuxtemps was a thorough master of his art. His Concertos are compositions worthy of the title they bear; they do not consist of a number of difficulties strung together without meaning, but are properly constructed works. He has written many Fantasias, all of which are the delight of good Violinists. His compositions being most difficult to render, they are chiefly known among artists, but in these days of rapid development in Violin-playing among amateurs, a new and wide field will certainly be opened for them.

From Belgium to Poland seems a wide step in my discourse, but it is really not so. Although the Polish Violinists retain much originality in their style of playing and compositions, it is to the French school that they belong. Lipinski, Wieniawski, and Lotto were all educated in the Paris school.

Lipinski has written a good deal for his instrument, and instructed many well-known players.

Henri Wieniawski was essentially a great artist. He was a marvellous Violinist, and displayed great genius as a composer for his instrument.

Adolphe Pollitzer settled in London many years since, and occupied a leading position among our resident Violinists.

Having lightly touched upon the various heads of the French school, I must again take up the thread of the English history of the instrument from about 1750, at which period we may trace a growing admiration for Violin-playing, notwithstanding the disparagement which this accomplishment received from different notabilities. Foremost among the revilers stands Lord Chesterfield, who considered playing upon any musical instrument to be illiberal in a gentleman. The Violin would seem to have been regarded by his lordship with a supreme amount of displeasure. His opinion of Violinists savoured greatly of that held by the framers of the statute passed in the reign of Elizabeth touching minstrels, who were to be included among "rogues, vagabonds, and sturdy beggars" wandering abroad. Lord Chesterfield says, "Music is usually reckoned one of the liberal arts, and not unjustly, but a man of fashion who is seen piping or Fiddling at a concert degrades his own dignity. If you love music, hear it; *pay Fiddlers to play for you, but never Fiddle yourself.*" Such was Lord Chesterfield's advice to his son. It is quite evident that he had no notion of the exquisite enjoyment derivable from being an executant in a quartette, the conversational powers of which have been so frequently noticed. That Lord Chesterfield's strictures discouraged the practice of the Violin in the higher circles of society is very probable, appearing as they do in a work which was held in the light of a textbook upon the conduct of a gentleman for some considerable time. Happily, the hollowness of much of his advice came to be recognised, and he who deemed cards and dice a necessary step towards fashionable perfection, and ordained that Fiddlers were to be paid to play for you as substitutes for your own personal degradation, came to be remembered, possibly, more on account of the laxity of his precepts than for any other reason.

In the days of Lord Chesterfield lived Michael Christian Festing, who was particularly zealous in the cause of music. He was a pupil of Geminiani, and wrote several solos. Festing still further carried out the idea of Britton, the "small-coal man," by bringing together a number of noblemen and gentlemen amateurs for the practice of concerted music. They met at the Crown and Anchor Tavern in the Strand, and named their society the "Philharmonic." So much for his furtherance of the art. It now remains to notice the great boon which Festing conferred upon his brother professors and their descendants. It is this which has given his memory lasting life in the annals of English music.

We are indebted to Festing as the chief instrument in the formation of the Royal Society of Musicians, which he may be said to have founded in the year 1738. This society derived its origin from the following curious circumstance. Festing being one day seated at the window of the Orange Coffee House, then at the corner of the Haymarket, observed a very intelligent-looking boy, who was driving an ass and selling brickdust. The lad was in a deplorable condition, and excited the pity of the kind-hearted musician, who made inquiries concerning him, and discovered that he was the son of an unfortunate professor of music. Struck with grief and mortification that the forlorn object before him should be the child of a brother musician, Festing resolved to attempt something for the boy's maintenance. Shortly after, with the help of other benevolently-disposed persons, he raised a fund for the support of decayed musicians and their families, and thus laid the foundation of the society, which is the first of its kind in Europe. Handel was one of its first and principal members, and left it a legacy of £1,000. Little did Festing and his supporters dream that their society, humble enough in 1738, would grow into a society possessing £80,000 in 1874—a sum which, however high-sounding, was all-insufficient to permit the committee to dispense the amount of good desired.

Returning again to our subject, we find that in Festing's lifetime there were several patrons of the art, the chief of whom were the Prince of Wales, the Duke of Cumberland, and the Earl of Mornington. Speaking of the Earl, the Hon. Daines Barrington says he "furnishes an instance of early attention to musical instruments. His father played well for a gentleman, on the Violin, which always delighted the child while in his nurse's arms, and long before he could speak." When he was nine years old, "an old portrait-painter came to the family seat, who was a very indifferent performer on the Violin, but persuaded the child that if he tried to play on that instrument, he would soon be able to bear a part in a concert. With this inducement he soon learned the two old catches of the 'Christ-Church Bells,' and 'Sing one, two, three, come follow me;' after which, his father and the painter accompanying him with the other two parts, he experienced the pleasing effects of a harmony to which he himself contributed. Soon after this he was able to play the second

Violin in Corelli's sonatas, which gave him a steadiness in time that never deserted him."

We may now glance at the period when Salomon came to England in 1781. Too much stress can scarcely be laid upon the good effected by Salomon's talents for the progress of music, and more particularly in behalf of instrumental music. We are deeply indebted to this musician for the spirit and enterprise which he displayed, in bringing to England, at no trifling pecuniary risk, the immortal Haydn. Salomon having established a series of twenty concerts in 1790, it occurred to him that to invite the famous musician to London would aid his enterprise. He communicated with Haydn, offering him the sum of fifty pounds for each concert. These terms were accepted, and Haydn set out for London, at the age of fifty-nine. He remained in England over a year, and composed the celebrated "Twelve Symphonies" known as the Salomon set. Salomon was one of the promoters of the Philharmonic Society, and led the orchestra at the first concert given by the society in 1813. Enough has been said to show the nature of the part he took in the development of music in England. Enjoying the friendship of those who moved in the higher circles of society, where his polished manners and high attainments ever made him a welcome guest, he was enabled to command such patronage as to make his laudable ventures successful.

Among the Violinists of Salomon's day, resident in England, were William and François Cramer, to whom severally were assigned the leadership of the Ancient Concerts and of the Opera.

The next Violinist who gained some celebrity was Nicholas Mori, born in London in the year 1796. He was associated with the formation of the Royal Academy of Music, in Tenterden Street, and became the principal instructor on the Violin at that institution. Paolo Diana (a Cremonese known under his adopted name of Spagnoletti) and Kieswetter each contributed his share towards the advancement of the instrument during their stay in this country.

The names of Dando and Henry Blagrove bring us to the players of our own time. These thoroughly representative English Violinists have done much to raise the standard of the public taste. In the year 1835, the "Concerti da Camera" were established (in imitation of those given in Paris by Pierre Baillot), and served to extend our knowledge of classical chamber music. The formation of the Musical Union still further increased our knowledge and taste in the same direction. The long roll of celebrated Continental artists introduced at the Society's concerts sufficiently stamps its character. All that remained to be done was to make the Quartette popular, and to bring it within the reach of all. This has been achieved by the indefatigable labours of Mr. Chappell in his *Monday Popular Concerts*. For some time the public failed to appreciate Mr. Chappell's scheme, but the enterprising director, nothing daunted, continued his course, and had ultimately the gratification of being besieged in his citadel at St. James's Hall, from the commencement of the season to its close.

Before closing our remarks on the progress of Violin-playing in England, we have still to mention a few other names in connection with this subject. Henry C. Cooper was a Violinist who ranked with the chief representatives of the English Soloists, and during a long professional career achieved much success. He set on foot, together with his coadjutors, M. Sainton, Hill, and Signor Piatti, the Quartette Association, the concerts of which were given at Willis's Rooms during several seasons. The career of Mr. John Carrodus was watched by his brother artists with much interest. As a pupil of Herr Molique, he gave early signs of exceptional talents; it was felt that he must inevitably come to the front; all that was predicted, and even more, in due time came to pass. He achieved a commanding position among the foremost Violinists of our time, both as a soloist and leader. With the names of Messrs. Henry and Alfred Holmes, I come to a close of the English branch of the subject. The brothers Holmes attracted the notice of Spohr, who was so delighted with their abilities that he composed and dedicated to them three Duets for two Violins.

The first name of any note in connection with the Violin in Germany is that of Graun, who was born in the year 1700. He became concertmaster to the King of Prussia, and excelled as a Violinist. His pupil, Francis Benda, next claims attention. Dr. Burney says of him: "His manner was neither that of Tartini nor of Veracini, nor that of any other leader; it was purely his own, though founded on the several models of the greatest masters;" and Hillar tells us that "his tones were of the finest description, the clearest and most euphonious that can be imagined." Benda published studies for his instrument, and also several solos and other works, all of which are admired for their good and *cantabile* style.

About this period appeared the admirable compositions for the Violin of that great master of his art, John Sebastian Bach—works differing essentially from those of his contemporaries.

"He was not of an age, but for all time."

To describe the character and beauties of Bach's Violin writings is within neither my province nor capacity. As an amateur Violinist and an observer of all that relates to the Violin, I may refer, however, to the vast amount of good which the compositions of Bach have exercised upon the cultivation of Violin-playing, and the marvellous development that they have received at the hands of many of our leading Violinists. For this happy state of things we are largely indebted to Herr Joachim; but for him these treasures might have remained hidden behind a cloud of *airs variés*, fantasias, and what not, for many a year to come. Herr Joachim has made the Sonatas of Bach familiar to thousands who a few years since scarcely knew of their existence. The difficulties which abound in these solid writings could only have been written by a master perfectly acquainted with the capabilities of the instrument. Many a tyro who plunges into the stream of Bach's crotchets and quavers soon finds himself encompassed by a whirlpool of seeming impossibilities, and is frequently heard to exclaim that the passages are impracticable. Vain delusion! Bach was himself a Violinist, and never penned a passage the rendering of which is impossible. The ease and grace with which a Joachim makes every note heard and felt, induces many a one to wrestle with Bach, the more so when it is found that the great author has confined himself to the lower positions of the instrument. Vain delusion number two! Bach exacts more on *terra firma* than many later writers have claimed in their wildest aerial flights.

From Bach to Handel is an easy step in our discourse. They were born within a year of each other, and were possessed of minds of similar calibre, though differently exercised. It would not, perhaps, be over-strained to call them respectively the Nelson and Wellington of music. The compositions of Handel materially advanced the Violin. His Overtures, Trios, Sonatas, and Concertos, were all received with the utmost attention, and led on to works by later composers, which would probably have never existed but for Handel's example.

We now reach the time when the Symphony was perfected by Haydn, who, following the steps of Bach, brought this branch of the art to a degree of perfection hitherto unknown. The influence of this composer on the progress of the Violin cannot be over-estimated. The Quartettes of Haydn are too well known to need more than mention here. The Quartettes of Giardini and Pugnani were laid aside to give place to these inspired compositions. The following amusing comparison, drawn by a lady, between the Quartettes of Haydn and the speech of articulate humanity appears in Bombet's "Letters on Haydn," and, though pretty well known, will lose nothing by repetition:—

"In listening to the Quartettes of Haydn, this lady felt as if present at a conversation of four agreeable persons. She thought that the first Violin had the air of an eloquent man of genius, of middle age, who supported a conversation, the subject of which he had suggested. In the second Violin she recognised a friend of the first, who sought by all possible means to display him to advantage, seldom thought of himself, and kept up the conversation rather by assenting to what was said by the others than by advancing any ideas of his own. The Alto was a grave, learned, and sententious man. He supported the discourse of the first Violin by laconic maxims, striking for their truth. The Bass was a worthy old lady, rather inclined to chatter, who said nothing of much consequence, and while she was talking the other interlocutors had time to breathe. It was, however, evident that she had a secret inclination for the Alto, which she preferred to the other instruments."

It may be said that the foregoing extract is more funny than just. Probably this is the case; however, I make use of it as throwing some light on the enjoyment derivable from listening to a Quartette, without reference to its critical bearings.

Resuming our subject again: Haydn wrote eight easy Sonatas for Violin and Pianoforte, but they are not of sufficient importance to cause them to be much played. Haydn used frequently to take the Tenor parts in his Quartettes.

Leopold Mozart, born in 1719, the father of the illustrious musician, was a Violinist, and wrote a "Method" for his instrument. He died in 1787.

To the great Mozart Violinists owe much; his compositions for the instrument raised its standing considerably. It is unnecessary to give here a detailed list of those of his writings in which the Violin takes part—they are happily known to most players. Mozart played the Violin from boyhood, and was taught by his father. It is gratifying to know that nearly all the great composers played upon stringed instruments, if not with proficiency, yet enough to enable them to make pleasurable use of their acquirements. Sebastian Bach, Handel, and Schubert were Violin-players; Haydn and Mendelssohn could take their Tenor part in a Quartette; and lastly, Beethoven used to amuse himself with the Double-Bass. Their compositions evidence a practical knowledge of stringed instruments, as distinct from theory. The glorious compositions of Beethoven for the Violin need no comment here; their beauties have formed the theme of the ablest critics; and I have no desire to contribute my humble mite to their exhaustive remarks.

With Fesca we again come amongst the Violinists. He was born at Magdeburg, in 1789. His Quartettes are very pleasing compositions; they are chiefly "Solo Quartettes."

The next Violinist claiming attention is the highly gifted Louis Spohr, the greatest composer for the Violin that ever lived, who combined in his own person high executive powers with a rare fecundity of classical composition. The Concertos of Spohr belong to an entirely different class from those of Viotti, Kreutzer, and others, inasmuch as Spohr's music is written so as not only to display the beauties of the instrument, but also to give the noblest specimens of its orchestration. His Duets for two Violins, his Tenor and

Violin Duets and Quartettes, are all too well known to need more than passing mention.

From Spohr has grown up a school of Violin-playing of a very distinctive character. Bernard Molique was endowed with great powers, both as a performer and a composer for his instrument. His Concertos are compositions of the highest character, and require for their rendering a finished artist.

Joseph Mayseder was a Violinist of an order distinct from that of Spohr or Molique. His style was exceedingly brilliant. Mayseder may also be said to have created a school of his own, and, owing to the circulation that his compositions obtained in England, his style was introduced among a great number of our countrymen. Kalliwoda wrote and played very much in the Mayseder manner. His Airs and Variations are especially brilliant compositions; his Overtures are also much admired for their sparkling and dramatic character.

I come now to notice one of the greatest artistes of our time—Herr Ernst—whose playing was impassioned in the highest degree. He made the Violin express his innermost thoughts in tones of delicious tenderness, such as his hearers can never forget. By nature noble, generous, and affectionate, the shade and substance of each trait was faithfully reflected in his exquisite playing. His compositions are among the finest solo writings we have. To mention his "Otello," "Airs Hongrois," "Le Prophète," and his "Studies," will be sufficient to call to the mind of most Violinists the high character of his compositions.

It now only remains for me to briefly allude to the German artists each Concert Season makes us familiar with. First and foremost, the mighty Herr Joachim, a host in himself. His able coadjutor, Herr Strauss, was justly admired for his intellectual rendering of the great masters, and the artistic spirit he invariably displayed. Herr Wilhelmj was regarded as one of the first players of our time, his executive powers being of the highest order.

SECTION XV

Anecdotes and Miscellanea connected with the Violin

"The Squire, in state, rode on before,
. . . . . .
The Trophy-Fiddle, and the case
Leaning on shoulder, like a mace."

HUDIBRAS AND THE CHAMPION CROWDERO.

The important part played by the renowned Champion Crowdero in Butler's inimitable satire has never failed to give keen enjoyment to all lovers of wit and humour. This being so, his exploits should be doubly appreciated by the votaries of the Fiddle, since it was he who valiantly defended the cause of Fiddling against the attacks of Hudibras—

"When civil dudgeon first grew high,
And men fell out, they knew not why;
When hard words, jealousies, and fears
Set folks together by the ears,
And made them fight, like mad or drunk.
. . . . . .
Then did Sir Knight abandon dwelling,
And out he rode a-colonelling."

The absurdities into which the genius of Cervantes hurried Don Quixote and Sancho served to moderate the extravagances of knight-errantry. The adventures of Hudibras and Ralpho, undertaken to extinguish the sports and pastimes of the people, aided greatly in staying the hand of fanaticism, which had suppressed all stage plays and interludes as "condemned by ancient heathens, and by no means to be tolerated among professors of the Christian religion."

With Crowdero we are taken back upwards of two centuries in the history of the Violin; from times wherein it is held in the highest esteem and admiration, to days when it was regarded with contempt and ridicule. Crowdero (so called from *crowd*, a Fiddle) was the fictitious name for one Jackson, a milliner, who lived in the New Exchange, in the Strand. He had served with the Roundheads, and lost a leg, which brought him into reduced circumstances, until he was obliged to Fiddle from one alehouse to another for his existence. Hudibras—

"On stirrup-side, he gaz'd about
Portending blood, like blazing star,
The beacon of approaching war.
. . . . .
Ralpho rode on, with no less speed
Than Hugo in the forest did;
But far more in returning made,
For now the foe he had survey'd
Rang'd, as to him they did appear,
With van, main battle, wings, and rear.
I' th' head of all this warlike rabble,
Crowdero marched, expert and able.
Instead of trumpet and of drum,
That makes the warrior's stomach come,
Whose noise whets valour sharp, like beer
By thunder turn'd to vinegar;
(For if a trumpet sound, or drum beat,
Who has not a month's mind to combat?)
A squeaking engine he apply'd
Unto his neck on north-east side,[1]
Just where the hangman does dispose,
To special friends, the knot or noose;
For 'tis great grace, when statesmen straight
Dispatch a friend, let others wait.
His warped ear hung o'er the strings,
Which was but souse to chitterlings;[2]
For guts, some write, ere they are sodden,

Are fit for music, or for pudding;[3]
From whence men borrow ev'ry kind
Of minstrelsy, by string or wind.
His grisly beard was long and thick,
With which he strung his Fiddle-stick;
For he to horse-tail scorned to owe
For what on his own chin did grow.

. . . . .

And now the field of death, the lists,
Were enter'd by antagonists,
And blood was ready to be broach'd,
When Hudibras in haste approach'd
With Squire and weapons, to attack 'em;
But first thus from his horse bespoke 'em,
'What rage, O citizens! What fury
Doth you to these dire actions hurry?

. . . . .

In name of King and Parliament
I charge ye all—no more foment.

. . . . .

           ... first surrender
The Fiddler as the prime offender,
Th' incendiary vile, that is chief
Author and engineer of mischief;
That makes division between friends
For profane and malignant ends.[4]
He and that engine of vile noise
On which illegally he plays,[5]
Shall (*dictum factum*) both be brought
To condign punishment, as they ought.'

. . . . .

This said he clapped his hand on sword,
To show he meant to keep his word.

. . . . .

He drew up all his force into
One body and into one blow.

. . . . .

The Knight, with all its weight, fell down

. . . . .

Like a feather bed betwixt a wall
And heavy brunt of cannon ball.

. . . . .

Crowdero only kept the field,

Not stirring from the place he held;
Though beaten down and wounded sore,
I' th' Fiddle, and a leg that bore
One side of him—not that of bone,
But much its better, th' wooden one.
He spying Hudibras lie strew'd
Upon the ground, like log of wood,
. . . . .

In haste he snatch'd the wooden limb
That, hurt in th' ankle, lay by him,
And, fitting it for sudden fight,
Straight drew it up, t' attack the Knight;
. . . . .

Vowing to be reveng'd, for breach
Of Crowd and skin, upon the wretch,[6]
Sole author of all detriment
He and his Fiddle underwent.
. . . . .

When Ralpho thrust himself between,
He took the blow upon his arm,
To shield the Knight from further harm,
And, joining wrath with force, bestow'd
On th' wooden member such a load,
That down it fell and with it bore
Crowdero, whom it propp'd before.
To him the Squire right nimbly run,
And setting his bold foot upon
His trunk, thus spoke: 'What desp'rate frenzy
Made thee, thou whelp of sin, to fancy
Thyself, and all that coward rabble,
To encounter us in battle able?
How durst th', I say, oppose thy curship
'Gainst, arms, authority, and worship,
And Hudibras or me provoke,
. . . . .

       ... but first our care
Must see how Hudibras doth fare.'
This said, he gently rais'd the Knight,
. . . . .

To rouse him from lethargic dump,
He tweak'd his nose with gentle thump,
Knock'd on his breast, as if't had been
To raise the spirits lodg'd within;

They, waken'd with the noise, did fly
From inward room to window eye,
And gently op'ning lid, the casement,
Look'd out, but yet with some amazement.
This gladded Ralpho much to see,
Who thus bespoke the Knight; quoth he,
Tweaking his nose, 'You are, great sir,
A self-denying conqueror;
As high, victorious, and great
As e'er fought for the churches yet.

. . . . . .

... The foe, for dread
Of your nine-worthiness, is fled;
All, save Crowdero, for whose sake
You did th' espous'd cause undertake;
And he lies pris'ner at your feet,
To be disposed as you think meet,
Either for life, or death, or sale,
The gallows, or perpetual jail;
For one wink of your powerful eye
Must sentence him to live or die;
His Fiddle is your proper purchase,
Won in the service of the Churches;
And by your doom must be allow'd
To be or be no more, a *Crowd*.'

. . . . . .

... The Knight began to rouse,
And by degrees grew valorous;
He stared about, and seeing none
Of all his foes remain, but one,
He snatch'd his weapon that lay near him,
And from the ground began to rear him,
Vowing to make Crowdero pay
For all the rest that ran away.
But Ralpho now, in colder blood,
His fury mildly thus withstood.
'Great sir,' quoth he, 'your mighty spirit
Is raised too high; this slave doth merit
To be the hangman's business sooner
Than from your hand to have the honour
Of his destruction; I, that am
A nothingness in deed and name,
Did scorn to hurt his forfeit carcase,

Or ill entreat his Fiddle or case;
. . . . .

Will you employ your conq'ring sword
To break a Fiddle, and your word?
. . . . .

    ... I think it better far
To keep him prisoner of war.'
. . . . .

He liked the squire's advice, and soon
Resolved to see the business done.
. . . . .

Ralpho dispatched with speedy haste,
And having ty'd Crowdero fast,
He gave Sir Knight the end of cord,
To lead the captive of his sword.
. . . . .

The Squire in state rode on before,
And on his nut-brown whinyard bore
The Trophy-Fiddle, and the case
Leaning on shoulder, like a mace.[7]
The Knight himself did after ride,
Leading Crowdero by his side,
And tow'd him if he lagg'd behind,
Like boat against the tide and wind.
Thus grave and solemn they march on,
Until quite thro' the town th' had gone,
At further end of which there stands
An ancient castle, that commands[8]
Th' adjacent parts; in all the fabric
You shall not see one stone nor a brick
But all of wood, by powerful spell
Of magic made impregnable.
. . . . .

Thither arriv'd, th' advent'rous Knight
And bold Squire from their steeds alight
At th' outward wall, near which there stands
A bastile, built t' imprison hands;
. . . . .

On top of this there is a spire
On which Sir Knight first bids the Squire
The Fiddle, and its spoils, the case,[9]
In manner of a trophy, place.
That done, they ope the trapdoor gate,

And let Crowdero down thereat;
Crowdero making doleful face,
Like hermit poor in pensive place.
To dungeon they the wretch commit,
And the survivor of his feet,
But the other that had broke the peace
And head of knighthood, they release,
Though a delinquent false and forged,
Yet b'ing a stranger, he's enlarged,
While his comrade that did not hurt
Is clapp'd up fast in prison for't;
So Justice, while she winks at crimes,
Stumbles on innocence sometimes."

1 Several explanations of this passage have been set forth by Butler's commentators. Dr. Grey asks, "Why the north-

east side? Do Fiddlers always, or most generally, stand or sit according to the points of the compass?" Dr. Nash suggests the poet may have had in view "a conceit," which is in Brown's "Vulgar Errors," viz., that the body of man is magnetical, and being placed in a boat will never rest till the head respecteth the north. Dr. Nash remarks, "Now, the body lying on its back with its head towards the north, or standing upright with the face towards the east, the reader will find the place of the Fiddle on the left breast to be due north-east."

2 Dr. Nash says, "Souse is the pig's ear, and chitterlings the pig's guts; the former alludes to Crowdero's ear, which lay on the Fiddle; the latter to the strings of the Fiddle, which are made of catgut."

3 Black pudding and sausages are placed in skins of gut.

4 This passage evidently refers to Violists meeting to make division to a ground, namely, in the words of Christopher Simpson, "A ground, subject, or bass (call it which you please) is prickt (written) down in two several papers, one for him who is to play the ground (upon an organ, harpsichord, or other instrument), the other for him who plays upon the Viol, who having the said ground before his eye (as his theme or subject) plays such variety of descant and division thereupon as his skill and present invention do then suggest to him." The poet's allusion to "Th' incendiary vile (Viol) that is chief author and engineer of mischief" humorously points to the popularity of the Viol. The poet's mention of persons meeting and performing on their Viols, thus making

> "   ... division between friends,
> For profane and malignant ends,"

is evidently a most humorous allusion to the case of the Royalist, Sir Roger L'Estrange, the friend of Butler, and to whom was given the names of the real persons shadowed under fictitious characters in the satire. Sir Roger, whilst in St. James's Park, heard an Organ being played in the house of one Mr. Hickson. His intense love of music prompted him to seek admittance. He found there a company of five or six persons, and being himself a good Violist, was prevailed upon to take a part. By-and-by Cromwell entered, without, Sir Roger explains in a pamphlet ("Truth and

Loyalty Vindicated," printed the year before the first part of Hudibras was published, in 1662), "the least colour of a design or expectation." Sir Roger went on making division with his Viol, apparently regardless of the presence of the Protector and thus earned for himself the title of Oliver's Fiddler, besides giving rise to the report that he solicited a private conference with Cromwell under the pretext of "making division" with his Viol. Dr. Johnson has truly said of Hudibras, "The manners, being founded on opinions, are temporary and local, and therefore become every day less intelligible and less striking.... Much, therefore, of that humour which transported the century with merriment is lost to us, who do not know the sour solemnity, the sullen superstition, the gloomy moroseness, and the stubborn scruples of the ancient Puritans, ... and cannot, but by recollection and study, understand the lines in which they are satirised. Our grandfathers knew the picture from the life; we judge of the life by contemplating the picture."

5 Alluding to an ordinance made in 1658: "And be it further enacted by the authority aforesaid, that if any person or persons, commonly called Fiddlers, or minstrels, shall at any time after the said first day of July (1657) be taken playing, Fiddling, and making music in any inn, alehouse, or tavern, or shall be taken proffering themselves, or desiring, or intreating any person or persons to hear them play, &c., &c., shall be adjudged ... rogues, vagabonds, and sturdy beggars."

6 Crowd, a Fiddle, and therefore for injury done by "breach," or cracks, to Crowdero's instrument.

7 The Fiddle-case referred to is one covered with leather, studded with nails, and with a lid opening at the end, and might be likened unto a mace.

8 "This is an enigmatical description of a pair of stocks and whipping-post. It is so pompous and sublime that we are surprised so noble a structure could be raised from so ludicrous a subject. We perceive wit and humour in the strongest light in every part of the description."—*Note by Dr. Grey.*

9 Dr. Nash suggests the following rendering: "His spoils, the Fiddle, and the case."

GEORGE HERBERT'S REFERENCES TO MUSIC.

George Herbert, poet and divine, said of music, "That it did relieve his drooping spirits, compose his distracted thoughts, and raised his weary soul so far above earth, that it gave him an earnest of the joys of heaven before he possessed them." His worthy biographer, Izaak Walton, tells us—"His chiefest recreation was music, in which heavenly art he was a most excellent master, and did himself compose many divine hymns and anthems, which he set and sung to his Lute or Viol; and though he was a lover of retiredness, yet his love to music was such that he went usually twice every week, on certain appointed days, to the Cathedral Church in Salisbury, and at his return would say, 'That his time spent in prayer and Cathedral music elevated his soul, and was his heaven upon earth.' But before his return thence to Bemerton, he would usually sing and play his part at an appointed private music meeting; and, to justify this practice, he would often say, 'Religion does not banish mirth, but only moderates and sets rules to it.'"

In walking to Salisbury upon one occasion to attend his usual music meeting, George Herbert saw a poor man with a poor horse that was fallen under his load. He helped the man to unload and re-load; the poor man blessed him for it, and he blessed the poor man. Upon reaching his musical friends at Salisbury they were surprised to see him so soiled and discomposed; but he told them the occasion, and when one of the company said to him "He had disparaged himself by so dirty an employment," his answer was, "That the thought of what he had done would prove music to him at midnight; and that the omission of it would have upbraided and made discord in his conscience whenever he should pass by that place; 'for if I be bound to pray for all that be in distress, I am sure that I am bound, so far as it is in my power, to practise what I pray for; and though I do not wish for the like occasion every day, yet let me tell you, I would not willingly pass one day of my life without comforting a sad soul, or showing mercy; and I praise God for this occasion; and now let us tune our instruments.'"

Herbert's love of imagery was often curious and startling. In singing of "Easter" he said—

"Awake my lute and struggle for thy part
        With all thy heart.
The Cross taught all wood to resound His name,
        Who bore the same.
His stretched sinews taught all strings, what key
Is best to celebrate this most high day,
Consort both heart and lute, and twist a song

>   Pleasant and long:
> Or since all music is but three parts vied
>   And multiplied,
> O let thy blessed spirit bear a part,
> And make up our defects with his sweet art."

The Sunday before the death of "Holy George Herbert," Izaak Walton says, "he rose suddenly from his bed, or couch, called for one of his instruments, took it into his hand and said—

> "My God, my God, my music shall find Thee;
>   And every string
> Shall have his attribute to sing."

And having tuned it, he played and sung—

> "The Sundays of man's life,
>   Threaded together on Time's string,
> Make bracelets to adorn the wife
>   Of the eternal, glorious King;
> On Sundays heaven's door stands ope,
>   Blessings are plentiful and ripe,
> More plentiful than hope."

The thought to which Herbert has given expression in his lines on Easter—that "All music is but three parts vied and multiplied"—was also in the mind of Christopher Simpson, who, in his work on "The Division Viol," 1659, uses it as a musical illustration of the doctrine of Trinity in Unity. He says: "I cannot but wonder, even to amazement, that from no more than three concords (with some intervening discords) there should arise such an infinite variety, as all the music that ever has been, or ever shall be, composed. When I further consider that these sounds, placed by the interval of a third one above another, do constitute one entire harmony, which governs and comprises all the sounds that by art or imagination can be joined together in musical concordance, *that*, I cannot but think a significant emblem of that Supreme and Incomprehensible Three in One, governing, comprising, and disposing the whole machine of the world, with all its included parts, in a most perfect and stupendous harmony."

It is interesting to notice an earlier and remarkable allusion to the union of sound from the pen of Shakespeare—

> "If the true concord of well-tuned sounds,
>   By unions married, do offend thine ear,
> They do but sweetly chide thee, who confounds

In singleness the parts that thou shouldst bear.
Mark how one string, sweet husband to another,
    Strikes each in each by mutual ordering,
Resembling sire and child and happy mother,
    Who, all in one, one pleasing note do sing."

VIOLINS FROM A MEDICAL POINT OF VIEW.

"Music and the sounds of instruments—says the lively Vigneul de Marville—contribute to the health of the body and the mind; they assist the circulation of the blood, they dissipate vapours, and open the vessels, so that the action of perspiration is freer. He tells the story of a person of distinction, who assured him that once being suddenly seized by violent illness, instead of a consultation of physicians, he immediately called a band of musicians, and their Violins played so well in his inside that his bowels became perfectly in tune, and in a few hours were harmoniously becalmed."—*D'Israeli's "Curiosities of Literature."*

Dr. Abercrombie recommends "Careful classification of the insane, so that the mild and peaceful melancholic may not be harassed by the ravings of the maniac. The importance of this is obvious; but of still greater importance," he continues, "it will probably be to watch the first dawnings of reason, and instantly to remove from the patient all associates by whom his mind might be again bewildered."

The following case, mentioned by Pinel, is certainly an extreme one, but much important reflection arises out of it:—

"A musician confined in the Bicêtre, as one of the first symptoms of returning reason, made some slight allusion to his favourite instrument. It was immediately procured for him; he occupied himself with music for several hours every day, and his convalescence seemed to be advancing rapidly. But he was then, unfortunately, allowed to come frequently in contact with a furious maniac, by meeting him in the gardens. The musician's mind was unhinged; *his Violin was destroyed;* and he fell back into a state of insanity which was considered as confirmed and hopeless."—*Abercrombie's "Intellectual Powers."*

"A MUSICIAN

is like an Echo, a retail dealer in sounds. As Diana is the goddess of the silver bow, so is he the Lord of the wooden one; he has a hundred strings in his bow; other people are bow-*legged*, he is bow-*armed*; and though armed with a bow he has no skill in archery. He plays with *cat*-gut and *Kit*-Fiddle. His fingers and arms run a constant race; the former would run away from him did not a bridge interpose and oblige him to pay toll. He can distinguish sounds as other men distinguish colours. His companions are crotchets and quavers. Time will never be a match for him, for he *beats* him most unmercifully. He runs after an Italian air open-mouthed, with as much eagerness as some fools have sought the philosopher's stone. He can bring a tune over the seas, and thinks it more excellent because far-fetched. His most admired domestics are Soprano, Siciliano, Andantino, and all the Anos and Inos that constitute the musical science. He can scrape, scratch, shake, diminish, increase, flourish, &c.; and he is so delighted with the sound of his own Viol, that an ass would sooner lend his ears to anything than to him; and as a dog shakes a pig, so does he shake a note *by the ear*, and never lets it go till he makes it squeak. He is a walking pillory, and crucifies more ears than a dozen standing ones. He often involves himself in dark and intricate passages, till he is put to a *shift*, and obliged to get out of a *scrape*—by scraping. His Viol has the effect of a *Scotch* Fiddle, for it irritates his hearers, and puts them to the itch. He tears his audience in various ways, as I do this subject; and as I wear away my pen, so does he wear away the strings of his Fiddle. There is no medium to him; he is either in a flat or a sharp key, though both are *natural* to him. He deals in third minors, and major thirds; proves a turncoat, and is often in the majority and the minority in the course of a few minutes. He runs over the *flat* as often as any Newmarket racehorse; both meet the same fate, as they usually terminate in a *cadence*; the difference is—one is driven by the *whip-hand*, the other by the *bow-arm*; one deals in *stakado*, the other in *staccato*. As a thoroughbred hound discovers, by instinct, his game from all other animals, so an experienced musician *feels* the compositions of Handel or Corelli.—Yours, TIMOTHY CATGUT, Stamford."—*Monthly Mirror.*

ORIGIN OF TARTINI'S "DEVIL'S SONATA."

The following interesting account of this marvellous composition was given by Tartini to M. de Lalande, the celebrated astronomer:—

"One night in the year 1713, I dreamed that I had made a compact with his Satanic Majesty, by which he was received into my service. Everything succeeded to the utmost of my desire, and my every wish was anticipated by this my new domestic. I thought that on taking up my Violin to practise, I jocosely asked him if he could play on that instrument. He answered that he believed he was able to pick out a tune; and then, to my astonishment, began to play a sonata, so strange and yet so beautiful, and executed in so masterly a manner, that I had never in my life heard anything so exquisite. So great was my amazement that I could scarcely breathe. Awakened by the violent emotion, I instantly seized my Violin, in the hope of being able to catch some part of the ravishing melody which I had just heard, but all in vain. The piece which I composed according to my scattered recollection is, it is true, the best of my works. I have called it the 'Sonata del Diavolo,' but it is so far inferior to the one I heard in my dream, that I should have dashed my Violin into a thousand pieces, and given up music for ever, had it been possible to deprive myself of the enjoyments which I derive from it."

In the "Reminiscences of Michael Kelly" we are told that in the year 1779 Kelly was at Florence, and that he was present at a concert given at the residence of Lord Cowper, where, he says, he had "the gratification of hearing a sonata on the Violin played by the great Nardini; though very far advanced in years, he played divinely. Lord Cowper requested him to play the popular sonata, composed by his master, Tartini, called the 'Devil's Sonata.' Mr. Jackson, an English gentleman present, asked Nardini whether the anecdote relative to this piece of music was true. Nardini answered that 'he had frequently heard Tartini relate the circumstance,' and at once gave an account of the composition, in accordance with that furnished by M. de Lalande."

DR. JOHNSON AND THE VIOLIN.

"Dr. Johnson was observed by a musical friend of his to be extremely inattentive at a concert, whilst a celebrated solo-player was running up the divisions and sub-divisions of notes upon his Violin. His friend, to induce him to take greater notice of what was going on, told him how extremely difficult it was. 'Difficult do you call it, sir?' replied the Doctor; 'I wish it were *impossible.*'"—*Seward's "Anecdotes of Dr. Johnson."*

"In the evening our gentleman farmer and two others entertained themselves and the company with a great number of tunes on the Fiddle. Johnson desired to have 'Let ambition fire thy mind' played over again, and appeared to give a patient attention to it; though he owned to me that he was very insensible to the power of music. I told him that it affected me to such a degree, as often to agitate my nerves painfully, producing in my mind alternate sensations of pathetic dejection, so that I was ready to shed tears; and of daring resolution, so that I was inclined to rush into the thickest part of the battle. 'Sir,' said he, 'I should never hear it if it made me such a fool.'"— Boswell's *"Life of Johnson."*

DR. JOHNSON ON THE DIFFICULTY OF PLAYING THE FIDDLE.

"*Goldsmith*: 'I spoke of Mr. Harris, of Salisbury, as being a very learned man, and in particular an eminent Grecian.'

"*Johnson*: 'I am not sure of that. His friends give him out as such, but I know not who of his friends are able to judge of it.'

"*Goldsmith*: 'He is what is much better; he is a worthy, humane man.'

"*Johnson*: 'Nay, sir, that is not to the purpose of our argument; that will as much prove that he can play upon the Fiddle as well as Giardini, as that he is an eminent Grecian.'

"*Goldsmith*: 'The greatest musical performers have but small emoluments; Giardini, I am told, does not get above seven hundred a year.'

"*Johnson*: 'That is indeed but little for a man to get, who does best that which so many endeavour to do. There is nothing, I think, in which the power of art is shown so much as in playing on the Fiddle. In all other things we can do something at first; any man will forge a bar of iron if you give him a hammer; not so well as a smith, but tolerably; and make a box, though a clumsy one; but give him a Fiddle and a Fiddlestick, and he can do nothing.'"—*Boswell's* "*Life of Johnson.*"

DR. JOHNSON'S EPITAPH ON PHILLIPS, THE WELSH VIOLINIST.

Johnson and Garrick were sitting together, when among other things Garrick repeated an epitaph upon Phillips, by a Dr. Wilkes, which was very commonplace, and Johnson said to Garrick, "I think, Davy, I can make a better." Then, stirring about his tea for a little while in a state of meditation, he, almost extempore, produced the following verses:—

"Phillips, whose touch harmonious could remove
  The pangs of guilty power or hapless love;
  Rest here, distress'd by poverty no more;
  Here find that calm thou gav'st so oft before;
  Sleep undisturbed within this peaceful shrine,
  Till angels wake thee with a note like thine!"

Boswell says, "Mr. Garrick appears not to have recited the verses correctly, the original being as follows. One of the various readings is remarkable, and it is the germ of Johnson's concluding line:—

"Exalted soul, thy various sounds could please
  The love-sick virgin, and the gouty ease;
  Could jarring *crowds*, like old Amphion, move
  To beauteous order and harmonious love;
  Rest here in peace, till angels bid thee rise,
  And meet thy Saviour's *concert* in the skies."

Boswell's "Journal of a Tour to the Hebrides" contains the author's letter to Garrick asking him to send the "bad verses which led Johnson to make his fine verses on Phillips the musician." Garrick replied, enclosing the desired epitaph.

Boswell remarks, "This epitaph is so exquisitely beautiful that I remember even Lord Kames, strangely prejudiced as he was against Dr. Johnson, was compelled to allow it very high praise. It has been ascribed to Garrick, from its appearing at first with the signature G.; but I heard Mr. Garrick declare that it was written by Dr. Johnson."

The epitaph of Phillips is in the porch of Wolverhampton Church. The prose part of it is curious:—

> Near this place lies
> Charles Claudius Phillips,
> Whose absolute contempt of riches,
> and inimitable performances upon the Violin,
> made him the admiration of all that knew him.
> He was born in Wales,
> made the tour of Europe,
> and, after the experience of both kinds of fortune,
> Died in 1732.

DR. JOHNSON'S KNOWLEDGE OF MUSIC.

He said he knew "a drum from a trumpet, and a bagpipe from a guitar, which was about the extent of his knowledge of music." He further tells us that "if he had learnt music he should have been afraid he should have done nothing else but play. It was a method of employing the mind, without the labour of thinking at all, and with some applause from a man's self." These remarks are better appraised and understood when we bear in mind Dr. Johnson's own estimate of his musical knowledge together with his having derived pleasure from listening to the sounds of the bagpipes. If a performance on those droning instruments was in the Doctor's mind when he said that the reflective powers need not be exercised in performing on a musical instrument, there might be some truth in the observation. The labour of thinking, however, cannot be dispensed with in connection with playing most musical instruments, and least of all the Violin.

DR. JOHNSON ON FIDDLING AND FREE WILL.

"*Johnson*: 'Moral evil is occasioned by free will, which implies choice between good and evil. With all the evil that there is, there is no man but would rather be a free agent, than a mere machine without the evil; and what is best for each individual must be best for the whole. If a man would rather be the machine, I cannot argue with him. He is a different being from me.'

"*Boswell*: 'A man, as a machine, may have agreeable sensations; for instance, he may have pleasure in music.'

"*Johnson*: 'No, sir, he cannot have pleasure in music; at least no power of producing music; for he who can produce music may let it alone; he who can play upon a Fiddle may break it: such a man is not a machine.'"—"*Tour to the Hebrides.*"

HAYDN IN LONDON.—A "SWEET STRADIVARI."

(BY PERMISSION OF MR. JOHN MURRAY.)

The following extracts, taken from "A Country Clergyman of the Eighteenth Century," a pleasant and entertaining book (consisting of selections from the correspondence of the Rev. Thomas Twining, M.A.), cannot fail to interest the reader. The Rev. Thomas Twining was born in 1735. He was an excellent musician, both in theory and practice, and a lover of the Violin. He had collected much valuable information with regard to music, with a view to writing a history of the subject. Upon learning that Dr. Burney was engaged on his History of Music, he not only generously placed his valuable notes at the service of the Doctor, but revised the manuscript of his friend's History. Dr. Burney, in the preface of his work, says: "In order to satisfy the sentiments of friendship, as well as those of gratitude, I must publicly acknowledge my obligations to the zeal, intelligence, taste, and erudition of the Rev. Mr. Twining, a gentleman whose least merit is being perfectly acquainted with every branch of theoretical and practical music."

The publication of the volume containing the interesting correspondence between Dr. Burney and his friend not only serves to enlighten us relative to the substantial aid given to our musical historian, but also makes us acquainted with an English eighteenth century amateur and votary of the Fiddle of singular ability and rare humility:—

"COLCHESTER, *February* 15, 1791.

"To DR. BURNEY,—

"... And now, my dear friend, let's draw our stools together, and have some fun. Is it possible we can help talking of Haydn first? How do you like him? What does he say? What does he do? What does he play upon? How does he play?... The papers say he has been bowed to by whole orchestras when he has appeared at the play-houses. Is he about anything in the way of composition? Come, come! I'll pester you no more with interrogations; but trust to your generosity to gratify my ardent curiosity in your own way. I have just—and I am ashamed to say but just—sent for his 'Stabat Mater.' Fisin[10] told me some quartetts had, not long ago, been published by him. He has written so much that I cannot help fearing he will soon have written himself dry. If the resources of any human composer could be inexhaustible, I should suppose Haydn's would; but as, after all, he is but mortal, I am afraid he must soon get to the bottom of his genius-box. My friend Mr. Tindal is come to settle (for the present at least) in this neighbourhood. He is going to succeed me in the curacy of Fordham. He plays the Fiddle well, the Harpsichord well, the Violoncello well. Now, sir, when I say 'well,' I can't be supposed to mean the wellness that one should predicate of a professor who makes the instrument his study; but that he plays in a very ungentlemanlike manner, exactly in time and tune, with taste, accent, and meaning, and the true sense of what he plays; and, upon the Violoncello, he has execution sufficient to play Boccherini's quintettos, at least what may be called very decently. But ask Fisin, he will tell you about our Fiddling, and vouch for our decency at least. I saw in one of the public prints an insinuation that Haydn, upon his arrival in London, had detected some forgeries, some things published in his name that were not done by him. Is that true? It does not seem very unlikely."

> 10 James Fisin was born in Colchester; was intimate with
> Dr. Burney, and well known as a Professor of Music.

. . . . .

Haydn left Vienna December 15, 1790, and arrived with Salomon in London on New Year's Day, 1791. The Rev. Thomas Twining's interrogations addressed to Dr. Burney respecting him were therefore made but a few weeks after Haydn's first arrival in England. Between the months of January and May much had been seen and heard of Haydn, information of which Dr. Burney gave to his friend, as seen in the following letter:—

"COLCHESTER, *May* 4, 1791.

"To DR. BURNEY,—

"How good it was of you to gratify me with another canto of the 'Haydniad'! It is all most interesting to me. I don't know anything—any musical thing—that would delight me so much as to meet him in a snug quartett party, and hear his manner of playing his own music. If you can bring about such a thing while I am in town, either at Chelsea, or at Mr. Burney's, or at Mr. Salomon's, or I care not where—if it were even in the Black Hole at Calcutta (if it is a good hole for music)—I say, if by hook or crook you could manage such a thing, you should be my Magnus Apollo for the rest of your life. I mention Salomon because we are a little acquainted. He has twice asked me to call upon him, and I certainly will do it when I come to town. I want to hear more of his playing; and I seem, from the little I have seen of him, to like the man. I know not how it is, but I really receive more musical pleasure from such private *cameranious* Fiddlings and singings, and keyed instrument playings, than from all the *apprêt* of public and crowded performances.

"I have lately had a sort of Fiddle mania upon me, brought on by trying and comparing different Stainers and Cremonas, &c. I believe I have got possession of a sweet Stradivari, which I play upon with much more pleasure than my Stainer, partly because the tone is sweeter, mellower, rounder, and partly because the stop is longer. My Stainer is undersized, and on that account less valuable, though the tone is as bright, piercing, and full, as of any Stainer I ever heard. Yet, when I take it up after the Stradivari it sets my teeth on edge. The tone comes out plump, all at once. There is a comfortable reserve of tone in the Stradivari, and it bears pressure; and you may draw upon it for almost as much tone as you please. I think I shall bring it to town with me, and then you shall hear it. 'Tis a battered, shattered, cracky, resinous old blackguard; but if every bow that ever crossed its strings from its birth had been sugared instead of resined, more sweetness could not come out of its belly. Addio, and ever pardon my sins of infirmity.

"Yours truly,

"T. T."

GAINSBOROUGH AS A MUSICIAN.

William Jackson, organist of Exeter Cathedral, was intimate with Gainsborough, and besides being a thorough musician, painted with ability. He was also the author of many essays. In one of these he makes us acquainted with the character of Gainsborough's musical abilities. He says, "In the early part of my life I became acquainted with Thomas Gainsborough, the painter, and as his character was perhaps better known to me than to any other person, I will endeavour to divest myself of every partiality, and speak of him as he really was. Gainsborough's profession was painting, and music was his amusement—yet, there were times when music seemed to be his employment, and painting his diversion.

"When I first knew him he lived at Bath, where Giardini had been exhibiting his then unrivalled powers on the Violin. His excellent performance made Gainsborough enamoured of that instrument; and conceiving, like the servant-maid in the *Spectator*, that the music lay in the Fiddle, he was frantic until he possessed the very instrument which had given him so much pleasure—but seemed much surprised that the music of it remained behind with Giardini. He had scarcely recovered this shock (for it was a great one to *him*) when he heard Abel on the Viol da Gamba. The Violin was hung on the willow; Abel's Viol da Gamba was purchased, and the house resounded with melodious thirds and fifths from 'morn to dewy eve!' Many an Adagio and many a Minuet were begun, but none completed; this was wonderful, as it was Abel's *own* instrument, and, therefore, *ought* to have produced Abel's own music!

"Fortunately my friend's passion had now a fresh object—Fischer's Hautboy[11]—but I do not recollect that he deprived Fischer of his instrument; and though he procured a Hautboy, I never heard him make the least attempt on it. The next time I saw Gainsborough it was in the character of King David. He had heard a Harper at Bath—the performer was soon Harpless—and now Fischer, Abel, and Giardini were all forgotten—there was nothing like chords and arpeggios! He really stuck to the Harp long enough to play several airs with variations, and would nearly have exhausted all the pieces usually performed on an instrument incapable of modulation (this was not a pedal Harp), when another visit from Abel brought him back to the Viol da Gamba. He now saw the imperfection of sudden sounds that instantly die away—if you wanted staccato, it was to be had by a proper management of the bow, and you might also have notes as long as you please. The Viol da Gamba is the only instrument, and Abel the prince of musicians! This, and occasionally a little flirtation with the Fiddle, continued some years; when, as ill-luck would have it, he heard Crosdill, but by some irregularity of conduct he neither took up nor bought the Violoncello. All his passion for the Bass was vented in descriptions of Crosdill's tone and bowing."

> 11 Fischer was a celebrated Oboe-player. He made his first appearance in London in 1768. Gainsborough painted two portraits of him, one of which is at Hampton Court.

Gainsborough's fondness for fresh instruments is alluded to by Philip Thicknesse, who says that during his residence at Bath, Gainsborough offered him one hundred guineas for a Viol da Gamba, dated 1612. His offer was declined, but it was ultimately agreed that he should paint a full-length portrait of Mr. Thicknesse for the Viol da Gamba. Gainsborough was delighted with the arrangement, and said "Keep me hungry; keep me hungry! and do not send the instrument until I have finished the picture." The Viol da Gamba was, however, sent the next morning, and the same day the artist stretched a canvas. He received a sitting, finished the head, rubbed in the dead colouring, &c., and then it was laid aside—no more was said of it or done to it, and he eventually returned the Viol da Gamba.

Jackson tells us that Gainsborough "disliked singing, particularly in parts. He detested reading; but was so like Sterne in his letters, that, if it were not for an originality that could be copied from no one, it might be supposed that he had formed his style upon a close imitation of that author. He had as much pleasure in looking at a Violin as in hearing it. I have seen him for many minutes surveying, in silence, the perfections of an instrument, from the just proportion of the model and beauty of workmanship. His conversation was sprightly; his favourite subjects were music and painting, which he treated in a manner peculiarly his own. He died with this expression—'We are all going to heaven, and Vandyke is of the party.'"

GARRICK AND CERVETTO.

Cervetto, the famous Violoncello-player, occupied the post of principal Violoncello at Drury Lane for many years. His fame as a performer was almost matched by the celebrity of his nasal organ, the tuberosity of which often caused the audience in the gallery to exclaim, "Play up, Nosey!" In Dibdin's "Musical Tour," 1788, we are told that "When Garrick returned from Italy, he prepared an address to the audience, which he delivered previous to the play he first appeared in. When he came upon the stage he was welcomed with three loud plaudits, each finishing with a huzza. As soon as this unprecedented applause had subsided, he used every art, of which he was so completely master, to lull the tumult into a profound silence; and just as all was hushed as death, and anxious expectation sat on every face, old Cervetto, who was better known by the name of 'Nosey,' anticipated the very first line of the address by—aw———a tremendous yawn. A convulsion of laughter ensued, and it was some minutes before the wished-for silence could be again restored. That, however, obtained, Garrick delivered his address in that happy, irresistible manner in which he was always sure to captivate his audience; and he retired with applause, such as was never better given, nor ever more deserved. But the matter did not rest here; the moment he came off the stage, he flew like lightning to the music-room, where he encountered Cervetto, and began to abuse him vociferously. 'Wha—why—you old scoundrel. You must be the most———' At length poor Cervetto said, 'Oh, Mr. Garrick! vat is the matter—vat I haf do? Oh! vat is it?' 'The matter! Why you senseless idiot—with no more brains than your Bass-Viol—just at the—a—very moment I had played with the audience—tickled them like a trout, and brought them to the most accommodating silence—so pat to my purpose—so perfect—that it was, as one may say, a companion for Milton's visible darkness.' 'Indeed, Mr. Garrick, it vas no darkness.' 'Darkness! stupid fool—but how should a man of my reading make himself understood by—a——— Answer me—was not the house very still?' 'Yes, sir, indeed—still as a mouse.' 'Well, then, just at that very moment did you not—with your jaws extended wide enough to swallow a sixpenny loaf—yawn?' 'Sare, Mr. Garrick—only if you please hear me von vord. It is alvay the vay—it is, indeed, Mr. Garrick—alvay the vay I go ven I haf the greatest *rapture*, Mr. Garrick.' The little great man's anger instantly cooled. The readiness of this Italian flattery operated exactly contrary to the last line of an epigram—the honey was tasted, and the sting forgot."

THE KING AND THE PLAYER.

George the Third was frequently at Weymouth, and often strolled about the town unattended. On the day of Elliston's benefit (at which His Majesty had expressed his intention of being present) he had been enjoying one of his afternoon wanderings, when a shower of rain came on. Happening to be passing the theatre door, in he went. Finding no one about, he entered the Royal box, and seated himself in his chair. The dim daylight of the theatre and slight fatigue occasioned by his walk, induced drowsiness: His Majesty, in fact, fell into a doze, which ultimately resolved itself into a sound sleep. In the meantime Lord Townsend met Elliston, of whom he inquired if he had seen the King, as His Majesty had not been at the palace since his three o'clock dinner, it being then nearly five. Elliston being unable to give his lordship any information, Lord Townsend sought His Majesty in another direction, and the comedian made his way to the theatre, in order to superintend the necessary arrangements for the reception of his Royal patrons. Upon reaching the theatre, Elliston went at once to the King's box, and seeing a man fast asleep in His Majesty's chair, was about recalling him to his senses somewhat roughly, when, happily, he discovered who it was that had so unexpectedly taken possession of the Royal chair. What was to be done? Elliston could not presume to wake His Majesty—to approach him—speak to him—touch him—impossible! and yet something was necessary to be done, as it was time to light the theatre, and, what was of still more importance, to relieve the anxiety of the Queen and family. Elliston hit on the following expedient: Taking up a Violin from the orchestra he stepped into the pit, and placing himself beneath his exalted guest, struck up *dolcemente*—

God save our no - ble King! Long live our gra-cious King!

The expedient produced the desired effect. The sleeper was loosened from the spell which bound him. Awakened, His Majesty stared at the comedian full in the face, ejaculated, "Hey, hey, hey!—what, what—oh, yes! I see—Elliston—ha, ha! Rain came on—took a seat—took a nap. What's o'clock?" "Nearly six, your Majesty." "Say I'm here. Stay, stay! This wig won't do—eh, eh! Don't keep the people waiting—light up; light up; let them in—fast asleep. Play well to-night, Elliston." The theatre was illuminated; messengers were despatched to the Royal party, which, having arrived in due course, Elliston quitted the side of the affable Monarch, and prepared himself for his part in the performance.

SIR WALTER SCOTT ON MUSIC AND FIDDLES.

"I do not know and cannot utter," said Sir Walter, "a note of music; and complicated harmony seems to me a babble of confused, though pleasing sounds; yet simple melodies, especially if connected with words and ideas, have as much effect on me as on most people. I cannot bear a voice that has no more life in it than a pianoforte or bugle-horn. There is in almost all the fine arts a something of soul and spirit, which, like the vital principle in man, defies the research of the most critical anatomist. You feel where it is not, yet you cannot describe what it is you want." Sir Joshua, or some other great painter, was looking at a picture on which much pains had been bestowed. "Why—yes," he said, in a hesitating manner; "it is very clever—very well done. Can't find fault, but it wants something—it wants—it wants—d—n me, it wants that!" throwing his hand over his head, and snapping his fingers. In talking of his ignorance of music, Scott said he had once been employed in a case where a purchaser of a Fiddle had been imposed on as to its value. He found it necessary to prepare himself by reading all about Fiddles in the encyclopædias, &c., and having got the names of Stradivari, Amati, &c., glibly on his tongue, got swimmingly through his case. Not long after this, dining at the Duke of Hamilton's, he found himself left alone after dinner with the Duke, who had but two subjects he could talk of—hunting and music. Having exhausted hunting, Scott thought he would bring forward his lately acquired learning in Fiddles, upon which the Duke grew quite animated, and immediately whispered some orders to the butler, in consequence of which there soon entered the room about half-a-dozen tall servants, all in red, each bearing a Fiddle case, and Scott found his knowledge brought to no less a test than that of telling by the tones of each Fiddle, as the Duke played it, by what artist it was made. "By guessing and management," said he, "I got on pretty well, till we were, to my great relief, summoned to coffee."[12]

12 Lockhart's "Life of Sir Walter Scott."

I have frequently heard of the Duke's passion for Violins, and also that he had a great number of them at Hamilton Palace. Among these instruments there appears to have been a singularly perfect Tenor by the brothers Amati. Signor Piatti has often spoken to me of having seen this instrument several years since in the possession of the family. The Hamilton collection of Fiddles was doubtless dispersed long before the rare MSS., the Beckford Library, the inlaid cabinets, and other treasures which served to make Hamilton Palace renowned throughout the world of art and letters.

Returning to the subject of Sir Walter Scott's references to music, it will be seen that his barristers possess among their gentlemanly embellishments a knowledge of stringed instruments. Who can forget that the young Templar,

Master Lowestoffe ("Fortunes of Nigel," chap. xvi. 138) "performed sundry tunes on the Fiddle and French Horn" in Alsatia; and that Counsellor Pleydell, on the eventful night, in "Guy Mannering" (chap. xlix. 255), being a "member of the gentlemen's concert in Edinburgh," was performing some of Scarlatti's sonatas with great brilliancy upon the Violoncello to Julia's accompaniment upon the harpsichord?

A CINDERELLA VIOLONCELLO.

A somewhat curious change in the ownership of a Violoncello occurred many years since. My father (Mr. John Hart) was walking along Oxford Street, when he heard the sounds of a Violoncello, a Violin, and a Cornet, which were being played in a side street. His curiosity being excited, he became one of the group of listeners. The appearance of the Violoncello greatly pleased him; it was covered with a thick coat of resin and dirt, but its author was clearly defined nevertheless. When the players had concluded their performance, Mr. Hart asked the wandering Violoncellist if he was disposed to sell his instrument. "I have no objection, if I can get enough to buy another and something over," was the answer. The terms not being insurmountable, a bargain was struck, and the dealer in Fiddles walked away, taking his newly-acquired purchase under his arm. The itinerant trio, having become a duet, gave up work for that day.

Reaching home with his charge, Mr. Hart was in the act of removing the accumulated dirt of many a hard day's work from the Violoncello, when Robert Lindley entered, and asked what might be the parentage of the instrument about which so much pains were being taken. "A Forster," was the reply; and at the same time the circumstances of the purchase were related. Lindley was much amused, and expressed a wish to possess the rescued instrument, though it had been much injured. The price was agreed upon, and the Violoncello thus passed from the most humble to the most exalted player in *one* day.

A STOLEN "STRAD."

It has often been remarked that to steal a valuable Violin is as hazardous as to steal a child; its identity is equally impregnable, in fact, cannot be disguised, save at the price of entire demolition. To use a paradox, Violins, like people, are all alike, yet none are alike. The indelible personality of the best Violins has been a powerful agent in the cause of morality, and has deterred many from attempting to steal them. We have, however, instances of undiscovered robberies of valuable instruments, and notably that of the fine Stradivari which belonged to a well-known amateur, an attaché at the British Embassy at St. Petersburg. The Violin in question was numbered with the Plowden collection. I disposed of it to the amateur above mentioned in 1868; it was a magnificent Violin, date 1709, in the highest state of preservation. In the year 1869 the owner of it was appointed to the Embassy at St. Petersburg, and removed thither. He was a passionate lover of the Violin, and an excellent player. One evening he was playing at a musical party. After he had finished he placed his "Strad" in its case as usual, which he closed, without locking it. The next day he was amusing himself with a parrot, which bit him on the lip; the wound appeared very unimportant, but exposure to the cold brought on malignant abscess, and he sank and died. In due course his representatives arrived in St. Petersburg, and took charge of his property, which was brought to England. Some twelve months afterwards a relative (Mr. Andrew Fountaine, of Narford), who took much interest in valuable Violins, was visiting the family of the deceased gentleman and asked to be allowed to see the Stradivari, 1709. The case was sent for and duly opened. When the Violin was handed to the visitor he remarked there must be some mistake, and suggested that the wrong case had been brought, the instrument he held having no resemblance whatever to the Stradivari, and not being worth a sovereign. Inquiries were set on foot, and it was satisfactorily proved that the case had never been opened since it had been brought to England; neither had it left the custody of the late owner's nearest relative, who had kept it secured in a chest. The next day after the occurrence of the event related above, I was communicated with, and asked if I could recognise the Stradivari in question. It is unnecessary to record my answer. I might, with an equivalent amount of reason, have been asked if I should know my own child. The double case was formally opened, and the Violin described above was taken out. "Is that the Stradivari?" I scarcely knew for the moment whether my interrogator was in earnest, so ridiculous was the question. It remains only to be said that the Russian authorities were memorialised and furnished by me with a full description of the instrument; but to this moment its whereabouts has never been discovered.

THE MISSING SCROLL.

It has often happened that portions of valuable instruments, detached from the original whole, have been once more recovered and reinstated in their proper place. The following is an amusing instance of this.

A well-known amateur, belonging to the generation now fast passing away, was the fortunate possessor of a Stradivari Violin, which he had occasion to take to the Fiddle doctor for an operation quite unknown to the students of the Royal College of Surgeons, but well understood by the members of the fraternity to which I have the honour to belong, namely, *decapitation*. This, in the Fiddle language, means the removal of the old neck, and the splicing of a brand-new one in its place. It is an operation wholly unattended with the horrors of human surgery. Again and again a time was appointed for the completion of this delicate insertion, but in vain—it was a case of hope deferred. The owner of the Stradivari becoming wearied with this state of things, determined to carry off his cherished instrument in its dismembered condition. Placing the several portions in paper, he left the Fiddle doctor's establishment, considerably annoyed and excited. Upon reaching his home his recent ebullition of temper had entirely passed away, and he calmly set himself to open the parcel containing his dissected "Strad," when, to his utter dismay, he failed to find its scroll. The anguish he suffered may be readily conceived by the lover of Fiddles. Away he started in search of his Fiddle's head, dead to all around him but the sense of his loss; he demanded of every one he met whether they had by chance picked up the head of a Fiddle. The answers were all in the negative; and many were the looks of astonishment caused by the strange nature of the question and the bewildered appearance of the questioner. At length he arrived at the house of the Fiddle doctor, whose want of punctuality had brought about the misfortune. Here was his forlorn hope! He might possibly have forgotten to put the scroll into the parcel. His doubts were soon at rest; the scroll had been taken with the other parts of the instrument. Completely overcome with sorrow and vexation, he knew not how to endeavour to recover his loss. He ultimately decided to offer a reward of five pounds and to await the result as contentedly as he could.

A few hours after the dejected owner of the Violin had left the shop of the Fiddle doctor, an old woman, the keeper of an apple stall in the neighbourhood, entered and offered for sale a Fiddle-head. The healer of Violins, taking it into his hands, was agreeably astonished to recognise in it the missing headpiece, and eagerly demanded of the seller whence she had obtained it, and what might be its price. "Picked it up in the gutter," she answered; and two shillings was the modest value she set upon her find. Without a moment's hesitation the money was handed to the vendor of Ribston pippins, and away she trudged in high glee at the result of her good luck. The Fiddle Æsculapius, equally gleeful at the course of events, resolved to avail himself of the opportunity afforded him of gratifying a little harmless revenge upon the fidgety amateur's haste in removing the "Strad" before the alterations had been completed. He therefore determined to keep the fact of the discovery to himself for a short time. Advertisements multiplied, and the reward rapidly rose to twenty guineas. Having satisfied his revengeful feelings, the repairer duly made known the discovery of the missing scroll, to the intense gratification of its owner. Finally, the repairer refused to accept any portion of the reward upon one condition, viz., that he was allowed to complete his work—a condition readily conceded.

ANOTHER WANDERING SCROLL.

Among the collection of valuable Violins belonging to the late Mr. James Goding, was a Stradivari Violin, dated 1710, which had been deprived of its original scroll, and bore a supposititious figure-head by David Tecchler, owing to a piece of vandalism perpetrated by an eccentric amateur. The original scroll had found its way to an Italian Violin of some merit, the value of which was considerably enhanced by the newly-acquired headpiece, which gave to the whole instrument an air of importance to which it could lay no claim till it carried on its shoulders a head belonging to the aristocracy of Fiddles. During a period of about twenty years this mongrel Fiddle became the property of as many owners, and ultimately fell into my hands. Leaving this instrument, we will follow the history of the Stradivari, date 1710. At the dispersion of Mr. Goding's collection by Messrs. Christie and Manson, in the year 1857, a well-known amateur purchased the Violin for the sum of seventy pounds, the loss of its scroll preventing the realisation of a higher figure. Sixteen years after this event the purchaser applied to me for a Stradivari scroll, that he might make his instrument complete. The mongrel Violin described above being in my possession, decapitation was duly performed, and the Stradivari received its head again. Here was a fortuitous course of circumstances! This exchange of heads took place without my being at all aware that the "Strad" scroll had returned to its original body; but on my mentioning the circumstance to my father, he informed me, to my astonishment and delight, that if the head of the mongrel Fiddle had been placed on the Stradivari, date 1710, from the Goding collection, it was now, as the effect of recent transmigration, on its own legitimate body.

A MONTAGNANA INSTRUMENT SHOT THROUGH THE BODY IN THE REVOLUTION OF 1848.

An enthusiastic amateur was playing the Violin in a house in one of the leading thoroughfares in Paris at the outbreak of the Revolution in 1848. His ardour was so great that the cannonading failed to interrupt him in his pleasurable pursuit; he fiddled on, regardless of all about him, as Nero is said to have done when his capital was in flames, and even left the window of his apartment open. Presently a whizzing noise, terminating in a thud above his head, arrested his attention. Upon his looking up he saw the mark of a bullet in the ceiling. Aroused to a sense of his danger, he closed the windows. Being about to put his Montagnana into its case, his astonishment may be imagined when he discovered a hole through the upper side, and a corresponding chink in the belly, both as sharply cut as though a centre-bit had done the work. His Violin bore witness to his miraculous escape; the bullet lodged in the ceiling had taken his Montagnana in its course. The instrument referred to in this anecdote has been in my possession more than once.

FIDDLE MARKS AND THE CREDULOUS DABBLERS.

It is said that a drowning man will clutch at a straw; the truth of the remark applies to the half-informed in Fiddle connoisseurship. It is very amusing to note the pile of nothings that these persons heap up under the name of "guiding points" in relation to Fiddles. I will endeavour to call to mind a few of these. I will begin with those little pegs seen on the backs of Violins near the button, and at the bottom; the position of these airy nothings without habitation or name "is deemed indisputable evidence of certain makers' handicraft." One is supposed to have put his pegs to the right, another to the left; another used three, four, and so on. I have frequently heard this remark—"Oh, it cannot be a Stradivari, because the pegs are wrong!"

The purfling also forms an important item in the collection of landmarks; certain makers are supposed to have invariably used one kind of purfling, no variation being allowed for width or material adopted. Original instruments are pronounced spurious and spurious original by this test. All Fiddles purfled with whalebone are dubbed "Jacobs," and no other maker is credited with using such purfling.

The back of a Violin is another very important item with these individuals. Particular makers are supposed to have only made whole backs, others double backs; others again are thought to be known only by the markings of the wood. There is another crotchet to be mentioned: some will tell you they will inform you who made your Violin by taking the belly off, and examining the shape of the blocks and linings. Rest assured if the maker cannot be seen outside, he will never reveal himself in the *inner consciousness* of a Fiddle. Measurement is another certain guiding point with these dabblers; the measuring tape is produced and the instrument condemned if it does not tally with their erroneous theory.

"GUARNERI" AT A DISCOUNT.

With what tenacity do persons often cling to the fond belief that undoubted Raffaeles, Cinque Cento bronzes, dainty bits of Josiah Wedgwood's ware, and old Cremonas, are exposed for sale in the windows of dealers in unredeemed pledges, brokers' shops, and divers other emporiums! It is the firm conviction of these amiable persons that scores of gems unknown are awaiting in such cosy lurking-places the recognition of the educated eye for their immediate deliverance to the light of day.

The quasi bric-à-brac portion of the general dealer's stock is dexterously arrayed in his window, and not allowed to take up a prominent position among the wares displayed. To expose treasures would be a glaring act of indiscretion, inasmuch as it would tend to the belief that the proprietor was perfectly cognisant of the value of his goods, whereas he is imagined by the hypothesis to be profoundly ignorant on the subject. Pictures, bronzes, china, and Fiddles, with their extremely modest prices attached, lie half hidden behind a mountain of goods of a diametrically opposite nature. There they may rest for days, nay, weeks, before the individual with the educated eye, for the good of all men, detects them. Sooner or later, however, he makes his appearance, and peers into every nook of the window, shading his eyes with his hands. Something within arrests his attention; his nose gets flattened against the glass in his eagerness to get near the object. He enters the establishment, and asks to be allowed to look at an article quite different from the one he has been so intent upon; his object being that the dealer may not awaken to a sense of the coveted article's value by a stranger seeming to be interested in it. After examining the decoy bird, he returns it, and carelessly asks to look at *the* article. Whatever the value set upon it may be, he tenders exactly the half, the matter being usually settled by what is technically known as "splitting the difference." Delighted with his purchase, he carries it home, and persuades his friends he has got to the blind side of the dealer, and is in possession of the real thing for the fiftieth part of what others give for it. He proceeds to enlighten his friends on the subject, telling them to follow his example, which they invariably do.

Scarcely a day passes without my hearing of a Cremona having been secured in the manner I have attempted to describe. My experience, however, teaches me that the whole thing is a delusion, and that the thoroughbred Cremona does not fall away from the companionship of its equals, once in the space of a lifetime, and that when this does happen, the instrument rarely falls to the bargain-hunter.

The following exceptional incident will, I hope, not be found wanting in interest as bearing on this theme. A votary of the Violin purchased an old Fiddle for some two or three pounds from a general dealer in musical instruments in his neighbourhood. He was well satisfied with his acquisition; and after subjecting it to a course of judicious regulation, so great were the improvements effected that the vendor regretted having sold it for such a trifling sum, and the more so when it was whispered about that the instrument was a veritable Amati—a report, by the way, very far wide of the mark, as it was simply an old Tyrolean copy.

Some little time after the occurrence related, the lover of Violins heard that the same instrument-seller from whom he purchased the imagined Amati, had secured a job lot of some half-dozen old Fiddles, the remnant of an old London music-seller's stock, and that he was offering them for sale. Our hero decided to pay another visit, and judge of the merits of the new wares, with a view to a second investment. Upon presenting himself to the local seller of Violins, he was at once informed that if he selected *any* instrument from the lot, he must be prepared to pay £10, the dealer having no intention of again committing his former error in selling a Cremona for some forty shillings. Upon this understanding the visitor proceeded to examine the little stock, which he found in a very disordered condition—bridgeless, stringless, and dusty. Among the whole tribe, however, was a Violin which seemed to elbow its way to the front of the group, and clamour for the attention of which it appeared to deem itself worthy. Unable to resist its seeming appeal, the intending purchaser decided to remove it from the atmosphere of its companions, and begged that he might be permitted to take the importuning Fiddle and string it in order to test its qualities. His request being acceded to, he carried it away. Upon reaching home, he took it from its case, and gently removed the dust of years. The varnish appeared to him as something very different from any he had ever seen before on a Violin; and being an artist by profession, qualities of colours were pretty well understood by him. With the Violin poised on his knee, somewhat after the manner seen in the well-known picture of Stradivari in his workshop, he thus communed with himself: "I have never seen the much-spoken-of Cremonese varnish, but if this instrument has it not, its lustre must indeed be more wondrous than my imagination has painted." After again and again examining the Violin, he retired to rest, but not to sleep. The Fiddle persisted in dodging him whichever way he turned on his couch. At the dawn of day—five o'clock—he was up, with the Fiddle again on his knee, thinking he might have been labouring under some infatuation the night before which the light of day might dispel. Convinced he was under no such delusion, he soon made for the music-seller's establishment, whom he delighted by paying the price demanded for the Violin. It was now time, he felt, to obtain professional advice on the matter; in due course he paid me a visit. Upon his opening the case I was unable to restrain my feelings of surprise, and demanded if he had any idea of the value of the Violin. "None whatever," he answered. Without troubling the reader further, I informed him that his Violin was an undoubted

Giuseppe Guarneri, of considerable value. He then recounted the circumstances attending its purchase, with which the reader is familiar.

DOMENICO DRAGONETTI—HIS GASPARO DA SALÒ.

Signor Dragonetti succeeded Berini as *primo basso* in the orchestra of the chapel belonging to the monastery of San Marco, Venice, in his eighteenth year. The procurators of the monastery, wishing to show their high appreciation of his worth, presented the youthful player with a magnificent Contra-Bass, by Gasparo da Salò, which had been made expressly for the chapel orchestra of the convent of St. Peter, by the famous Brescian maker.

Upon an eventful night, the inmates of the monastery retired to rest, when they were awakened by deep rumbling and surging sounds. Unable to find repose while these noises rent the air, they decided to visit the chapel; and the nearer they got to it the louder the sounds became. Regarding each other with looks of mingled fear and curiosity, they reached the chapel, opened the door, and there stood the innocent cause of their fright, Domenico Dragonetti, immersed in the performance of some gigantic passage, of a range extending from the nut to the bridge, on his newly-acquired Gasparo. The monks stood regarding the performer in amazement, possibly mistaking him for a second appearance of the original of Tartini's "Sonata del Diavolo," his Satanic Majesty having substituted the Contra-Basso for the Violin. Upon this instrument Dragonetti played at his chief concert engagements, and though frequently importuned to sell it by his numerous admirers, declined to do so; in fact, though for the last few years of his life he gave up public performance, he resolutely refused most tempting offers for his treasure—£800, to use an auctioneer's phrase, "having been offered in two places," and respectfully declined. In his youthful days he decided that his cherished Gasparo should return to the place from whence he obtained it, the Monastery of San Marco, and this wish was accordingly fulfilled by his executors in the year 1846. The occasion was one of much interest; it was felt by Dragonetti's friends and admirers that to consign the instrument upon which he had so often astonished and delighted them with the magic tones he drew from it, to the care of those who possibly knew nothing of its merits, was matter for regret.

Being desirous of furnishing the reader with all the information possible relative to Signor Dragonetti's instrument I communicated with Mr. Samuel Appleby, who was his legal adviser, and probably better acquainted with him than any other person in this country. He very kindly sent me the following particulars, which are interesting:—

"BRIGHTON, *July* 2, 1875.

"MY DEAR SIR,—

"Your letter of yesterday needs no apology, as it will afford me pleasure at any time to give you any information in my power respecting the late Signor Dragonetti, having known him well from 1796 to his death.

"His celebrated Gasparo da Salò instrument, or Contra-Basso, was left by his will to the Fabbricieri (or churchwardens) for the time being of the Church of St. Mark's, at Venice, to be played upon only on festivals and grand occasions. I was present on one of such festivals, which lasted three days, in July, 1852. I then saw the Basso, which was played on in Orchestra No. 1, there having been two bands for which music had been composed expressly.

"In April, 1875, being again in Venice, I inquired from the Verger of St. Mark's if Dragonetti's *Violone* was in the church, and I could see it. The reply was in the affirmative, but as the Fabbricieri had the care of the instrument, under lock and key, it would be necessary to see them and get their consent for its production. As this would cause me some little trouble, I left Venice without carrying out my intention.

"Dragonetti by his will left me his Amati Double-Bass, which is now in this house, and I believe the only one of that make in England, and consequently highly prized by

"Yours truly,
"SAMUEL APPLEBY.

"Mr. Hart."

THE BETTS STRADIVARI.

The Bibliophile tells us of Caxton, Aldine, and Baskerville editions having been exposed for sale by itinerant booksellers, men who in opening their umbrellas opened their shops. Collectors of pictures, china, and Fiddles, have each their wondrous tales to tell of bygone bargains, which are but the echoes of that of the Bibliophile. It is doubtful, however, were we to search throughout the curiosities of art sales, whether we should discover such a bargain as Mr. Betts secured, when he purchased the magnificent Stradivari which bears his name, for twenty shillings. About half a century since, this instrument was taken to the shop of Messrs. Betts, the well-known English Violin-makers in the old Royal Exchange, and disposed of for the trivial sum above-mentioned. Doubtless its owner believed he was selling a brand-new copy, instead of a "Stradivari" made in 1704, in a state of perfection.

Frequently importuned to sell the instrument, Mr. Betts persistently declined, though it is recorded in Sandys and Foster's work on the Violin, that five hundred guineas were tendered more than once, which in those days must have been a tempting offer indeed! Under the will of Mr. Betts it passed to his family, who for years retained possession of it.

About the year 1858 it became the property of M. Vuillaume, of Paris, from whom it was purchased by M. Wilmotte, of Antwerp. Several years later it passed to Mr. C. G. Meier, who had waited patiently for years to become its owner. The loving care which this admirer of Cremonese Violins bestowed upon it was such, that he would scarcely permit any person to handle it. From Mr. Meier it passed into my possession in the year 1878, which change of ownership brought forth the following interesting particulars from the pen of the late Charles Reade, the novelist and lover of Fiddles:—

"THE BETTS STRADIVARI.

"To the Editor of the 'Globe.'

"SIR,—As you have devoted a paragraph to this Violin, which it well deserves, permit me to add a fact which may be interesting to amateurs, and to Mr. George Hart, the late purchaser. M. Vuillaume, who could not speak English, was always assisted in his London purchases by the late John Lott, an excellent workman, and a good judge of old Violins.[13] The day after this particular purchase, Lott came to Vuillaume, by order, to open the Violin. He did so in the sitting-room whilst Vuillaume was dressing. Lott's first words were, 'Why, it has never been opened!' His next, 'Here's the original bass-bar.' Thereupon out went M. Vuillaume, half-dressed, and the pair gloated over a rare sight, a Stradivari Violin, the interior of which was intact from the maker's hands. Mr. Lott described the bass-bar to me. It was very low and very short, and quite unequal to support the tension of the strings at our concert pitch, so that the true tone of this Violin can never have been heard in England before it fell into Vuillaume's hands. I have known this Violin forty years. It is wonderfully preserved. There is no wear on the belly except the chin-mark; in the centre of the back a very little, just enough to give light and shade. The corners appear long for the epoch, but only because they have not been worn down. As far as the work goes, you may know from this instrument how a brand-new Stradivari Violin looked. Eight hundred guineas seems a long price for a dealer to give: but after all, here is a Violin, a picture, and a miracle all in one; and big diamonds increase in number; but these spoils of time are limited for ever now, and, indeed, can only decrease by shipwreck, accident, and the tooth of time.—I am, your obedient servant,

"CHARLES READE.

"19, ALBERT GATE, *May* 9, 1878."

13 The hero of Mr. Read's "Jack of All Trades, a Matter-of-fact Romance."

LEIGH HUNT ON PAGANINI.

"'I projected,' says Leigh Hunt, 'a poem to be called "A Day with the Reader." I proposed to invite the reader to breakfast, dine and sup with me, partly at home, and partly at a country inn, to vary the circumstances. It was to be written both gravely and gaily; in an exalted, or in a lowly strain, according to the topics of which it treated. The fragment on Paganini was a part of the exordium:—

"So played of late to every passing thought,
 With finest change (might I but half as well
 So write!) the pale magician of the bow," &c.

I wished to write in the same manner, because Paganini with his Violin could move both the tears and the laughter of his audience, and (as I have described him doing in the verses) would now give you the notes of birds in trees, and even hens feeding in a farmyard (which was a corner into which I meant to take my companion), and now melt you into grief and pity, or mystify you with witchcraft, or put you into a state of lofty triumph like a conqueror. The phrase of *smiting* the chord—

"He *smote*; and clinging to the serious chords
 With godlike ravishment," &c.

was no classical commonplace; nor, in respect to impression on the mind, was it exaggeration to say, that from a single chord he would fetch out—

"The voice of quires, and weight
 Of the built organ."

Paganini, the first time I saw and heard him, and the first time he struck a note, seemed literally to *strike* it—to give it a blow. The house was so crammed, that being among the squeezers in the standing-room at the side of the pit, I happened to catch the first glance of his face through the arm a-kimbo of a man who was perched up before me, which made a kind of frame for it; and there on the stage, in that frame, as through a perspective glass, were the face, bust, and the raised hand of the wonderful musician, with the instrument at his chin, just going to commence, and looking exactly as I have described him.

> "His hand
> Loading the air with dumb expectancy
> Suspended, ere it fell, a nation's breath.
>   He *smote*; and clinging to the serious chords
> With godlike ravishment, drew forth a breath
> So deep, so strong, so fervid, thick with love—
> Blissful, yet laden as with twenty prayers,
> That Juno yearned with no diviner soul,
> To the first burthen of the lips of Jove.
>   Th' exceeding mystery of the loveliness
> Sadden'd delight; and with his mournful look
> Dreary and gaunt, hanging his pallid face
> 'Twixt his dark flowing locks, he almost seemed
> Too feeble, or, to melancholy eyes,
> One that has parted with his soul for pride,
> And in the sable secret lived forlorn."

"'To show the depth and identicalness of the impression which he made upon everybody, foreign or native, an Italian who stood near me said to himself, after a sigh, "O Dio!" and this had not been said long when another person, in the same manner, uttered "O Christ!" Musicians pressed forward from behind the scenes to get as close to him as possible; and they could not sleep at night for thinking of him.'"—*Timbs's Anecdote Biography*.

THACKERAY ON ORCHESTRAL MUSIC.

"I wish I were a poet; you should have a description of all this in verse, and welcome. But if I were a musician! Let us see what we should do as musicians. First, you should hear the distant sound of a bugle, which sound should float away; that is one of the heralds of the morning, flying southward. Then another should issue from the eastern gates; and now the grand *réveille* should grow, sweep past your ears (like the wind aforesaid), go on, dying as it goes. When, as it dies, my stringed instruments come in. These to the left of the orchestra break into a soft slow movement, the music swaying drowsily from side to side, as it were, with a noise like the rustling of boughs. It must not be much of a noise, however, for my stringed instruments to the right have begun the very song of the morning. The bows tremble upon the strings, like the limbs of a dancer, who, a-tiptoe, prepares to bound into her ecstasy of motion. Away! The song soars into the air as if it had the wings of a kite. Here swooping, there swooping, wheeling upward, falling suddenly, checked, poised for a moment on quivering wings, and again away. It is waltz-time, and you hear the Hours dancing to it. Then the horns. Their melody overflows into the air richly, like honey of Hybla; it wafts down in lazy gusts, like the scent of the thyme from that hill. So my stringed instruments to the left cease rustling; listen a little while; catch the music of those others, and follow it. Now for the rising of the lark! Henceforward it is a chorus, and he is the leader thereof. Heaven and earth agree to follow him. I have a part for the brooks—their notes drop, drop, drop, like his: for the woods—they sob like him. At length, nothing remains but to blow the Hautboys; and just as the chorus arrives at its fulness, they come maundering in. They have a sweet old blundering 'cow song' to themselves—a silly thing, made of the echoes of all pastoral sounds. There's a warbling waggoner in it, and his team jingling their bells. There's a shepherd driving his flock from the fold, bleating; and the lowing of cattle. Down falls the lark like a stone; it is time he looked for grubs. Then the Hautboys go out, gradually; for the waggoner is far on his road to market; sheep cease to bleat and cattle to low, one by one; they are on their grazing ground, and the business of the day is begun. Last of all, the heavenly music sweeps away to waken more westering lands, over the Atlantic and its whitening sails."—"*An Essay without End.*"

ADDISON ON THE PERSONIFICATION OF THE LEADING INSTRUMENT.

In the pages of the *Tatler* (April, 1710), Addison with much ingenuity and humour personifies certain musical instruments. He says: "I have often imagined to myself that different talents in discourse might be shadowed out after the same manner by different kinds of music; and that the several conversable parts of mankind in this great city might be cast into proper characters and divisions, as they resemble several instruments that are in use among the masters of harmony. Of these, therefore, in their order; and first of the Drum.

"Your Drums are the blusterers in conversation, that with a loud laugh, unnatural mirth, and a torrent of noise, domineer in public assemblies; overbear men of sense; stun their companions; and fill the place they are in with a rattling sound, that hath seldom any wit, humour, or good breeding in it. I need not observe that the emptiness of the Drum very much contributes to its noise.

"The Lute is a character directly opposite to the Drum, that sounds very finely by itself. A Lute is seldom heard in a company of more than five, whereas a Drum will show itself to advantage in an assembly of five hundred. The Lutenists, therefore, are men of a fine genius, uncommon reflection, great affability, and esteemed chiefly by persons of a good taste, who are the only proper judges of so delightful and soft a melody.

"Violins are the lively, forward, importunate wits, that distinguish themselves by the flourishes of imagination, sharpness of repartee, glances of satire, and bear away the upper part in every *consort*. I cannot but observe, that when a man is not disposed to hear music, there is not a more disagreeable sound in harmony than that of a Violin.

"There is another musical instrument, which is more frequent in this nation than any other; I mean your Bass-Viol, which grumbles in the bottom of the *consort*, and with a surly masculine sound strengthens the harmony and tempers the sweetness of the several instruments that play along with it. The Bass-Viol is an instrument of a quite different nature to the Trumpet, and may signify men of rough sense and unpolished parts, who do not love to hear themselves talk, but sometimes break out with an agreeable bluntness, unexpected wit, and surly pleasantries, to the no small diversion of their friends and companions. In short, I look upon every sensible, true-born Briton to be naturally a Bass-Viol."

WASHINGTON IRVING ON REALISTIC MUSIC AND THE VIOLIN.

"Demi-Semiquaver to Launcelot Langstaff, Esq.

"SIR,—I felt myself hurt and offended by Mr. Evergreen's terrible philippic against modern music in No. 11 of your work, and was under serious apprehension that his strictures might bring the art, which I have the honour to profess, into contempt. So far, sir, from agreeing with Mr. Evergreen in thinking that all modern music is but the mere dregs and drainings of the ancient, I trust before this letter is concluded I shall convince you and him that some of the late professors of this enchanting art have completely distanced the paltry efforts of the ancients; and that I, in particular, have at length brought it almost to absolute perfection.

"The Greeks, simple souls, were astonished at the powers of Orpheus, who made the woods and rocks dance to his lyre—of Amphion, who converted crotchets into bricks, and quavers into mortar—and of Arion, who won upon the compassion of the fishes. In the fervency of admiration, their poets fabled that Apollo had lent them his lyre, and inspired them with his own spirit of harmony. What then would they have said had they witnessed the wonderful effects of my skill?—had they heard me, in the compass of a single piece, describe in glowing notes one of the most sublime operations of nature, and not only make inanimate objects dance, but even speak; and not only speak, but speak in strains of exquisite harmony?

"I think, sir, I may venture to say there is not a sound in the whole compass of nature which I cannot imitate, and even improve upon;—nay, what I consider the perfection of my art, I have discovered a method of expressing, in the most striking manner, that indefinable, indescribable silence which accompanies the falling of snow."

[Our author describes in detail the different movements of a grand piece, which he names the "Breaking up of the ice in the North River," and tells us that the "ice running against Polopay's Island with a terrible crash," is represented by a fierce fellow travelling with his Fiddle-stick over a huge Bass-Viol at the rate of 150 bars a minute, and tearing the music to rags—this being what is called execution.]

"Thus, sir, you perceive what wonderful powers of expression have hitherto been locked up in this enchanting art. A whole history is here told without the aid of speech or writing; and provided the hearer is in the least acquainted with music, he cannot mistake a single note. As to the blowing up of the powder-bank, I look upon it as a *chef d'oeuvre* which I am confident will delight all modern amateurs, who very properly estimate music in proportion to the noise it makes, and delight in thundering cannon and earthquakes.

"In my warm anticipations of future improvement, I have sometimes almost convinced myself that music will in time be brought to such a climax of perfection as to supersede the necessity of speech and writing, and every kind of social intercourse be conducted by the Flute and Fiddle. The immense benefits that will result from this improvement, must be plain to every man of the least consideration. In the present unhappy situation of mortals a man has but one way of making himself understood: if he loses his speech he must inevitably be dumb all the rest of his life; but having once learned this new musical language, the loss of speech will be a mere trifle, not worth a moment's uneasiness. This manner of discussing may also, I think, be introduced with great effect into our National Assemblies, where every man, instead of wagging his tongue, should be obliged to flourish a Fiddle-stick; by which means, if he said nothing to the purpose, he would at all events 'discourse most eloquent music,' which is more than can be said of them at present.

"But the most important result of this discovery is, that it may be applied to the establishment of that great desideratum in the learned world—a universal language. Wherever this science of music is cultivated, nothing more will be necessary than a knowledge of its alphabet, which, being almost the same everywhere, will amount to a universal medium of communication. A man may thus—with his Violin under his arm, a piece of resin, and a few bundles of catgut—fiddle his way through the world, and never be at a loss to make himself understood.—I am, &c.,

"DEMI-SEMIQUAVER."

SPOHR AND HIS GUARNERI.

"Shortly before my leaving Brunswick I had a case made worthy of the splendid Violin I had brought from Russia, viz., a very elegant one; and in order to protect this from injury, I had packed it up in my trunk, between my linen and clothes. I therefore took care that this, which contained my whole estate, should be carefully fastened behind the carriage with cords. But, notwithstanding, I thought it necessary to look out frequently, particularly as the driver told me several trunks had been cut down from behind carriages. As the carriage had no window at the back, this continual looking out was a very troublesome business, and I was therefore very glad when, towards evening, we arrived between the gardens of Göttingen, and I had convinced myself for the last time that the trunk was still in its place. Delighted that I had brought it so far in safety, I remarked to my fellow-traveller: 'My first care shall now be to procure a good strong chain and padlock, for the better security of the trunk.'

"In this manner we arrived at the town gate, just as they were lighting the lamps. The carriage drew up before the guard-house. While Beneke gave our names to the sergeant, I anxiously asked one of the soldiers who stood round the carriage, 'Is the trunk still secured?' 'There is no trunk there,' was the reply. With one bound I was out of the carriage, and rushed out through the gate with a drawn hunting-knife. Had I with more reflection listened awhile, I might perhaps have been fortunate enough to hear and overtake the thieves running off by some side-path. But in my blind rage I had far overshot the place where I had last seen the trunk, and only discovered my over-haste when I found myself in the open field. Inconsolable for my loss, I turned back. While my fellow-traveller looked for the inn, I hastened to the police-office and requested that an immediate search might be made in the garden houses outside the gate. To my astonishment and vexation I was informed that the jurisdiction outside the gate belonged to Weende, and that I must address my request there. As Weende was half a league from Göttingen, I was compelled to abandon for that evening all further steps for the recovery of my Guarneri. I passed a sleepless night, in a state of mind such as, in my hitherto fortunate career, had been wholly unknown to me. Had I not lost my splendid Guarneri, the exponent of all the artistic excellence I had till then attained, I could have lightly borne the loss of the rest. On the following morning the police sent to inform me that an empty trunk and a Violin-case had been found in the fields behind the gardens. Full of joy I hastened thither, in the hope that the thieves might have left the Violin in the case, as an object of no value to them; but, unfortunately, it did not prove so. The bow of the Violin, a genuine Tourte, secured in the lid of the case, had remained undiscovered."—*Spohr's Autobiography.*

SPOHR AND THE COLLECTOR.

When Louis Spohr was in London in 1820, he tells us, in his Autobiography, he received a letter couched in the following terms: "Mr. Spohr is requested to call upon Dr. —— to-day at four o'clock." "As I did not know the name of the writer," he proceeds to relate, "nor could ascertain from the servant the purpose for which my attendance was requested, I replied, in the same laconic tone, 'At the hour named I am engaged, and cannot come.' The next morning the servant reappeared, bearing a second and more polite note: 'Mr. Spohr is requested to favour Dr. —— with a visit, and to appoint the hour when it will be convenient for him to call.' The servant had been instructed to offer me the use of his master's carriage, and having in the meantime discovered that the gentleman was a celebrated physician, a patron of music, and a lover of Violins, I drove to his house. A courteous old gentleman with grey hair met me on the stairs. Unfortunately he neither understood French nor German, consequently we were unable to converse together. We stood for a moment somewhat embarrassed, when he took my arm and led me into a large room, on the walls of which hung a great number of Violins. Other Violins had been removed from their cases and placed on the tables. The Doctor gave me a Violin-bow, and pointed to the instruments. I now perceived that he was desirous of having my opinion of the instruments. I, therefore, played upon them, and placed them in order, according to my idea of their merit. When I had selected the six most valuable ones, I played upon them alternately in order to discover the best of the half-dozen. Perceiving that the doctor cast upon one instrument glances especially tender whenever I played upon it, I gladly afforded the good old man pleasure by declaring it to be the best Violin. When I took my hat to leave, the old gentleman, with a kind smile, slipped a five-pound note into my hand. Astonished, I looked at it, and also at the Doctor, not knowing at first what he meant; but suddenly it occurred to me that it was intended as a fee for having examined his Violins. I smilingly shook my head, laid the note on the table, pressed the Doctor's hand, and descended the stairs. Some months later, upon the occasion of my benefit concert, the Doctor procured a ticket, for which he sent a ten-pound note."

THE ETTRICK SHEPHERD AND THE VIOLIN.

"But the pleasantest part of our fellowship is yet to describe. At a certain period of the night, our entertainer (the renowned Timothy Tickler) knew by the longing looks which I cast to a beloved corner of the dining-room what was wanting. Then with, 'Oh, I beg your pardon, Hogg, I was forgetting,' he would take out a small gold key that hung by a chain of the same precious metal to a particular button-hole, and stalk away as tall as the life, open two splendid Fiddle-cases, and produce their contents, first the one, and then the other; but always keeping the best to himself; I'll never forget with what elated dignity. There was a twist of the lip, and an upward beam of the eye, that were truly sublime. Then down we sat, side by side, and began—at first gently, and with easy motion, like skilful grooms, keeping ourselves up for the final heat, which was slowly but surely approaching. At the end of every tune we took a glass, and still our enthusiastic admiration of the Scottish tunes increased—our energies of execution redoubled, till ultimately it became not only a complete and well-contested race, but a trial of strength, to determine which should drown the other. The only feeling short of ecstasy that came across us in these enraptured moments were caused by hearing the laugh and joke going on with our friends, as if no such thrilling strains had been flowing. But if Tim's eye chanced to fall on them, it instantly retreated upwards again in mild indignation. To his honour be it mentioned, he has left me a legacy of that inestimable Violin, provided that I outlive him. But not for a thousand such would I part with my old friend."—*Altrine Tales.*—*Hogg's Reminiscences of Former Days.*

THE FIDDLE TRADE.

"There is, for instance, Old Borax, whom those who want to know whereabouts to look for—within the shadow of St. Martin's Church.

"Borax makes but little demonstration of his wealth in the dingy hole that serves him for a shop, where a Double-Bass, a couple of Violoncellos, a Tenor or two hanging on the walls, and half-a-dozen Fiddles lying among a random collection of bows, bridges, coils of catgut, packets of purified resin, and tangled horsehair in skeins, serve for the insignia of his profession. But Borax never does business in his shop, which is a dusty desert from one week's end to another. His warehouse is a private sanctum on the first floor, where you will find him in his easy chair reading the morning paper, if he does not happen to be engaged with a client. Go to him for a Fiddle, or carry him a Fiddle for his opinion, and you will hardly fail to acknowledge that you stand in the presence of a first-rate judge. The truth is, that Fiddles of all nations, disguised and sophisticated as they may be to deceive common observers, are naked and self-confessed in his hands. Dust, dirt, varnish, and bees'-wax are thrown away upon him; he knows the work of every man, of note or of no note, whether English, French, Dutch, German, Spaniard, or Italian, who ever sent a Fiddle into the market, for the last two hundred years; and he will tell you who is the fabricator of your treasure, and the rank he holds in the Fiddle-making world, with the utmost readiness and urbanity—on payment of his fee of one guinea.

"Borax is the pink of politeness, though a bit of a martinet after an ancient and punctilious model. If you go to select a Fiddle from his stock, you may escape a lecture of a quarter of an hour by *calling* it a Fiddle, and not a Violin, which is a word he detests, and is apt to excite his wrath. He is never in a hurry to sell, and will by no means allow you to conclude a bargain until he has put you in complete possession of the virtues, and failings, if it have any, of the instrument for which you are to pay a round sum. As his Fiddles lie packed in sarcophagi, like mummies in an Egyptian catacomb, your choice is not perplexed by any *embarras de richesses*; you see but one masterpiece at a time, and Borax will take care that you *do* see that, and know all about it, before he shows you another. First unlocking the case, he draws the instrument tenderly from its bed, grasps it in the true critical style with the fingers and thumbs of both hands a little above the bridge, turning the scroll towards you. Now and then he twangs, with the thumb of his left hand, the third or fourth string, by way of emphasis to the observations which he feels bound to make—instinctively avoiding, however, that part of the strings subject to the action of the bow. Giving you the name of the maker, he proceeds to enlighten you on the peculiar characteristics of his work; then he will dilate upon the remarkable features of the specimen he holds in his hand—its build, its model, the closeness and regularity of the grain of the wood of which the belly was fashioned: the neatness, or, wanting that, the original style of the purfling—the exquisite mottling of the back, which is wrought, he tells you, 'by the cunning hand of nature in the primal growth of the tree'—*twang*. Then he will break out in placid exclamations of delight upon the gracefulness of the swell—*twang*—and the noble rise in the centre—*twang*—and make you pass your hand over it to convince yourself; after which, he carefully wipes it down with a silk handkerchief. This process superinduces another favourite theme of eulogium—namely, the unparalleled hue and tone (of colour) imparted by the old Italian varnish—a hue, he is sure to inform you, which it is impossible to imitate by any modern nostrums—*twang*. Then he reverts to the subject of a Fiddle's indispensables and fittings; discourses learnedly on the carving of scrolls, and the absurd substitution, by some of the German makers, of lions' heads in lieu of them; hinting, by the way, that said makers are asses, and that their instruments bray when they should speak—*twang*. Then touching briefly on the pegs, which he prefers unornamented, he will hang lingeringly upon the neck, pronounce authoritatively upon the right degree of elevation of the finger-board, and the effects of its due adjustment upon the vibration of the whole body-harmonic, and, consequently, upon the tone. Then, jumping over the bridge, he will animadvert on the tail-piece; after which, entering at the *f*-holes—not without a fervent encomium upon their graceful drawing and neatness of cut—*twang*—he will introduce you to the *arcanum mysterii*, the interior of the marvellous fabric—point out to you, as plainly as though you were gifted with clairvoyance, the position and adaptation of the various linings, the bearings of the bass-bar, that essential adjunct to quality of tone—*twang*—and the proper position of the sound-post. Lastly, he will show you, by means of a small hand-mirror throwing a gleam of light into its entrails, the identical autograph of the immortal maker—Albani, Guarneri, or Amati, as the case may happen—with the date printed in the lean old type and now scarcely visible through the dust of a couple of centuries, '*Amati* Cremonæ fecit 1645,' followed by a manuscript signature in faded ink, which you must take for granted.

"Borax has but one price; and if you do not choose to pay it, you must do without the article. The old fellow is a true believer, and is accounted the first judge in Europe; Fiddles travel to him from all parts of the Continent for his opinion, bringing their fees with them; and for every instrument he sells, it is likely he pronounces judgment upon a hundred. It is rumoured that the greatest masterpieces in being are in his possession.

"A dealer of a different stamp is Michael Schnapps, well known in the trade, and the profession too, as a ravenous Fiddle-ogre, who buys and sells everything that bears the Fiddle shape, from a Double-Bass to a dancing-master's pocketable Kit. His house is one vast warehouse, with Fiddles on the walls, Fiddles on the staircases, and Fiddles hanging like stalactites from the ceilings. To him the tyros resort when they first begin to scrape; he will set them up for ten shillings, and swop them up afterwards, step by step, to ten or twenty guineas, and to ten times that amount if they are rich enough and green enough to continue the experiment. Schnapps imports Fiddles in the rough, under the designation of toys, most of which are the production of his peasant-countrymen bordering on the Black Forest; and with these he supplies the English provinces and the London toy and stationers' shops. He is, further, a master of the Fiddle-making craft himself, and so consummate an adept in repairing that nothing short of consuming fire can defeat his art. When Pinker, of Norwich, had his Cremona smashed all to atoms in a railway collision, Schnapps rushed down to the scene of the accident, bought the lot of splintered fragments for a couple of pounds, and in a fortnight had restored the magnificent Stradivari to its original integrity, and cleared 150 guineas by its sale. But Schnapps is a humbug at bottom—an everlasting copyist and manufacturer of dead masters, Italian, German, and English. He has sold more Amatis in his time than Amati himself ever made. He knows the secret of the old varnish; he has hidden stores of old wood—planks of cherry-tree and mountain-ash centuries old, and worm-eaten sounding-boards of defunct Harpsichords, and reserves of the close-grained pine hoarded for ages. He has a miniature printing press, and a fount of the lean-faced, long-forgotten type, and a stock of the old ribbed paper torn from the fly-leaves of antique folios; and, of course, he has always on hand a collection of the most wonderful instruments at the most wonderful prices, for the professional man or the connoisseur.

"'You vant to py a Pfeedel,' says Schnapps. 'I sall sell you de pest—dat ish, de pest for the mowny. Vat you sall gif for him?'

"'Well, I can go as far as ten guineas,' says the customer.

"'Ten kinnis is good for von goot Pfeedel; bote besser is tventy, tirty, feefty kinnis, or von hunder, look you; bote ten kinnis is goot—you sall see.'

"Schnapps is all simplicity and candour in his dealings. The probability is, however, that his ten-guinea Fiddle would be fairly purchased at five, and that you might have been treated to the same article had you named thirty or forty guineas instead of ten.

"I once asked Schnapps if he knew wherein lay the excellence of the old Italian instruments.

"'Mein Gott!—if I don't, who de teifil does?'

"Then he went on to inform me that it did not lie in any peculiarity in the model, though there was something in that; nor in the wood of the back, though there was something in that; nor in the fine and regular grain of the pine which formed the belly, though there was something in that; nor in the position of the grain running precisely parallel with the strings, though there was something in that; nor in the sides, nor in the finger-board, nor in the linings, nor in the bridge, nor in the strings, nor in the waist, though there was something in all of them; nor yet in the putting together, though there was much in that.

"'Where does it lie, then, Mr. Schnapps?'

"'Ah, der henker! hang if I know.'

"'Has age much to do with it, think you?'

"'Not mosche. Dere is pad Pfeedels two hunder years ole as vell as goot vons; and dere is goot Pfeedels of pad models, vitch is made fery pad, and pad Pfeedels of de fery pest models, and peautiful made as you sall vish to see.'

"This is the sum total of the information to be got out of Schnapps on that mysterious subject. On other matters he can pronounce with greater exactness. He knows every Cremona in private or professional hands in the whole kingdom; and where the owner bought it, if he did buy it; and what he gave for it, or from whom he inherited it, if it came to him as heir-loom. Of those of them which have passed through his hands, he has got fac-similes taken in plaster, which serve as exemplars for his own manufactures. Upon the death of the owner of one of these rarities, Schnapps takes care to learn particulars; and if the effects of the deceased come under the hammer, he starts off to the sale, however distant, where, unless some of his metropolitan rivals in trade have likewise caught the scent, he has the bidding all his own way, and carries off the prize.

"The inundation of German Fiddles, which may be bought new for a few shillings, has swamped English makers of cheap instruments, of which there are by this time five times as many in the market as there is any occasion for. Hence it is that Fiddles meet us everywhere; they cumber the toy-shop; they house with the furniture dealer; they swarm by thousands in the pawnbrokers' stores, and block out the light from his windows; they hang on the tobacconists' walls; they are raffled at public-houses; and they form an item in every auctioneer's catalogue.

"Meanwhile the multiplication of rubbish only enhances the value of gold; and a Fiddle worthy of an applauding verdict from old Borax is more difficult of acquisition than ever. So I shall keep my Cremona."

THE PRINCE AND THE FUGAL VORTEX.

A Royal amateur and British Admiral, a lover of the Violin and patron of music, happened whilst at Malta to be leading Mozart's charming Quartet in G major—

The opening movement, together with the Minuet, Trio, and Andante having been rendered with pleasure and satisfaction, the Finale was entered upon with due determination.

Its fugal subject—

Molto Allegro.

was well under way, and speedily in full sail. Ere long an evident indecision of purpose manifested itself, the motive or subject failing to elicit other than dubious answers to its calls; it was emphasised with loudness, not without signs of impatience, but to no purpose; all became hopelessly involved and incoherent, until at length, like the ice described by the "Ancient Mariner"—

"The *fugue* was here, the *fugue* was there,
    The *fugue* was all around;
 It cracked and growled and roared and howled
    Like noises in a swound."

The second Violin, overcome by the surging counterpoint, ceased playing, and with the adroitness of a Raleigh turned to the Prince and said, "Pardon me, your Royal Highness, I fear we have been carried away by the vortex of the melody." The execution of chamber compositions belonging to the higher walks of counterpoint is frequently disappointing, but seldom or never is the failure so gracefully and agreeably accounted for.

SALE OF CREMONESE INSTRUMENTS AT MILAN, AT THE END OF THE LAST CENTURY.

(Extracted from the "Gazetta di Firenze," 1790.)

The following instruments were offered for sale at Milan, by Signor Francesco Albinoni, in March, 1790:—

1. Violin by Antonio and Girolamo Amati, Cremona   1616
2. Violin by Niccolò Amati   1647
3. Violin by Niccolò Amati   1667
4. Violin by Andrea Guarneri   1657
5. Violin by Giuseppe Guarneri, figlio   1705
6. Violin by Antonio Stradivari   1708
7. Violin by Antonio Stradivari   1719

8.	Violin by Giovanni Ruggeri	1653
9.	Violin by Francesco Ruggeri	1670
10.	Tenor by Antonio and Girolamo Amati	1617
11.	Tenor by Antonio and Girolamo Amati	1618
12.	Tenor by Francesco Ruggeri	1619
13.	Violoncello by Amati, Cremona	1622
14.	Violoncello by Andrea Guarneri	1692

The above announcement cannot fail to make one reflect on the different degree of interest excited by a sale of Cremonas a century ago and one at the present time. The sale conducted by Signor Albinoni, in 1790, at Milan, doubtless passed with but little, if any, display of enthusiasm, and were it now possible to learn the prices realised, they would certainly give occasion for surprise when compared with those now obtained. As regards the increased interest taken in rare Violins, the sale of the Gillott collection, in 1872, furnishes an instance of comparatively recent date. The announcement of Messrs. Christie and Manson served to bring together in King Street, St. James's, a legion of Violin votaries. So unusual was the excitement that the *Graphic* had one of its pages occupied by an excellent representation of "Viewing the Violins." In Paris, in the year 1878, the sale of a Stradivari Violin, at the Hôtel Drouot, gave rise to an unusual display of interest. The first bid was for ten thousand francs, and the Stradivari, dated 1709, was knocked down for the large sum of twenty-two thousand one hundred francs. When the biddings at the Hôtel des Ventes had reached eighteen thousand francs, a casualty, which might have led to unpleasant results, lent additional zest to the proceedings. There was a great pressure among the crowd to obtain a sight of the Stradivari. Two or three of the more adventurous spirits clambered on to a table to gain a clear prospect of the precious Fiddle, causing the legs of the table to give way and the enthusiasts to be precipitated to the ground. A cry of terror—less for the fallen than for the Fiddle—arose from the throng; but soon the voice of the auctioneer was heard proclaiming, in reassuring accents, "Do not be alarmed, gentlemen; the Stradivari is safe!"

AN INDEFATIGABLE VIOLINIST.

"Puppo, the Violinist, being in Paris in 1793, was summoned before the Committee of Public Safety on suspicion, when the following interrogatories were put to him: 'Your name?' 'Puppo.' 'What were you doing during the time of the tyrant?' 'I played the Violin.' 'What do you do now?' 'I play the Violin.' 'And what will you do for the nation?' 'I will play the Violin.'"

A WISH.

"Busts, cameos, gems—such things as these
    Which others often show for pride,
I value for their power to please
    And selfish churls deride;
One Stradivari, I confess.
Two meerschaums, I would fain possess."

—Extract from Oliver Wendell Holmes' Lines on Contentment.

LIVING STRADIVARIS.

A passionate lover of Fiddles, being in Milan, made the acquaintance of an Italian who, like himself, was a lover of the bow. They had not long met before the theme of their mutual delight was broached; the beautiful features in the works of the great masters were dwelt upon, their respective points of genius discriminated, until the freemasonry of Fiddle-connoisseurship was exhausted. Inquiries were exchanged as to the whereabouts of remarkable specimens, when suddenly the Italian's face brightened, and gave indication that a happy thought had crossed his mind. "By the way, I can introduce you to a friend who has in his possession some choice Stradivaris, of various dates, and having heads of a very marked character." His companion was on his feet before he finished speaking, eagerly demanding where these choice "Strads" were to be seen. The distance being but a few streets off, it was agreed that they should start at once. On arriving at a house in the Via Meravigli, the Italian inquired of the servant if his master was at home. Being assured of this, the Fiddler-connoisseurs were shown into an apartment, where they anxiously awaited the host. Presently he entered, and the usual exchange of courtesies having been gone through, the Italian, with the utmost gravity, inquired after the Stradivaris, and received answer that they never were better; his companion, who was burning to feast his eyes on them, begged that he might have the pleasure of seeing them. The host, flattered by the interest taken in his "Strads" by his visitor, acquiesced, left the room, and brought in his collection, which, if not unique, was in every way original.

It consisted of five *Stradivaris*—three boys and two girls. Unable longer to restrain his laughter, the Italian broke forth into one of those hearty peals which terminate only when the risible faculties are completely exhausted. Signor Stradivari, the happy parent of the collection just ushered into the room, regarded his visitor with astonishment, in which he was joined by the specimens of various dates. Ultimately the countenance of Signor Stradivari began to assume anything but a pleased appearance, as he had failed to comprehend what there was about his cherished ones to excite such ungovernable mirth. When the joke was explained, it is needless to say that the wit's friend, the connoisseur, suffered some disappointment, but soon heartily joined in the laugh raised at his expense. Signor Stradivari and his family were not long kept behind the curtain, and soon added their laugh to that of the rest of the company.

PLEASURES OF IMAGINATION.

A lady belonging to Covent Garden Theatre, who had never heard Paganini, requested leave to be present at one of the rehearsals of his concerts. It happened that Paganini did not bring his Violin with him, but borrowed one from a member of the orchestra, and, instead of playing, made a kind of *pizzicato obbligato*. After the rehearsal was finished, the lady addressed Mr. Cooke: "Oh, dear, Mr. Cooke, what a wonderful man he is! I declare, I may say, that till this morning I never knew what music was capable of." Cooke replied, "Indeed, madam, he is truly wonderful; but allow me to observe that on this occasion you are indebted rather to your imagination than your ears for the delight you have experienced." "How, Mr. Cooke?" "Why, madam, this morning Paganini has not played at all—he has not even touched a bow." "Extraordinary!" exclaimed the lady; "I am more than ever confirmed in my opinion of him; for if *without* playing he can affect one in such a manner, how much more wonderful are the sensations he must produce when he *does* play!"

A ROYAL AMATEUR.

"Francis the First, Emperor of Austria, was a passionate lover of music, and played admirably on the flute. His greatest pleasure was to perform the Trios and Quartetts of the old masters. One of the household physicians of the court excelled on the Tenor. As imperial etiquette did not permit a simple physician to accompany the Emperor in his pieces unless he had the *entrée* at court, Francis first created his doctor a baron, and then a privy councillor, thus giving him his *petites* and *grandes entrées*. By the help of his Tenor-playing our medical musician insinuated himself so successfully into the good graces of the Emperor, that he became almost the rival of Metternich, and all the other ministers courted his friendship. Such was the rise of the celebrated Baron Still. But for his Tenor, this all-powerful favourite of Francis the First would have lived and died an obscure physician."—*Critique Musicale.*

POPE PIUS IX. AND THE MUSICIAN.

"An Italian composer, named Peregrini, was a fellow-student of Mastai Ferretti, now the occupant of the Papal chair. Since their quitting college, Fortune abandoned the *maestro*, whilst she smiled upon the priest. One day Pius IX. received the following letter:—'Most Holy Father,—I know not if you recollect that I had the honour of being your fellow-student at College, and that your Holiness has done me the honour of playing duos with me on the Violin; and that the execution of them was not always irreproachable, at least on my part, which so displeased your Holiness at the time that you deigned to apply certain corrections to my fingers. I have taken the liberty of revealing myself to your recollection, and to pray you to take under your protection one who can never cease to remember the happy moments he has passed with him whose apostolic virtues have raised him to the throne of St. Peter.' The Pope replied, 'I have never forgotten your name, my son; come to me at Rome, and we will again play duets together, and if you have not progressed in your studies, I shall know how again to correct you.'"—*Hogarth's Musical Herald.*

OLE BULL AND FIDDLE VARNISH.

"A man who had a patent varnish for Violins, brought his invention to Ole Bull, and begged him to try it. He said that it gave ordinary instruments the sweet quality of a Cremona Fiddle. Ole Bull tried it, and found that it improved the tone, and promised to use a Violin prepared with it at a concert he had to give at the house of the Duke of Riario. There was a great deal of fashionable company at this concert, and the heat of the room melted this famous varnish, which was really a preparation of asafoetida. The smell which it exuded was so maddening that an ordinary man would have stopped and excused himself; but Ole Bull merely closed his eyes, turned his face away, and played with an energy which became more frenzied the more intolerable the stink became. He enjoyed an overwhelming success, and the Duke rushed forward to seize his hand in congratulation. The appalling odour of asafoetida struck him in the face, and Ole Bull had to explain in what agony he had been performing."—*Ole Bull's* "*Breve i Uddrag*," *by Jonas Lie, Copenhagen*, 1881.

ON THE TREATMENT OF THE VIOLIN.

In a Letter from the celebrated Tartini.

The letter here presented to my readers was translated and published by Dr. Burney, in 1779, under the following title: "A Letter from the late Signor Tartini to Signora Maddalena Lombardini (afterwards Signora Sirmen). Published as an important lesson to performers on the Violin.

"PADUA, *March* 5, 1760.

"'MY VERY MUCH ESTEEMED SIGNORA MADDALENA,

"'Finding myself at length disengaged from the weighty business which has so long prevented me from performing my promise to you, a promise which was made with too much sincerity for my want of punctuality not to afflict me, I shall begin the instructions you wish from me by letter; and if I should not explain myself with sufficient clearness, I entreat you to tell me your doubts and difficulties, in writing, which I shall not fail to remove in a future letter.

"'Your principal practice and study should, at present be confined to the use and power of the bow, in order to make yourself entirely mistress in the execution and expression of whatever can be played or sung, within the compass and ability of your instrument. Your first study, therefore, should be the true manner of holding, balancing, and pressing the bow lightly but steadily upon the strings; in such a manner as it shall seem to breathe the first tone it gives, which must proceed from the friction of the string, and not from percussion, as by a blow given with a hammer upon it. This depends on laying the bow lightly upon the strings at the first contact, and on gently pressing it afterwards, which, if done gradually, can scarcely have too much force given to it, because, if the tone is begun with delicacy, there is little danger of rendering it afterwards either coarse or harsh.

"'Of this first contact and delicate manner of beginning a tone you should make yourself a perfect mistress in every situation and part of the bow, as well in the middle as at the extremities; and in moving it up as well as in drawing it down. To unite all these laborious particulars into one lesson, my advice is, that you first exercise yourself in a swell upon an open string—for example, upon the second string; that you begin *pianissimo*, and increase the tone by slow degrees to its *fortissimo*; and this study should be equally made with the motion of the bow up and down, in which exercise you should spend at least an hour every day, though at different times, a little in the morning and a little in the evening; having constantly in mind, that this is, of all others, the most difficult and the most essential to playing on the Violin. When you are a perfect mistress of this part of a good performer, a swell will be very easy to you; beginning with the most minute softness, increasing the tone to its loudest degree, and diminishing it to the same point of softness with which you began, and all this in the same stroke of the bow. Every degree of pressure upon the string which the expression of a note or passage shall require will by this means be easy and certain; and you will be able to execute with your bow whatever you please. After this, in order to acquire that light pulsation and play of the wrist, from whence velocity in bowing arises, it will be best for you to practise every day one of the *Allegros*, of which there are three in Corelli's Solos, which entirely move in semiquavers. The first is in D, in playing which you should accelerate the motion a little each time, till you arrive at the quickest degree of swiftness possible; but two precautions are necessary in this exercise—the first is, that you play the notes *staccato*, that is, separate and detached, with a little space between every two, for though they are written thus—

they should be played as if there was a rest after every note, in this manner—

The second precaution is, that you first play with the point of the bow; and when that becomes easy to you, that you use that part of it which is between that part and the middle; and when you are likewise mistress of this part of the bow, that you practise in the same manner with the middle of the bow; and, above all, you must remember in these studies to begin the *Allegros* or flights sometimes with an up-bow; and sometimes with a down-bow, carefully avoiding the habit of constantly practising one way. In order to acquire a greater facility of executing swift passages in a light and neat manner, it will be of great use to you if you accustom yourself to skip over a string between two quick notes in divisions, like these—

Of such divisions you may play extempore as many as possible, and in every key, which will be both useful and necessary.

"'With regard to the finger-board, or carriage of the left hand, I have one thing strongly to recommend to you, which will suffice for all; and that is, the taking a Violin part, either the first or second of a concerto, sonata, or song—anything will serve the purpose—and playing it upon the half-shift, that is, with the first finger upon G on the first string, and constantly keeping upon this shift, playing the whole piece without moving the hand from this situation, unless A on the fourth string be wanted, or D upon the first; but in that case, you should afterwards return again to the half-shift, without ever moving the hand down to the natural position. This practice should be continued till you can execute with facility upon the half-shift any Violin part not intended as a solo, at sight. After this, advance the hand on the finger-board to the whole-shift, with the first finger upon A on the first string, and accustom yourself to this position till you can execute everything upon the whole-shift with as much ease as when the hand is in its natural situation; and when certain of this, advance to the double-shift, with the first finger upon B, on the first string; and when sure of that likewise, pass to the fourth position of the hand, making C with the first finger upon the first string; and indeed this is a scale in which, when you are firm, you may be said to be mistress of the finger-board. This study is so necessary, that I most earnestly recommend it to your attention.

"'I now pass to the third essential part of a good performer on the Violin, which is the making of a good shake, and I would have you practise it slow, moderately fast, and quick; that is, with the two notes succeeding each other in these three degrees of *adagio, andante,* and, *presto*; and in practice you have great occasion for these different kinds of shakes; for the same shake will not serve with equal propriety for a slow movement as for a quick one; but to acquire both at once with the same trouble, begin with an open string, either the first or second, it will be equally useful; sustain the note in a swell, and begin the shake very slow, increasing in quickness, by insensible degrees, till it becomes rapid, in the manner following:—

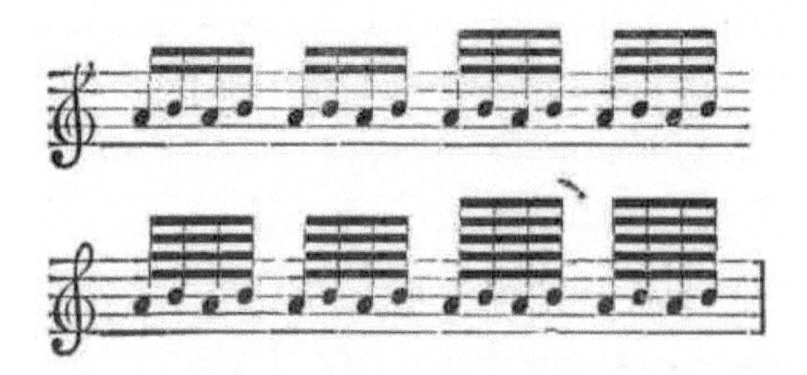

But you must not vigorously move immediately from semiquavers to demisemiquavers, as in this example, or from these to the next in degree—that would be doubling the velocity of the shake all at once, which would be a skip, not a graduation; but you can imagine between a semiquaver and a demisemiquaver intermediate degrees of rapidity, quicker than the one, and slower than the other of these characters; you are therefore to increase in velocity by the same degrees in practising the shake, as in loudness when you make a swell. You must attentively and assiduously persevere in the practice of this embellishment, and begin at first with an open string, upon which if you are once able to make a good shake with the first finger, you will with the greater facility acquire one with the second, the third, and the fourth, or little finger, with which you must practise in a particular manner, as more feeble than the rest of its brethren. I shall, at present, propose no other studies to your application: what I have already said is more than sufficient, if your zeal is equal to my wishes for your improvement. I hope you will sincerely inform me whether I have explained myself clearly thus far; that you will accept of my respects, which I likewise beg of you to present to the Prioress, to Signora Teresa, and to Signora Chiara, for all whom I have a sincere regard; and believe me to be with great affection,

"'Your obedient and most humble servant,
"'GIUSEPPE TARTINI.'"

Milton Keynes UK
Ingram Content Group UK Ltd.
UKHW030902151124
451262UK00006B/1078